"Engaging and distinctive. Christman brings intelligence, wit, and insightful honesty to her personal experiences with motherhood, womanhood, and girlhood, to abuse and its legacies, to the search for joy, creative expression, and love. Moving, beautifully written, and often quite funny."

—MEGAN HARLAN, author of *Mobile Home: A Memoir in Essays*

"Within these striking essays, Christman wrestles with her penchant for worry and her fear and shame of failing others, yet she also claims the power and beauty of her own body, both as a twenty-year-old girl and a forty-something woman, mother, wife, professor, early morning spinning class front-rower, and essayist. But Christman is not simply an essayist, she's an Essayist's Essayist. Every time I read her work, I learn so much about essay writing—not only from the essays themselves, but in the moments when she explains how she thinks about the essay and even how she teaches the essay in her classroom."

—JILL TALBOT, *Fourth Genre*

"At once fierce and exquisitely tender, *The Heart Folds Early* is a breathtaking journey into the mind of a mother grappling with an impossible choice. Jill Christman has written a profoundly generous book, offering her story with open palms and, in doing so, affirming the right of every woman to be the authority on her own body and life."

—NICOLE GRAEV LIPSON, author of *Mothers and Other Fictional Characters*

"This book is a continuous wonder, a compulsively readable story told with keen wisdom and nerves of steel about the fierce desire to grow and birth babies from a full life of one's own. Christman plows right through the pastel curtain around labor and delivery, revealing exactly why the mother and creator of life must wield the power to control this dangerous, bloody, and powerful act and to choose a future for herself and her children."

—SONYA HUBER, author of *Voice First: A Writer's Manifesto*

"*The Heart Folds Early* is a brilliant, breathtaking memoir about the dignity and necessity of our choices, and how everybody bears griefs unforeseen that, at times, hardly seem survivable. Jill Christman writes about the toughest matters of human existence with a directness, empathy, and humor that is the closest thing I'll ever know to love born from a page. I'm so grateful for this book, for this narrator's wisdom, for her heart."

—BROOKE CHAMPAGNE, author of *Nola Face: A Latina's Life in the Big Easy*

Praise for Jill Christman's *If This Were Fiction: A Love Story in Essays*

Winner of the 2023 Book of the Year Award from the Chicago Writers Association for traditional nonfiction

Finalist for the 2023 Heartland Booksellers Award

Silver Winner of the 2022 Foreword INDIES Book Award for autobiography and memoir

Winner of the 2023 Quill & Ink Award for nonfiction

"Christman's writing is moving and poetic, and she has a knack for imbuing profundity into everyday activities, whether slicing an avocado or climbing a hill. Fans of the personal essay shouldn't miss these intimate encounters."

—*Publishers Weekly*, starred review

"Eloquent and probing, Christman's essays examine the profound ways relationships can—for better or worse—transform an individual life and provide glimpses into the complexities of the human heart. A warmly wise, intimate memoir."
—*Kirkus Reviews*

"*If This Were Fiction: A Love Story in Essays* gives you what you didn't know you needed: sloths and loss and Swedish Fish candy, alligators and avocados and bird girls, pain and loss and hard traveling back to confront that pain, googly eyes and wayward skirts and lipsticks uncapped in purses, electric eye contact with a fetching poet across a dive bar, all woven with joy."
—SONYA HUBER, *Brevity*

"Christman has paid profound attention to her life, her relationships, to experiences ordinary and cataclysmic, to who and what she's loved and lost. And this makes her a generous writer: with the attention she brings her subjects comes the prospect that the reader's stories might matter if we dare to consider ourselves just as keenly. Attention itself is just a form of love, and Christman grants her audience plenty of both in this work. . . . However she might characterize her thoughts, I'd follow them anywhere."
—BROOKE CHAMPAGNE, *The Rumpus*

"Reading these essays is like hanging out with a true friend, someone who isn't afraid to be real. Jill Christman writes about love, loss, trauma, fear, parenthood, and the strange wonder of our past and former selves with deep understanding, humor, and so much beauty."
—BETH (BICH MINH) NGUYEN, author of *Stealing Buddha's Dinner*

"*If This Were Fiction* is the collection I wish I had the talent and skill to write. Christman's words shine with unusual beauty and hard-earned brilliance."
—ASHLEY C. FORD, author of *Somebody's Daughter*

"What is more complex than love, marriage, motherhood, and family? Probably nothing, but Jill Christman takes the deep dive with intelligent, intense, intimate essays that will catch you off guard and leave you wanting more. *If This Were Fiction* is a piercing book by a brilliant, gutsy writer."
—DINTY W. MOORE, author of *To Hell with It*

The Heart Folds Early

AMERICAN LIVES
Series editor: Tobias Wolff

The Heart Folds Early

A Memoir

Jill Christman

University of Nebraska Press
Lincoln

© 2026 by Jill Christman

Acknowledgments for the use of copyrighted material appear on pages 275–279, which constitute an extension of the copyright page.

All rights reserved

The University of Nebraska Press is part of a land-grant institution with campuses and programs on the past, present, and future homelands of the Pawnee, Ponca, Otoe-Missouria, Omaha, Dakota, Lakota, Kaw, Cheyenne, and Arapaho Peoples, as well as those of the relocated Ho-Chunk, Sac and Fox, and Iowa Peoples.

Publication of this volume was assisted by the Virginia Faulkner Fund, established in memory of Virginia Faulkner, editor in chief of the University of Nebraska Press.

For customers in the EU with safety/
GPSR concerns, contact:
gpsr@mare-nostrum.co.uk
Mare Nostrum Group BV
Mauritskade 21D
1091 GC Amsterdam
The Netherlands

Library of Congress Control Number: 2025029484

Designed and set in Garamond Premier Pro by L. Welch.

For Ella and Henry

Now cracks a noble heart. Good night sweet prince:
And flights of angels sing thee to thy rest!
Why does the drum come hither?

WILLIAM SHAKESPEARE
Hamlet, V, ii

Contents

Prologue *1*
1. Sweet Home Alabama *5*
2. Grief Is the Gorilla *10*
3. Long Prairie Road and Highway 101 *22*
4. I Can't Make You Love Me *25*
5. Tongue and Groove *44*
6. Feminist Fury: An Interlude *54*
7. Testing Begets Testing *60*
8. Becoming the Mother I Am *79*
9. Ways of Seeing *95*
10. Nothing's Going to Change My World *107*
11. Moona's Story *125*
12. The Secret of Secrets *135*
13. The Eighteen-Week Ultrasound *140*
14. Choice *151*
15. Chicago *164*
16. Between Heaven and Earth *173*
17. What If It's a Myth? *194*
18. Painting Faces *204*
19. The Heart Folds Early *211*
20. L.B. *222*
21. Vagina Will Find Vagina *242*
22. The Angel and the Umbilical Rope *252*
23. Give Me Your Hands *264*

Acknowledgments *275*

The Heart Folds Early

Prologue

What is the new book about? someone will occasionally ask, and I am no good with this part of writing, the part where I'm expected to talk. I could say anything, right? "Grief," I sometimes say. "Love," I try instead. Or "All the things there are to be afraid of," I might say, and then turn the question around, because redirection is my superpower: "What are *you* most afraid of?"

I really am curious. Also, grief, love, and fear tangle like a silver chain hidden at the bottom of the jewelry box: lay the chain on a tray, drizzle on some oil, and use a needle to loosen each knotted link. The heart's holy trinity. They're all here, but—I want to see if I can say it at the beginning and not flinch—at heart center, this book is about abortion. Specifically, it's about a second-trimester abortion. My own.

I was thirty-seven years old and six days shy of twenty weeks pregnant. Because I never thought I would make that choice. Because I didn't see it coming. Because the late-term abortions no one wants to think about need to be part of the national conversation.

This book is also about the abortion you got when you were in college and you thought, *one time, just one time*, and you were caught up in the moment. Or your girlfriend's abortion when you were both still in high school and your moms drove you, together—so you would be there for support—over state lines to a clinic. Didn't you write a song for her? Also your roommate's abortion the fall after that summer when she hid her growing belly under loose

T-shirts because she was so afraid of her father and when she got back to college, to you, she lifted that T-shirt to expose her belly, told you she hadn't had a period all summer. Did you think she might be pregnant? You did. Also? Your mother's abortion. Your aunt's abortion. Your teacher's abortion.

This book is about your daughter's abortion.

My life. Their lives. The infinite number of choices we make every day and how way leads on to way, how we are crushed and rebuilt.

Three years ago I put this book away. Too depressing, the marketing folks at the publishing houses said. How would we position this memoir? How would it sell? It's certainly not a baby-shower book. Nobody wants to read about babies dying. You'll scare pregnant women. It's depressing.

You're damn right it's fucking depressing.

I was tired. My living children were navigating a pandemic, anxiety, guns in schools. They needed me to show up every day for them with whatever I had left in the tank. I needed to look forward, not back. Or so I told myself because I was scared and spent and just barely hanging on. I know you know.

Well. Things have gotten scarier, haven't they?

Time matters.

What are the moments you remember with terrifying clarity?

On June 24, 2022, I was in a second-floor Airbnb in Glenwood Springs, Colorado, up before my family, coffee in hand, feet up on the couch, looking through a plate glass window over the construction site of a hot springs development, the Colorado River, the train tracks, and beyond all of that, a glorious mountain, looking as if she hadn't a single fuck left to give, rising up and making everything else—the bulldozers, the passenger train, the strip of condos, and even the mighty Colorado River—look small. Glowing red in the morning sun, she wore a shawl of green against the early morning chill, looking for all the world like the mother of us all.

And then I picked up my phone and saw the notification. I knew this was coming, we all knew this was coming, but as with those other great disasters—JFK's assassination, the Challenger explosion, the second plane hitting the second tower—this was a jolt to the nerve center, and I will always remember where I was and what I was doing when I read the news: the Supreme Court had overturned Roe v. Wade. Our right to an abortion in the United States—our right to access medical care for our own bodies—was no longer protected. We all knew this day was coming, I had seen this day coming, and yet, when it did, I felt the news, so small, the size of a phone screen, like a kick to the stomach. Like a cramp, my uterus contracting like a fist. The coffee in my mouth turned bitter. I flipped my phone face-down on the couch, as if I could hit pause, mute, reject call.

Was the mountain trembling? Did I see her shake? If she had been a volcano, she would have blown.

We both would have blown.

So, yeah, this book is about choice. About choices.

1   Sweet Home Alabama

Before we lost the baby—correction: before we chose to end my pregnancy and let our broken-hearted baby die—Colin's accident was the grief story at the center of my life on this planet, almost burning me to ashes as he had been burned. Like all stories of grief, this one began with love. One year after we met, Colin dropped to his knee in the sand and asked me to marry him. I can still see his face looking up at me: earnest and in love, but also mischievous, sparkling, confident, pretty sure he had this locked in. There were drops of water in his dark hair catching the last of the day's soft light. Mist. On the Oregon coast, there is always mist. I said yes, and then, less than a month after Colin's proposal, the phone rang in the house we shared with his sister. Again, a lifetime later, if I listen, I can hear the phone, the scream, the sound coming out of the dark with the news that Colin was dead.

I know this is how accidents happen: suddenly, randomly, crushingly. In the slow months after Colin's death, my heart took in this knowledge like a sea change. I could love a breathing someone, and then, like that, he could be gone.

This understanding felt like a rearranging of my cells, a restructuring of molecular code, a rewiring of my brain. There are some people who never leave us. One way or another, we carry them with us, and—if we can, if we choose—we keep going.

AFTER COLIN DIED, what were my choices? On the most basic level, keep living or die, so once I decided *against* dying—and that took a while—I was in for this life on earth, but this wasn't a one-time choice and there were many choices nested inside. I could have stopped loving and letting myself be loved. I could have given up on figuring out what I wanted to do. Despite what I had lost, *because* of what I'd lost, I wanted love and I wanted purpose—which has always felt like some combination of paying attention, staying curious, and attempting to make sense of it all—but I needed a plan. I needed a way through my grief to the other side, and I was tired. So tired. For years, every day felt like reaching my hand down into the writhing nest as a new baby snake punctured the soft egg with its needle tooth, emerging whole but tiny, a new life sliding through my fingers like water, a fresh serpent to be reckoned with. *Hello, grief, what do you have for me today?*

Follow me through time, space, and choices of every description to eight years post-accident, eight years of Colin dead, thousands of miles away from that misty Oregon coast, way down in Alabama now, where I first ignored the bad advice of the classmate in my MFA program who slapped down the first chapter of the true thing I was writing (I didn't know to call the thing a memoir then), sneered across the seminar table at me, and said, "Who do you think you are? Frank Zappa's daughter?"

"Moon Unit? No, asshole, I think I'm Frank friggin' Zappa."

Okay, so I said nothing. I stayed silent because, because, because those were the rules—of both survival and workshop.

But I found the anger I needed to shake him off. The haters gonna hate—and thus it has always been. I chose, instead, to hear my teacher who shared a smoke with me outside the flapping doors of the English Department building when the class was over. *Keep writing, Jilly.*

Keep writing, Jilly.

You never know in this world when someone's going to come

along and save your life, or how they're going to accomplish the job of pulling you up just when you think you're going down for the last time. This teacher was one of those people at one of those moments. I didn't know what I was doing, but the pages stacked up on the corner of my ravaged desk—stories about abuse (and art), accidental death (and love), eating disorders (and survival). Somewhere in the last months of writing this first book, I figured out the question I hadn't even known I was asking: In a crazy, dangerous world where wars are fought, and children are neglected and starving, in a world where six-year-olds are raped and dogs are abandoned in paper bags, in a world where beloved young men ignite on highways and beautiful young women want so desperately to take up less space in a world that has handled them so roughly that they stick their fingers down their throats to purge out all that is wrong and bad—in a world like this, *can I really have a baby?*

This was a complicated question. Heeding Rilke's advice to his young poet, I surrendered my need for order and answers and tried to *love the questions themselves.* Three hundred pages later, I was nowhere near my answer, but I was beginning to understand my questions. *Really? After this? And knowing this? But considering this? Can I really have a baby?*

IN GRAD SCHOOL, in Alabama, I was nobody's mother—unless you count my dog, Tango, which I kind of do. But even then—again, not consciously, not really, because I was still such a mess—I knew I wanted to be a mother, and so in my first extended literary effort I wrote with my windows open through the long, fragrant mornings of a southern magnolia bloom, past my lunchtime run, and back to my desk, sweating now, until the darkening shadows took me to the bar where I would spin out the demons and angels of a long day writing. This was lonely business. In my mind, there was no sense of audience, not even the reading shadow of my mother or teachers or Colin. My business was solitary. I felt as if I were physically constructing a Jill I could understand, a Jill with a body I could live inside—out of words.

I wrote to imagine a space where my children could be conceived, carried, and born to live with me and their adoring father (who would he be? where would I find him? how would I know he would stay?). I wrote to believe in the possibility that good things happen and love can flourish and be safe in a world that sometimes seemed to be imploding—a submarine under the weight of the sea, down with creatures I could only imagine, collapsing in on itself, deep in the darkest place on the planet.

IN MY REAL, off-the-page life, just as I was finishing that first book, and emerging into the pink light of a Tuscaloosa spring, I was breaking up with the man I'd dated for most of my graduate school career. On the verge of graduation, my romantic choices seemed two-pronged: marry or get the hell out.

The man I left was a good man. I couldn't live with him, but I did love him, and he gave me many good things I carry with me. He gave me the title of my first book, for one—*Darkroom*, which is the perfect one-word title for that book and demonstrates that he was paying close attention, that he saw me—as well as a better understanding of both the periodic sentence and all things competitive sports. But possibly the most important thing he left me with when we broke up, as clean a break as I've ever known, was a life-altering question that jerry-rigged some lost connection between my heart and brain like a carefully chewed wad of gum wedged into just the right place. Still holding.

I was having a tantrum in the tiny living room of his apartment, low down on the futon couch, somewhere between a tiny version of a bulked-up Mark McGwire on the TV, seven to twelve remote and game controls, and that morning's impeccably penciled-in *New York Times* crossword puzzle. "I can't have a baby!" (Did I stop before the end of that sentence? Before the *with you*?)

"I can't have a baby! What if the baby *died*?"

And he turned his full attention on me, not like the Yale-educated guy with the inexplicable passion for fantasy football that I knew him to be, but more like a spiritual guide from one of the hippie potlucks of my youth and he said, "You would give up the thing you want most in this world because you're *afraid*?"

I can't remember what I said in return, but I have never forgotten the question. His voice was low and angry, and I was startled. I'd heard another version of this question from a channeled angel going by the earth name of Divine Grace in the months after Colin's death. She had advised me to make decisions out of love, not fear, and here was this reminder from the most unexpected place.

Would I give up the thing I wanted most in the world because I was afraid?

2   Grief Is the Gorilla

I was not a protected child—loved, and loved dearly, but not protected. My mother trusted us to take care of ourselves, and it should be said that she didn't have a lot of choice in the matter. She left my father when I was two, driving north from Miami in a van and ending up on the coast of Massachusetts with two kids, a hopeful heart, and no money. As she now rightly points out, the climate was different in the seventies. There was not so much fear. Don't get me wrong: There were still plenty of things *to* fear. It's just that my mother—and a lot of mothers just like her—didn't know to be afraid of them. No seatbelts, no sunscreen, no bike helmets. The list goes on and on, but we need to take my mom's point: It was a different time and we played by different rules. Or no rules.

    She let my brother and me go, giving the world to us—and us to the world. Let go and let learn was her philosophy. Plus, she was a single mom and she had to go to work. There were no babysitters or money for babysitters even if she could find one. We were the last house before a nature preserve on a little island, and I know the pleasure of being a child left alone to wander through sand dunes without schedules or restrictions. I gathered beach grasses into bouquets and toasted them in the sun, I dug a spot for myself in the warm sand near a pungent bayberry bush and read *The Black Stallion* straight through in one glorious afternoon, I poked a branch into a sticky nest hanging from a tree and pulled it back dangling with fuzzy caterpillars like a prize. I grew myself, I suppose, into an artist.

We twenty-first-century parents know the problem with this picture. The world can be a dangerous place, and an unsupervised child is an at-risk child. My mother has no reason to feel bad: Her two kids are grown, employed, and living in loving families—all in all, we're okay. My mother, working mostly alone, did not fail us.

That needs to be said—and then it needs to be repeated that my brother and I were often unwatched and vulnerable. Between the ages of six and twelve, I was molested by a neighbor. My mother never knew. Between the ages of thirteen and nineteen, I inflicted abuses upon myself: relentless bulimia, blackout drinking, risky sex. She never knew. I never told her, and I did everything I could to appear normal. I was not a difficult child or even a defiant teenager. I wanted to be good, and good enough. I wanted her to love me—and love me she did, always.

I was the teenage girl who would break a mother's heart, but I didn't want my mother's heart to break, and so I was another girl as well, the one my mother could see. In the end, I turned out all right. Maybe better than all right.

QUITE FAIRLY, you may be thinking: *Hold on, girlfriend. I thought you said this book was about abortion?* And it is. When I think about abortion, I think about all the years and the moments in between that led up to that choice in May 2006. What life has been like inside this female body of mine. What this body has accumulated—and what has been taken away. How this body has been ill-used by the world and how she has triumphed. What I have learned from being on the inside looking out through blue eyes I have sometimes used in love and sometimes used as a kind of weapon. I am not so perfect—and fuck it, I shouldn't have to be.

I MET COLIN when I was nineteen—a baby, right?—but I felt as if I'd been grown for a long, long time, and by many measures (sex, alcohol, independence: What *are* the measures?), I had been operating as an adult woman. With Colin, I was becoming less afraid. He made me feel safe, cherished enough to remember the bedrock abuse of my childhood without risk of dissolution, to dig through the memories as my recovery required without the fear that no one would ever love me, such damaged goods.

I loved him like crazy, and he loved me even though I was.

I think back to our time together, and I can't remember if I worried about losing Colin.

When did I start being afraid of everyone I love dying?

AFTER COLIN'S ACCIDENT, I was dismantled. Grief was a fog. Grief was a deep well. Grief was concrete shoes. Grief was sticky, a clear, immobilizing syrup. Grief was a thick plate of bulletproof glass like the kind they put up between us and the gorillas at the zoo, the one the alpha male gazes through placidly or throws his body against in a fit of caged frustration. The sound is concussive, the glass shakes, but it doesn't come down. There is the side of the world where we live in grief, pretty much alone, and there is the other side of the world you can see but can no longer join. On that other side, people set alarms and take showers and put on clothes they have washed and folded and put in drawers. They go to work or school. The people on the other side of the glass go to coffee shops and order lattes or they ride past on bicycles or, my god, they reach for each other in front of a bookstore window, squeeze hands, and laugh. What? What was happening? How did they *do* that? Didn't they know?

From my side of the glass, in the early weeks after Colin died, I stopped leaving the house I still shared with his sister Diane and her two little girls. Diane's grief was different from mine. Her grief didn't own the luxury of dismantlement. She'd returned to finish her degree after marrying and having children young; now, she had two little girls, she was going through an ugly divorce, and her baby brother was dead. The final clause did not make the first two disappear. She had to keep moving and I did not. I withdrew from all my classes; Diane did not. At first, I was still considering dying, but I also tried to be useful. I know this doesn't make sense. Without classes or a job, I could help with Diane's girls. I would be the fun aunt—making mouse pancakes for breakfast and overseeing the painting of a giant Grinch on the sliding glass doors, but I made a mess. I was a mess. Diane couldn't bear the sound of my crying. Who could blame her? Her baby brother was dead. She knew that and she had no choice but to keep moving, and there I was, in her house, hoping to die.

I experimented with language: Colin died. My fiancé died. Colin was killed. My friend Colin was killed. There was an accident. Colin was in an accident. He was DOA—dead on arrival. That doesn't mean Colin arrived anywhere, that means the first responders arrived and Colin was already dead. Colin passed away. They wouldn't let me see his body. Colin is gone. He is gone he is gone he is gone.

There were no words. There are no words. And even these words have become cliché in the script of grief.

Here is the truth: Where Colin had been, there was now nothing. No. Not nothing. There was a wallet stuffed with bloody money, an engagement ring, a leather bomber jacket that smelled just like him, his lucky fucking rock.

Grief is the gorilla, throwing shit against the glass.

I'M DOING THE THING where we write the space the beloved left behind without writing the beloved in life. Let me do Colin some small justice.

Colin loved guitars, girls, and dogs. He liked long walks, sleeping late, and fast cars. Loved to drive. Loved to get in the car, open the sunroof, and go. He was a California boy through and through—hated the rain, loved the sun, and enjoyed these clear preferences with no sense that life couldn't be perfect for as long as he was here living it. This seems like it would be annoying, right? But Colin's love of beauty and brightness lifted me up. He was a tease and a jokester. Six foot two with a mop of dark hair and chocolate brown eyes, he paused and looked toward the sun when he stepped outside, waiting for the tickle, and then the sneeze. I loved to rest with my head on his chest, listening to his heart beating. He would kiss me anywhere, in front of anyone. When we went out to eat, we sat on the same side of the booth so we could touch legs and hold hands under the table. My favorite drink that summer was a greyhound and he'd buy the grapefruit and squeeze the juice fresh, leaving a few sections in perfect wedges for me to find at the bottom of my glass, something to hold on my tongue.

What he didn't like was school—it wasn't for him. He'd dropped out of San Diego State to move north, closer to me, starting a job with a British dirigible company that was testing out airships in Washington and Oregon. This was how Richard Branson was spending some of his money in the late eighties. When asked, Colin would say he was a blimp babysitter. At the time of Colin's death, we'd known each other only a year. Some years pass and we barely notice. Other years break us down to our molecules. For me, and for Colin, 1989 was such a year.

IT WAS FALL 1988, my sophomore year at the University of Oregon, and my new best friend, Diane—a friend who is *still* my best friend—invited me to Thanksgiving with her family in San Rafael. We drove down from Oregon to California with her daughters, Haley and Courtney, sleeping in the back, and everyone was in bed when we arrived. So it wasn't until Thanksgiving morning that I first saw Colin—whom I'd heard about, but not considered, not really, as I'd never really considered death or dying or the hereafter.

Wearing cut-off jeans and a T-shirt, my bed-messed hair skewered in place with a pencil, I was ascending the spiral staircase, following the sound of voices and the smell of coffee, when I first saw him. *My god.* It doesn't seem possible that I truly remember the quality of light in this first picture of Colin, but I feel as if I do. Thanksgiving morning, late November, but we were in Northern California, in San Rafael, and later in the day we would take a hike with the dog across a sunny mountaintop, so maybe I'm not too far off when I tell you the light was golden, when I tell you that in my first vision of Colin he was gleaming. Almost too beautiful to be real. I remember what he was wearing, too: faded Levi's. Nothing else.

One flexed bronzed arm held Haley's squirming four-year-old body, all baby powder smell in soft pajamas, against his side. The long guitar-playing fingers of his other hand curled around a coffee mug. Here was everything I wanted from a morning, posed at the top of the stairs, waiting for me.

I can't speak to the love—like the golden light, that seems unfair to claim outright (although I'd like to do that and have it be true)—but the lust was immediate. Later, Colin and I would discuss how the attraction between us buzzed. Our lust made a *sound*. Maybe it was the element of surprise. Maybe it was two spinning spheres coming close enough to touch, locking in—a kind of Venn diagram of desire.

"Hi," I said, loading the word with more sex than I intended.

"Hi," he answered, bending his knees and lowering Haley's feet towards the solid ground without unlocking the grip of his eyes from mine. His eyelashes were long like a girl's, his hair so dark it was almost black, everything about him disheveled. Everything about him asking to be taken back to bed.

I swallowed and licked my lips. "I'm Jill," I said. Haley's swinging feet gained purchase and she trotted down the hall, toward kitchen noises and bacon. Colin and I were alone at the top of the stairs.

"I figured. I'm Colin."

"Yeah. I figured. Diane told me about you. Sort of."

"Yeah. Me too. I mean, she did too. Told me about you." He paused. "Sort of. Umm. Coffee?"

"That'd be great."

It was Thanksgiving Day 1988, only 8:30 a.m., and Colin and I were already feeling grateful. By midnight, Diane would hear a ruckus and think that somebody was spinning an unbalanced load in the washer. This wasn't like me, and it wasn't like Colin either, this shameless leap into the sheets, his bed made up on the floor of his mother's office and me in it, but we both seemed to know our time was set to expire, the sand in our hourglass running.

WHEN I MET COLIN, I was broken. While the simplest thing to say is that Colin saved me—and this is true—the older I get the more I can see how the rescue worked in both directions. When we first met, I may have been the one more obviously crushed by the sexual abuse of my childhood and the determined self-destruction that had followed me deep into my teenage years, but Colin himself was unmoored. He was looking for purpose, and for better or worse, he found that in me—a reason to quit smoking pot, a home base, a vision for the future. Babysitting those blimps, Colin stood on the ground holding the ropes, watching the sky. In a way, my very existence provided the same steadiness from the ground for him. Colin was the baby in a big family of seven kids, but he was a caretaker and a nurturer. He needed to be needed, and in this way, we came together and filled in the other's broken bits. The problem with this picture that we couldn't see then is that we didn't always feel *separate* the way two people need to be, coming together in love but also floating apart, catching some air. We merged. Who knows how long we could have lived like that? We never moved beyond that first stage of love, the one that never feels quite real, the one that feels floaty, dirigible-like. We were emotional airship testers and we'd risen up, alone and together, above the earth, floating in a layer of calm air where there were lots of long mornings in bed and car rides along the coast, wind in our hair, like lovers in a movie.

Our life together didn't feel completely real, and so, when it was gone, when *he* was gone, I had to wonder whether it had been. Real, I mean. Sometimes I still do. The universe never asked us to test the flexibility of our bond. The universe required something else.

Colin was crushed, disappeared, and I spent years trying to find the ground.

A MONTH OR SO after the accident, I left Diane and the girls to piece together their lives without the sounds of my keening and moved back in with my mom. She kept me alive—feeding and sheltering and loving me. In the beginning, when I was physically incapacitated by grief, she even bathed me. How do we shape the experience of grief? Is there any way to make grief less lonely? My mother tried. And then, before long, I must have understood I needed to leave. The same meticulous mother-care that had sustained me was starting to disable me. I didn't need to live for myself because she was doing it for me.

My mother tells me that taking me to the airport and watching me get on a plane to San Jose, Costa Rica, was one of the hardest things she has ever done. I can't remember how the plan came about, but somehow I bought a one-way ticket to San Jose to meet up with Colin's older brother, Sean, and Sean's river-guide girlfriend to backpack through Central America and Mexico, eventually making our way back up through California. Unbelievably, the girlfriend's brother had also died violently that fall. Murdered. We were ragged, a wreck. A wandering wound.

Who decided our grieving trio was a good idea? There's no way *I* came up with the plan, but why would they want me there with them? Two days after Colin had died, I'd gone to the University of Oregon's campus for the last time, visiting the health center first—where they shot me in the ass with a sedative and gave me some pills—and then I must have been calm enough for my mother to walk me across the street to the small office of a kind woman with a soft voice who did some kind of magic to withdraw me from all my classes and refund my tuition, sending me on my way with the message that the school would be there when I was once again ready. Two months later, at the beginning of January, I was in no way ready. I was still spending my afternoons on the floors of Eugene bookstores, suspended in melancholy clouds of sandalwood and the bending notes of a sitar, flipping pages in the most woo-woo metaphysical texts I could find in search of some kind of portal to the spirit world—and Colin. If I managed to shower and eat on any given day of that dark winter, I was doing great. So there's no way Central America was my idea.

On the dark day of my departure, my mother followed me as far as she could—which, back then, was past check-in, through security, and all the way to the mouth of the gangway. How fragile I must have looked to her, a twenty-year-old daughter, numb and glassy-eyed with grief, reeling, made small again by this new knowledge of death. How much like her baby tottering toward the edge of the stairs, a cliff. My mother tells me now that she wanted to hold onto me. She wanted to hold onto me—or go with me.

But she said nothing. Instead, she helped me hoist my backpack onto my bent shoulders and checked the straps on the rolled sleeping sheet she'd sewn to protect me from dirty beds. Then she let me go. She cradled her leather pocketbook and watched me stumble down the gangway. I turned at the bottom and blew her a kiss. *Bye Mom bye.*

During a time when I didn't have the capacity to carry my own fear, my mother loved me enough not to give me hers to hold instead, choosing what I needed over what she needed. What she needed was to hold onto me, keeping me close and alive, no matter the cost—but what she did was let me go.

I have tried to take this lesson into my life as a mother, a responsibility that feels many lifetimes away from the broken girl I was at the bottom of that gangway, blowing kisses to my mom, heartbroken and terrified, not knowing whether I would ever come back to her. Did I reach up to touch the side of the plane as I moved through the door, the way I do now, for luck? No. I'm sure not. I wasn't looking for luck.

AFTER COLIN WAS DEAD, I prayed to be pregnant. I prayed to have made something, some*one*, together, with our bodies, before he was gone. I told myself then I would have carried the pregnancy, birthed our baby, raised that child with the love and help of Colin's mom and dad, brothers and sisters. The scenario was not beyond imagining. No matter the precautions, wherever there is heterosexual sex, there is always a chance of pregnancy, wanted or not. Before I was twenty-one, I might have been a mother. By the time I met Mark, I would have had a ten-year-old kid, but of course that kid would have changed the trajectory of my life in ways we can't see from here looking back. I would have never met Mark. The kids sleeping in this house right now would have been unmade.

I knew pregnancy was a possibility, and in my reeling mind I told myself I would absolutely carry and keep the baby we'd made together. Statistically, most of us aren't killed on the way across town to pick up pizza after work. The very fact that Colin had died in that way made anything feel possible. The power of probability to either comfort or terrorize was diminished for me. Until the thing happened, anything could happen. Minute to minute we don't know what the next minute will bring.

In my mind I was *sure* I would have kept that baby, but now, of course, I understand I have no way of really knowing what I would have done because a couple of weeks after Colin died, my period came. My circumstances required me to make no choice. I cried and cried, the death of another possibility, one I carried only in my mind. There was never a pregnancy. I am telling you a specific story about my grief (so young, so sure) and my strange wish, but also I am telling you something bigger, a story I have in common with every other person with a womb on this planet—and regrettably, ridiculously, a fair number of people without a womb who therefore have zero grounds for speculation regarding a choice they're so certain they would make regarding a pregnancy they will never carry. At age twenty, my limbs numbed by the shock of Colin's death, I was flailing for something solid the way a drowning person will grab onto anything, even another drowning person, to keep from going under, to somehow stay in the air, lips burbling the surface. Here is what I thought: *If I am pregnant, I will not have an abortion. I will carry this baby. I will keep this baby.*

For years, I believed this. I could believe this still. But it doesn't matter, does it? There was no pregnancy; therefore, there was no decision. Both question and answer are moot.

Moot.

Moot, the word, once defined a female debater (isn't *that* interesting?), and in the legal arena, a purely hypothetical argument. But also: a moat, that dangerous barrier of water with which we protect our castles, the best of which are filled with snapping crocodiles. And molt. The shedding of skin or hair to make space for the new.

Here is another statement, also ridiculous: *If I am pregnant, I will have an abortion.*

Why do we pretend we know? We do not know, we cannot know, unless we are, in fact, carrying a pregnancy in a particular time with every factor and set of circumstances that precise moment holds. An imagined choice is not a choice. A theoretical choice is a thought experiment, nothing more. The choice has to be a real choice, and then the decision needs to result in one or the other: an abortion or not an abortion.

During the same month I was wishing the blood away, Diane had the opposite experience. In a fling with a guy whose name and face I remember, but whose personality I do not, Diane peed on a stick and found out she was pregnant. This was just weeks after Colin died. I don't think we know whether the sex that landed her in this condition happened before or after Colin's death—in that reckless time before or in that time right after when she was trying to feel something, even for a moment, that wasn't horror and sadness. Regarding the abortion, Diane never expressed any hesitation. Nothing about her life or circumstances said it was time to have a baby—and furthermore, she said, she wasn't going to have that man's baby. She said some other choice things I won't repeat here. In that time, at that place, Diane's choice was abortion. Both her marriage and her brother were dead. She had two little girls to raise already in this world and a degree to finish so she could get a job that would give them the life she wanted for them. She was broke. Diane decided to end the pregnancy, found a clinic, pulled together the money, and had the abortion. She made an actual choice.

3   Long Prairie Road and Highway 101

I haven't told you how Colin died.

The accident happened at a crossroads in Tillamook, a small town on the coast of Oregon most famous for cheddar cheese. Colin was staying in Tillamook during the week to work. How was I to know when I let him go on that final Monday morning that this tiny, wet city would be so prone to burning?

What's notable about Tillamook historically is also the thing that brought Colin and his workmates, all young men, to the dark crossroads where they died that night: During World War II, the Navy built the two largest free-standing wooden structures in the world in Tillamook, hangars massive enough to play six games of football simultaneously—in each one. On that soggy day in November, Colin and his friends had been in one of those giant hangars preparing a Virgin lightship for the next day's planned inflation. The blimps were a pet project of British entrepreneur Richard Branson, extreme adventurer and would-be knight. I don't blame Branson for what happened to Colin—I mean, maybe I do a little bit—but whenever I hear about his high-risk attempts in balloons or speedboats or spaceships, I think: *Sir Richard, were the brakes good on that company van? Was your guy okay to drive? Did you leave some men behind on life's grand adventure?*

Colin has been dead longer than he was alive, I am easily old enough to be mother to the young man he was when he died, and the scope of that perspective looks to me like a cavernous, wood-framed building, a wonder of engineering and the last structure Colin ever stood in, a space big enough to fly a jet plane through. Three young men died that night, two British and one American—Colin—and a second American survived, diminished. I wonder now if they felt small in that looming, covered air, or whether the sense of sheer enormity—I remember Colin stretching his long arms, fingers up and open, as if he were trying to carry a cloud, trying to explain to me the size, the *hugeness*—made these young men feel bigger, more invincible, as they climbed into the minivan, not bothering with seatbelts, and headed down the road for a pizza.

Before I was a mother, I never thought about this detail of the tragedy, but now? It makes me so sad to know they died hungry.

COLIN WAS IN THE BACKSEAT of the white Chrysler company van when they were broadsided by a tow truck going highway speed. It seems that the driver of Colin's van failed to obey the stop sign, failed to yield in any way, and drove into the path of the truck without a flicker of a brake light.

In tragedy and grief, how many ways can we say *why*? We scream, we whisper, we moan. We beg, we question, we accuse. The same word, a million times. *Why?* How did it happen? When someone we love dies, there are always more questions than answers. *Why* didn't the driver brake? Was he checking traffic in the wrong direction because he was British? But then, crossing a two-lane highway, wouldn't it be necessary to look both ways? Were the brakes faulty in some way the investigators missed? Did he smash down the pedal and get only mush? Or maybe the truck startled him and in his urgency he missed the pedal? Or, the worst, was he playing chicken with the tow truck? With a vanload of twenty-something young men as his audience, did he think he could make it to the other side before the truck got to them? Did his bravado outweigh caution? If he had made it, if the tow truck driver had laid on his horn and glared at the stupid boys in the white van as it flashed away into the darkness, if Colin had turned his head on his neck, one arm thrown casually over the back of the bench seat, to look back and say, "Man, you idiot, that was a close one," maybe even in an admiring way, and then turned back to the front, laughed with his three friends, that would have been that: a moment forgotten, never mentioned, nothing.

But that's not what happened. The other thing of an infinite number of options happened. Colin's head was crushed. They wouldn't let me see his body. When I insisted, they told me that, the thing they were going to protect me from—"unviewable," they said. The driver and the man sitting beside him both died. There was one survivor, another young man, this one from Michigan but also engaged to be married. He was sitting next to Colin and he lived. Sometimes I think about this man and the woman he'd planned to make his wife, and I wonder if their lives took a path resembling the one they'd envisioned before that night. I doubt it. His name is Chris. Before Colin died, we'd met on several occasions, but he never contacted me after the accident and I've never reached out to him either. What would I say that would mean anything? What would I ask that wouldn't be cruel?

Before the accident, before it was too late, I don't remember being afraid of Colin dying. I don't remember being cognizant of such an accident being *the worst thing*, but then the van was flattened, and not far from that place where he got down on his knees, Colin died. Colin was dead.

Our beginning was also our end, the middle squeezed to almost nothing. "Life doesn't come with plot," I remind my memoir-writing students.

I was twenty years old and I needed to begin again.

4 I Can't Make You Love Me

Time is playing her old trick with narrative. Somehow I have never done this math, but I realize now that when my young poet walked into that seminar I was auditing on the sprung novel with visiting writer John Keeble in fall 1998, exactly ten years has passed since Colin and I had met on that spiraling staircase in California. So much time and distance. Those ten years had been another lifetime. I'd navigated three, three-year romantic relationships in those ten years and moved from a Psychology lab in Oregon to a writing workshop in Alabama. I wasn't unhappy and I was never lonely, but I was still searching for the way I wanted to begin the next story.

In the decade of my twenties, why didn't I simply let myself be *alone* for a couple years? Just as our relationship to freedom and safety for our children has changed radically in recent decades, so has our relationship to *relationships*. I lived my twenties in the nineties—the first five years in Eugene, Oregon, all flannel and DiFranco and ultimate frisbee, and the second half in Tuscaloosa, Alabama, where my mind was being blown by pretty much everything—from Faulkner and cheese grits to feminist theory and all things race. I had never lived anywhere with more than a handful of Black people and now my white neighbors were flying a Confederate flag and calling me, and I (almost) quote: an N-word-"lovin' Yankee bitch" across the low fence dividing our fire-ant-infested yellowing lawns. Amid all this stuff going on in my head, I was living in a body that was very interested in being a body in communion with other bodies.

These were the days before dating apps and selfies, before social media and profiles. I lived out the decade of my twenties in the nineties, and in those days we walked into spaces with other people—classrooms, farmers' markets, ultimate frisbee fields, bars and shows and warehouse after-parties—in a kind of simmering stew of pheromones and sexual attraction. I don't know how to describe it. There was a lot of eye contact. Much of it was, just as I'm sure it is today, gross and dangerous, and some of it was kind of sparkly and great. We didn't have cell phones. We exchanged landline numbers and you either wrote all the digits down in the right order or you didn't. You either lost the scrap of paper he tore off the fridge at the house party to write his name on or you didn't. Sometimes there was a number you really did want to call, but then you found a wad of paper in the back pocket of your favorite jeans, well-laundered and now no bigger than a spit ball, and that was that. Waiters wrote their numbers on checks. The guys in the band would pass their numbers down from the stage—you suspected they had some written out before the show, a kind of boy-in-the-band business card. In all these cases, the chance that you'd never see that person again was high. And that felt okay.

I have never been young and looking for love in the digital age, so I can't speak to whatever joy might come of swiping right, but I *can* describe the tactile experience of nascent romance in the eighties and nineties. We didn't have the phrase then, but lordy, the FOMO was peak. If you weren't there, you weren't there. You missed it. Unlike today, you didn't know *what* you were missing—at the party or on the hike or at the lake—but staying home always felt like a risk, the possibility of a missed opportunity.

The flirting was my favorite part. First there was the eye contact. Sometimes something touching, fingers on a bar, a not-so-accidental bump, hipbones wedging through a party, a firm hand on the back of your hand to steady the lighter, your faces inches apart, illuminated by the tiny flame at the tip of your cigarette—crackle, ember, inhale, exhale. And then there was the exchange of telephone numbers, not with tiny, sleek computers pulled out of our pockets, but with whatever paper and writing implement you could scrounge, a common goal that threw the two of you into a shared activity from the beginning. The matchbook cover is cliché for a reason, but also, of course, receipts, the bottom of an English paper, a bookmark, even a corner of a page in a book. If that book was something good—say, *The Death of Ivan Ilych* or *Frankenstein*, all the better.

Or sometimes the first connection would be all eye contact and no speaking. This sort of thing usually happened if you were hanging out in a coffee shop writing or stopping by the mainstage to dance for a bit at the Saturday Market—a few days later, in the free weekly *What's Happening*, there was a "missed connection" section wherein the besotted could perform some gentle stalking, which seems way creepier now than it did then. For example: *Java House. Tues morning. You, writing at the corner table, auburn hair shining like a penny. Me, a shaggy blond, tongue-tied at the counter. Your eyes blue, mine green. Call me?* And then they'd put their actual number. A landline, of course.

In this dating pool, I was—I suppose—what might be considered successful. I had some demons, to be sure, but I was shining a light on them. I had long brown hair and blue eyes with a golden corona around the pupil. I was ridiculously fit from running and endless crunches and teaching a class called power aerobics. I was also outdoorsy, a child of hippies and artists, who'd spent time in a marijuana-growing community, riding a horse named Moona to a one-room schoolhouse. So my backstory was excellent. I was just enough tragic. Smart, but conditioned to behave in a way that wasn't threatening. A little shy, but in the right crowd with just the right amount of liquid relaxer, I made people laugh. Also, I have always been a pretty *nice* person, and kindness can sometimes be misread as attraction.

I never knew whether the guys who pursued me were interested in me or sex with me, and I never reached a level I'd call comfortable with that, but what I'm saying is that I never had trouble getting a date. Being, and staying, alone would have required a level of self-possession I did not possess. Even after Colin's love and death had pulled me, miraculously, out of the most destructive version of the self-hatred stewed into my blood, bones, and flesh during my preteen years in that smoky garage, I had not found what felt to me like the wisdom to believe that someone loved me for *me* and not for my body. Loved me for something more than my usefulness to them as an object of desire.

NOW THAT I'M MIDDLE-AGED, I understand something new: It wasn't that I was too wounded to feel loved for all of me, for who I was; the fact is—and I am sorry to say this because of what it says about the state of our world and the unrelenting insistence of the fucking patriarchy—that my value to most men was indeed my sexuality. But here's what I now know for sure: Not being loved for *me* didn't mean there was something wrong with *me*, that I needed to continue to make myself sexier or more beautiful or less threatening. Nope. Men did love me for sex; when they loved me *only* because of the sex, it was not because of some fundamental flaw in me or my character or my intelligence, but because of some fundamental flaw in *them*. Young people, hear this, in all things sex and love: Don't ask yourself *What's wrong with me?* . . . Ask yourself *What's wrong with them?* And then adjust your relationships accordingly.

A lifetime ago, on a sunny Saturday afternoon in Eugene, a long-haired, bearded employee in a garden store pretty much dissolved when I, dirt smudged and sun kissed, wearing only a sports bra under my overalls, laid the pitchfork I wanted to buy on the counter. He cracked and asked me for my number right there at the cash register. I smiled, shook my head—ridiculously, I never wanted to hurt anyone's feelings—and told him, honestly, that I was in a relationship. This guy I remember specifically because he looked so crushed and desperate. *You don't even know me*, I remember thinking. *You don't even know me. You're . . . ridiculous. Also? Fuck you. I just came in here for a pitchfork. Don't make me use it.*

IN THE DECADE after Colin died, the decade of my twenties, in the nineties, I tried to be alone. I thought being alone would be good for me, getting to know myself for myself with no one else there to hold up a mirror of their own design—and I'm sure it's true. But I rarely stayed that way for long. After Colin, I filled my life, as safely as I could, with a series of monogamous relationships, the gaps in between well-mortared. My first post-Colin boyfriend claimed I wouldn't leave a relationship until I had the next one waiting in the wings. He wasn't wrong.

After Colin, I wonder, was I afraid of being alone? Or of something else entirely?

Three seemed to be my magic number. Beginning when I was fourteen years old, I had my first three-year relationship, a partnership so strange and inappropriate I may give the story of post-abuse teenage sexuality its own book. After that, I remained single for one tumultuous, dangerous year—my first year of college, the year I was eighteen. Then I got together with Colin: one year. Then not quite a year of solitary grieving. Then a series of three three-year relationships in the nine years between 1990 and 1999. Then my husband—and that has been that.

How normal is this pattern? This rarely alone? An early marriage would result in the same dynamic: a move from the family house to the marriage house with no freedom in between. A 2022 Pew

Research Center study found that over that 34 percent of young adult women and 63 percent of men were not in committed relationships. That's wild to me. All those single people!

I am well past the middle of my life. I never learned how to be alone.

AFTER COLIN DIED, during the time I was traveling with my ragged trio in Central America, my body transformed, putting on twenty pounds or so, mostly in avocado weight. When I'd met Colin, I'd been living as a hardcore bulimic for over six years—all of my teen years. Treatment programs hadn't worked, talk therapy hadn't worked, medication with what was then a brand-new antidepressant—Prozac—hadn't worked. I had basically accepted that my eating disorder would eventually kill me, and this seemed to me like fair payment in exchange for the sense of control my disease purported to offer me over both my mind and body.

Colin disagreed. He wanted me alive in this world. In the months before his death, Colin was doing everything he could do to help me heal with an urgency that seemed eerily prescient after the accident. Together, we'd revisited the trauma of my childhood sexual abuse. It was clear to both of us that my eating disorder—bulimarexia—was a symptom of that bedrock violation, something we needed to cure from the ground up, and my healing did feel like a team effort, his and mine.

Colin made me feel safe, safer than I'd ever felt, and from this place of safety I could visit the darkest places in my brain and return to the light to tell about it. It was exhausting labor and Colin was always there to hold me and listen. Until he wasn't.

While Colin was alive, I made progress. I was still throwing up, but not every day, and certainly not the six to eight times a day I was purging before we'd met.

But after Colin's death? I was cured. I'm not exaggerating. I wish this were an overnight treatment I could offer to other sufferers, but such a cure requires a rewiring of the brain. Such a cure requires a shift of seismic proportions.

In the days right after the accident, I didn't think about food or puking. I didn't think about the size of my body or the sharpness of my bones. Numb to the world, I simply existed. I somehow managed not to die, neither feeling nor not feeling. But then one night, a couple weeks into this first winter of grief, I lay in a cooling bath, watching my hands and toes floating above the surface of the remaining scrim of bubbles like pale human flotsam, thinking, *Huh, if I wanted, I don't right now, but if I wanted, I could send a message from my brain to my hand and lift up one of those fingers.* In other words, I noticed I was living in a body.

I'd vomited a lot since the accident—from shock and trauma, nobody tells you about that part of loss—but not on purpose. Now, a couple weeks in, I was starting to eat again, and with eating came that old urge to rid myself of whatever I had swallowed, to be fully empty. But on that night, as the thought (*maybe you should vomit*) came into my quiet head, Colin came in right after. *I don't even have a body*, he said, among other things, but that was the argument that found purchase in my broken brain. *I don't even have a body.* The spirit of Colin—was it really him I heard? Or some manifestation of him I created because I knew him so well? Had I, in fact, *swallowed* him?—achieved in less than a minute what over six years of secret suffering and a year of outpatient eating-disorder therapy and a failed experiment with medication had failed to do: get me to understand that living in a body that basically worked was a gift not to be fucked up by self-harm. I needed to take care of myself, not-there Colin explained. Protecting the body I was so lucky to have was now on me. Frankly, he seemed a little annoyed. *I don't even have a body.*

And then? Just like that? I did what Colin wanted. I didn't make myself throw up that night—or ever again. I simply stopped.

From here in the timeline, I can see the miracle.

AT THE BEGINNING of the summer of 1990, with my visa counting down the days, I returned from Central America, washing up on the banks of the Rogue River in southern Oregon and taking a job as a cook at a kayak school. I did not know how to cook, not really, but I excel at following written instructions, and that turned out to be all I needed to make the kind of lasagnas (fresh pasta!), baked salmon, and cookie bars that hungry kayak students gobbled up after a day on the water. My signature uniform was Patagonia quick-dry shorts and a sports bra with an apron. It was *hot* in that kitchen.

I was curvy again, tanned, and very, very sad. I set up my tent down below the river house, put down an old rug, rolled out a futon, made a tiny bookshelf with two cement blocks and a board. I ran an orange extension cord down from the main house, so I had power for a lamp, a fan, and a boom box on which I played an endless rotation of the handful of CDs I'd brought with me: Tracy Chapman's self-titled first album, Indigo Girls self-titled first album, Ani DiFranco's self-titled album, Sinéad O'Connor's *I Do Not Want What I Haven't Got*, Tom Petty's *Full Moon Fever*, Sarah MacLachlan's *Touch*, Paul Simon's *Graceland*, Bonnie Raitt's *Nick of Time*, Prince's *Purple Rain*, 10,000 Maniacs' *In My Tribe*, Melissa Etheridge's *Brave and Crazy*, and Michelle Shocked's *Short Sharp Shocked*. I'm guessing I still know every word of every song on every album—and it bugs me when I hear a song on Spotify because I want the next song to be the right song in the right order. If you know those albums, I'm guessing you have an absurdly clear picture of me and that time in my life. What's that the kids say these days? If you know, you know. Part of my lore.

My romance with S began in that kitchen when he brought me a tiny bouquet of wildflowers and osprey feathers and moved, probably too quickly, to my tent. Colin had been gone for only eight months. I wasn't ready, not really, but I wanted to feel something other than sad, and so we began. Somehow we kept it going for three years. S was a kayaker and a potter. He took me out onto the water, teaching me how to do a combat roll, and into the woods where we pitched tents on the rims of alpine lakes. He insisted we get a dog, and together we chose Tango, a wrinkled Ridgeback puppy with ears like crushed velvet, the canine love of my life, the best girl. All of which is to say—where S is involved, I have no regrets, and we might have made a more permanent match, but we were so young, feeling our way through sexuality, vocation, and geography in the kind of hydraulic swirl you might find on the downriver side of a big boulder at high water.

Also, S *needed* to be alone. He required freedom to a point young Jill considered pathological. If, say, I wanted to make a couple's date with friends the next night at a brewery, S would shrug: Maybe he'd be there, maybe not. How could he possibly know twenty-four hours in advance? Refusing to make plans that might bind him to a particular course, S sparked impulsivity like a live wire in a storm. If snowfalls or creeks rose to levels that sent regular people running for their houses, S would get a gleam in his eyes and take off with his skis or his kayak to throw his body over ridges or off waterfalls. Surfing the knife-edge of death made S feel alive.

Risk is what S *needed*—and this I could not bear. I could not let that happen again. I could not receive another predawn call and I wanted to live inside the illusion that I had control over that. S had come into my life—blond, curly-haired, lithe—like some kind of water sprite bearing flowers to the river-house kitchen. He lived in a perpetual state of desire—always seeking the next thing, whether it be a challenge, a feeling, or simply something beautiful he'd never seen before. This is not, at its most fundamental level, a bad thing, and I loved S, but our timing was terrible. S felt Colin like a ghost between us in our bed—those were his words exactly. He worried I would always be saving my best and truest love for a dead man—perfect, adored, unchanging—and this tension ripped us apart.

When S left, moving alone to a teepee in the woods, Tango stayed with me.

Always, always keep the dog.

WITHIN A COUPLE OF WEEKS, I let T, the Brit from work with whom I'd been shamelessly flirting, spend the night. In this brief affair, I was badly behaved. First, he was a doctoral student and I was his supervisor in the psychology lab at the university. To be clear, I'd just graduated with a BA, and T was both older than me *and* male, so at the time I didn't recognize my abuse of power, but my overstep became clear when I broke off the relationship after a month or so and the poor guy packed up his face-recognition experiments and left town. Working near me was too painful, he told our shared mentor. I was ashamed.

Why had I let it happen? *How* had I let it happen? Email was brand new. Social media wasn't yet a thing. T's carefully composed messages gave me a tiny shot of dopamine when they popped open on my screen. How distracted he'd been by my neck or thigh or hair during our morning lab meeting, the places he wanted to take me, what he would do to me if we were ever alone. T used words like "pudding," "jumper," "biscuit," and "boot" to describe none of those things as I had known them previously, and the novelty of this, ridiculously, charmed me. T adored me—fiercely, irrationally, completely—in just the way I needed at a time when S was pretty much done with me. What did I even want?

One night T rode his bicycle to my house, and fine, S was gone, so I let T go down on me. Well. That was nice, so I let him spend the night. I let him watch me while I slept and run his hands over the soft curve of my waist and hips as if I were some kind of sculpture. A tenderness I found almost annoying. I can't remember touching him, only the feeling of his hands on me. I let him make coffee in the kitchen I had shared with S and bring it to me in bed—and then I made him leave. More than anything, I was exercising my power. Unluckily, this was the morning S had decided to come by the house early to pick up some of his things. He saw T's bike chained to the porch railing of the little house we had shared, over the patch of dirt where our scarlet runner beans had grown up the previous summer, stretching ever closer to the sun. S had left *me* but here I'd invited another man into our bed within weeks, or maybe even days. I honestly can't remember.

Then, when T pedaled home, after a night away with me, he found his cat, left outside for the night, dead in the road.

Everything was terrible. Everybody was sad.

COLIN'S SISTER, Diane, my BFF, proposed I throw a tequila party in my little house to cheer myself up. My mom invited a young friend of hers who worked at the natural foods store where she was a cashier. She thought he was cute—but *not for you*, she'd later clarify, protectively. *I never thought he was good for YOU.*

Surely T must have been there too? In any case, so it began, a flirtation with green-eyed M who was wrong for me in every way a man can be wrong for a woman except physically. I have no excuse for myself. Or maybe I do. From thirty years in the future, I want to do some psychoanalysis on the twenty-three-year-old woman I was: My life up to this point hadn't offered me a lot of opportunity to have senseless fun and nothing about M made sense. M pulled me into his charismatic orbit with a sleight of hand. Literally.

He carried a Zippo in the front pocket of his jeans and the way he reached into his jeans, pulling it out and holding the warm metal in his long fingers, flicking open the top with a deft rotation of his wrist. We met in 1993. His favorite movie was *Reservoir Dogs*, and while it should have been a warning bell for me that he found inspiration in depraved killers—cinematic or otherwise—I was taken in by his lighter tricks. M could do the Mr. White thing, flicking open the lighter and then rotating the wheel with a finger snap, the flame rising like magic—hot and ready.

I can report this worked on me.

M was a tall, handsome, slithering snake in the grass, somehow standing upright and moving through the world on meticulously shod feet. He didn't like to be barefoot and was the worst kind of vegetarian: the morally superior sort in the presence of whom good dogs cowered. And yet, and yet, based on those nimble fingers and his skill with a lighter, I guess? I let him move into my little house, and then—how had I not learned my lesson in those two years?—when it was time to leave for graduate school, I took him with me in a Ryder truck all the way across the country from Oregon to Alabama.

Again: Was this more fear? Was I that afraid of being alone? Did I think—with me—he would change and become, you know, a completely different person? Can you imagine how Colin must have been rolling in his grave? My point is this: Sometimes, in sex and in love, we make some strange decisions. I puzzle over those miserable years with M: I mean, how could the sea change that was Colin's death cure me of my eating disorder—like really, and permanently—but still allow me to undervalue myself *and my dog* to the point of being with M? Friends, in the house we rented in Tuscaloosa, he had a media room where he'd watch Tarantino movies in a seemingly endless rotation, the sounds of gunfire reverberating off the walls of a room Tango was not allowed to enter. A room that was, and I quote, "a no-dog zone."

Y'all, he wasn't *nice*. Tango would sometimes hide behind me to get away from him.

Watch the dog. The dog knows.

He was not my people. And yet there I was, having sex with him with more frequency than we did anything else, buying myself multiple weekly lottery tickets for a pregnancy neither of us wanted. Actually, I don't really know how M felt about fatherhood. We didn't talk much. I was not then, nor was I ever, a fertility risk taker, but whenever we engage in any activity that brings a viable sperm into the vicinity of a viable egg, we're rolling one of those fancy D&D dice with an impossible number of sides, no matter what he tells you right before he puts it in. Every invisible-to-the-naked-eye sperm is a teeny tiny possibility. I dry swallowed a single pill popped from the round blister pack with meticulous regularity before I brushed my teeth each night, and while this method never failed, as I think about abortion across my life span, I play a mind experiment: What if I'd gotten pregnant with M? Okay, gross. But seriously. What? I have no answer. I want to pretend I have an answer. I would have had the baby and raised the child alone!—on a grad-student stipend, thousands of miles away from any family. Or I would have hurried to the nearest clinic and ended the pregnancy immediately, without a word to M. Or I would have accepted the miracle of this baby who made it past my careful BCP popping to build a real relationship with M who must have had more depth than I'm giving him credit for, right?

I can't even pretend to imagine, honestly, and it doesn't matter: I never got pregnant. There was no decision. It isn't real.

Fortunately for me, M made the dissolution of our relationship easy—if by "easy" I mean treacherous and dirty, but also completely unignorable. During our first winter together in Alabama, M started sneaking around with the assistant cook at the natural foods café he managed, and after nine months in Alabama and exactly three years of us, he headed back west in an old beater he bought for that purpose, a fucking Vanagon.

I'm ashamed to tell you I was heartbroken. Jesus. I'm embarrassed for myself. He left me alone in the three-bedroom house we'd rented too far away from the campus (so he would be close to the café) on a lot with a chain-link fence and red ant hills as high as my waist. I shit you not. During the breakup we'd sit out on the cement stairs at the back of the house, shoulder to shoulder, smoking American Spirits he'd light with his fucking Zippo and watching Tango tiptoe around the ant hills, while M lied and lied and lied.

Until the end, M pinned his departure on Alabama and the humidity, never fessing up to his infidelity.

He was not terribly smart.

I Googled him just now and got just two hits. It would appear he's a fifty-six-year-old CrossFit instructor in Oregon.

SO THERE I WAS: twenty-six-years old, a mere pup, alone with my beautiful hound dog in Ala-friggin-bama. Regular M has moved out and a guy from my MFA program begins courting me, parking his car outside my rented house in that residential neighborhood and coming in with a six-pack of beer and a rented movie. Our first date. I have no memory of the movie—perhaps because we never watched it. Things got weird mighty quick.

We're going to be forced to call this guy Frank because his real name also begins with an M, and that's too many Ms. Also, I've already referenced them, but I need to say more about my neighbors on Springbrook Circle—an elderly couple and their adult son Tut Hodo. Now I'm using real names because I can't resist and because the story I'm going to tell you is one hundred percent true. Living next to the Hodos burned images, both visual and auditory, into my brain that I can never erase, most of which became material for bad poems destined for the trash bin because I had no earthly idea how to handle the material they offered up from across the chain-link fence. The senior Hodo beat Mrs. Hodo regularly. I know this because I would hear the yelling, screaming, and crashing. Sometimes I would call the police. Sometimes someone else would. Nothing ever came of these calls. I never saw Mr. Hodo led away in handcuffs or anything like that. Once, I met Mrs. Hodo by the fence while she was taking out the Styrofoam tray from fresh chicken parts, and while we stood talking over the waist-high chain-link fence that separated our driveways, she explained that Mr. Hodo didn't mean nothing by it and she hoped they weren't bothering me. The white tray cracked in her fidgeting hands, leaking and streaking her sinewy forearms with thin, red chicken blood. This is the image of Mrs. Hodo I carry to this day. A couple of months later she was dead. Cancer, they said.

By the end of my first year in Tuscaloosa, Mrs. Hodo and M were both gone. So it must have been a weekend night in early September when Frank pulled his car in behind mine in the driveway and came inside. Apparently, Tut thought it was too soon for me to be taking new gentlemen callers. Apparently, Tut believed *he* should be my next boyfriend.

Note for the record that Tut and I had never spoken a word. Not even hello.

Frank and I had settled onto the couch, but we hadn't even finished our first beers when we heard Tut in the front yard, bellowing like an animal. I hurried to both doors, front and back, checking the locks. What the hell was happening? At first, we couldn't make out the words. Was he even using words? I turned off the lights in the living room and Frank and I crouched on either side of the front window, peeking out through the crack. Tut was drunk, that was clear. Really drunk. By now it was completely dark, so it was hard to see what exactly was happening.

In memory, what unfolded next took a long time, hours, but logically that doesn't make sense. Tut wasn't alone out there in my yard and he was wielding a wooden bat, swinging it around and screaming, we were finally able to make out, threats. Not at me. At Frank. He was calling Frank out for a fight. The phrase "motherfucking pussy"—but slurred and in a deep southern accent—was the general theme of Tut's discourse. You will not be surprised to learn that Frank did *not* join Tut in the front yard.

Tut wanted Frank to join him in the yard. Tut wanted—seemingly—to beat the shit out of Frank with that bat. Frank's failure to appear drove Tut deeper into his rage. Tut jumped up on the hood of Frank's car. Again, it was really dark, and we were crouched on the floor peeking through the tiniest of cracks, so all of this happened in shadow. It was so creepy and weird, it was hard to hang onto reality. For me, at least. I mean, this is my *life*? I could feel my mind sneaking backward out of my body. Somebody had to *do* something. I fought to hang on, to stay present in the dark smashing screaming.

And then Tut thought of a new strategy. He would wail on Frank's car with the bat until Frank came out to try to stop the damage, to save the car. Again, not Frank's first choice. Instead, Frank crawled over to the phone and called 911. Tut's rage seemed to be growing. I checked all the locks again. The dispatcher said she would send out a car. And when the cops arrived, Tut jumped down off Frank's car. He talked to the police, we heard laughter, and then we saw Tut and his crowd move back over to his side of the fence. No arrests. The police came to the door, I opened it, and they were still smiling like there was some joke we couldn't understand. There was nothing to be afraid of, they assured me. Tut was just having a little fun.

That was the first night I spent with Frank. After the police left without taking a report, he was too afraid to walk out to his car. Weird that I can't remember the make and model of that car, something a little strange—a Volkswagen Dasher? It was an older model, silver, and after Tut, the front end was pretty dinged up.

In retrospect, ours was an inauspicious beginning.

THE NEXT AFTERNOON, when I pulled into my driveway in the bright, hot light of the Alabama afternoon, Tut ran out the door of his house. That day, I had bought a fresh canister of pepper spray for moments just like this one and I kept one hand on the handle of the car door and thrust the other down into my bag, wrapping my fingers around the trigger. Then I froze. I couldn't move. I couldn't speak. Tut ran to the fence and wrapped his fingers around the top of the chain link. His eyes darted back and forth like two scared dogs behind a fence.

We stayed like that for a minute.

Now that he had me outside, and so close, was Tut deciding on the best way to kill me? The girl next door his father had called a N-word-"lovin' Yankee bitch" when he found out I was teaching writing at the University of Alabama?

No. No, it turns out, he was not. Not yet anyway.

Tut wanted to apologize.

"Sorry about last night," he began.

I stayed frozen.

Tut continued. "Do you want to be my girlfriend?"

I did not, in fact, want to be Tut Hodo's girlfriend, but neither did I want to say that out loud and clearly in that moment at the chain-link fence. My fingers uncurled and curled again around the pepper spray canister. I was a rabbit. I was a rabbit, frozen under the hedgerow while the dogs sniffed the edges.

Did I shake my head? Did my eyes grow wide? I didn't move.

"Aww, c'mon," Tut said. "You ain't mad at me, are you?"

My memory stops here. Later, in retelling, this was everybody's favorite part. *You ain't mad at me, are you?* The story ended here because I couldn't remember what happened next, or how I unfroze. I can't remember if I said yes or no or are you out of your fucking mind? I had already found a roommate and we'd rented a house way over on the other side of town, just on the edge of campus. The next morning, a small crew of helpers—not including Frank—showed up to help me load the U-Haul I then drove across the city in a winding fashion, stopping and turning and looping around, just in case I was being followed.

You know the strangely comforting advice about running in a zigzag if you're being chased by a crocodile? So the croc can't gain the advantage of straight-line momentum? At age twenty-six, I'd lived in this world long enough to know for certain I didn't want to leave a clear trail.

I didn't want Tut to find me.

WHEN I CONSIDER my serial monogamy years, I wonder if consecutive relationships are a series of frantic compensations for whatever came before. Let's stay with the crocodile trope but put the crocs in a more safely contained area of our imaginations—and give them names. So. Finding a romantic relationship I wanted to live inside during my twenties was like trying to balance on a wire over a moat thrashing with crocodiles with names like Loneliness and Inadequacy or Undeserving of Love and Daddy Issues. Arms out to the side, oop! A little this way and then a little this way. Steady on now.

Frank was—and is, I presume—a Yale-educated fiction writer. His mastery of grammar and syntax was superb. Of the three surviving three-year boyfriends, I'd vote Frank most likely to read this book and never reach out to tell me about it—which, for the record, is the good and right thing to do. So, hello, Frank. After the emotional tyranny of M, Frank felt safe and good. Frank was thoughtful and kind. Frank made lattes and brought them to me in bed. Frank did the Sunday *New York Times* crossword with alarming efficiency.

Frank was never going to hurt me, so what did I do? I hurt him. Remember, I was balancing on that beam. Then, three more years on the calendar, and nearing the end of my twenties, it felt like time to either marry Frank or move on.

I did that terrible thing we do. I told him the thing: *I love you but I'm not* in *love with you*. Which was true, and no doubt incredibly painful to hear. This was something I knew clearly by my midtwenties. To quote Bonnie Raitt from one of those albums I played on repeat in the river house the summer after Colin died: *You can't make your heart feel something it won't*. Here is a true thing: You can't make someone love you. Neither can you make yourself love someone. You do or you don't. As we've established, Frank was no fool. He knew a tautology when it was standing in front of him, so again, he did the right thing. He left without a fuss. After three years together, he made one last visit to my front porch with a box of my things—toothbrush, underwear, ice cream maker—and I traded him for a box of his things, and that was that. I never heard from Frank again. Our break was the cleanest I've ever known.

5   Tongue and Groove

After Frank? Well. There was a brief flurry of indecision and excitement. I knew Mark: He was that hot guy in the literature class I was auditing. Children of mine, if you're reading this, flip forward a few pages. What I'm going to say next might gross you out. Nobody wants to hear the story of their own conception.

The timing is a little fuzzy. Frank and I split up a couple weeks before the holidays, in the waning weeks of 1998. I remember this because I had a Christmas party at the big house I rented with another grad school classmate. We served eggnog and cookies like real grown-ups. Mark was having a party that same night, hosted with his girlfriend in their house just up the road. Our party started earlier, so folks came to us first and then moved on over to Mark and his girlfriend's house. None of that is particularly interesting except for the part where Mark showed up at *our* party, even though there was much to do at his house in preparing for *their* party—which must have been exceedingly annoying to the girlfriend in question during a time, I now understand, when much of what Mark did or didn't do sparked her ire. Anyway, Mark showed up, and he stood on my big front porch in a black leather jacket and Levi's, leaning against a pillar with a Marlboro in one hand and glass of well-spiked eggnog in the other, and let me tell you, he was smoking. Also, he was a poet and he had come in on a schmancy fellowship that released him from any teaching in his first year. So he was a hot, smart poet with time to read big novels, and he couldn't stay long, he explained, but he wanted to make sure I was planning to come up to his place when things wrapped up at my place.

Which is exactly what I did. There was much flirting. At one point, some idiot let their dogs out of the room they were closed into for safety and Mark's girlfriend was pissed—which, again, I understand. It was a little scary, but also the first time I got a good look at Walt, all shaggy eyebrows and wolfhound heft. Again I want to claim love at first sight, because, my god, I would come to love that good boy with all my heart.

But also, since I had already broken up with Frank, I'd dipped my toe back into the dating pool—urr, the moat—almost immediately, and I'm not proud of this, but I was already sleeping with a *different* guy from our MFA program, an Arkansan lawyer-turned-fiction-writer with whom I had possibly nothing in common beyond our love of a good party, wit, good humor, and comparative attractiveness. We were operating under the I-look-good-you-look-good-lets-f&*# philosophy of hookups, and since our meetings were clandestine—executed under cover of darkness and completed before the sun rose on another Tuscaloosa winter morning—nobody knew except the two of us. This complete secrecy was not my idea—although perhaps it should have been. The sneak clause was all Arkansas, and young people out there, if you should ever be in any kind of relationship wherein the other party wants to keep said relationship secret? Be wary. Be very wary. In our case, however, we were playing out that Bob Seger classic. I used him, he used me, and neither one cared.

Still, I wonder. *Why* did he want to keep me a secret? Could there have been any reason that wasn't ugly or, at best, yucky? Here's a life tip that can be broadly applied to all manner of situations that make us sad, insecure, afraid, or perpetually pissed off: When someone in any kind of relationship behaves poorly and defends that poor behavior by waving the "it's complicated" flag? It's rarely complicated. Nine times out of ten, it's ridiculously simple, but as I said, in this case? We were working on those night moves. Simple.

And now? My whole lucky life points outward from our shared duplicity because if Mark had believed me to be with Arkansas, well, he might have set his sights elsewhere when he and Walt moved out and got their own bachelor pad. The story is a long one, and this is not the first time I've told it, so I'll cut to the chase—like, the actual chase. Tell it fresh.

LATER THAT SPRING, there were more parties. Another one at my house. This time, it was a disco party. The invitation, photocopied zine-style onto quarter sheets of paper, featured the iconic Charlie's Angels photo, skintight pants, guns raised, but my roommate and I replaced the Angels' faces with ours—Melissa's, mine, and Tango's. In those days, this alteration involved scissors and glue. This time, we served Jell-O shots and deviled eggs on borrowed deviled egg plates. Melissa and I both wore fabulous bell-bottomed pantsuits, and the stereo blasted the Bee Gees and Donna Summer, ABBA and Gloria Gaynor. If it's possible to sing "I Will Survive" with *too* much enthusiasm, I did it that night. I did not plan to crumble. I would *not* lay down and die.

Our friend Don had come dressed as Evil Knievel, and at one point someone got the foolish idea to build a ramp, set it on fire, lay out some party guests in the road as obstacles, and have Knievel jump his souped-up, beribboned bicycle over the whole flaming, drunken mess. Naturally, everyone involved was injured, but none seriously. I found some bandages in the medicine cabinet and passed them around. Arkansas squeezed himself into an extra pantsuit we'd bought at the Goodwill. Mark stuck with his standard uniform of Levi's and a white T-shirt. He smelled *amazing*. Somewhere there's a Polaroid that included Knievel, Arkansas, Mark, and a few others. I hope I find it someday because I remember looking at the photo and thinking: *Here, among these men and boys, there is one obvious choice.*

I'd like to see that photo with my middle-aged eyes. Maybe one day it will emerge from a box in the back of the attic closets we've jointly owned now for over two decades. Isn't the passing of time a *trip*?

At the end of the evening, which was also the wee hours of the morning, I stepped out onto the porch to say good night to Mark and he said, "You should probably give me a call sometime." As if the future were written. As if he knew I would. Arkansas had snuck into my room where he was passed out in my bed, still wearing the jumpsuit. Honestly, it wasn't the best look.

"Yeah," I said, smiling and touching the shoulder of that leather jacket. What was that *smell*? Leather, smoke, cold air, and this Markness. "Yeah, I probably should."

HERE AGAIN, the timeline gets a little fuzzy, but not long after the disco party, maybe two weeks at the most, there was another party at the house of an assistant professor in literature who had become my friend almost immediately upon moving into the house next door to ours. The previous fall, Libbie had seen me out in the garden, picking the last of my tomatoes, and, she later reported, ran inside to tell her husband that there was a pretty girl in the back, *outside*, wearing only overalls and a *bra*. I mean, it was a sports bra, but yeah, accurate.

This next party was a post-reading reception for visiting poet Gerald Stern, and thus it was considerably more sophisticated. Nary a Jell-O shot. This matters because I used the occasion as an excuse to bake cheese straws with scratch-made puff pastry. Sparing you the literal days I spent rolling, folding, and nurturing that buttery dough as if I were the mother and she my dough baby, I will simply report that the resulting straws were light and crispy, the

Parmigiano-Reggiano divine. When I lay my golden twists against the sloping walls of a wooden bowl, the result was magnificent.

I was proud.

I was standing right there—alone? why would I have been alone?—when Arkansas approached the food table. He made a greedy grab for one of my twists and shoved it into his mouth as a dog would a bone. And then, imagine my horror when he coughed and spit the giant bite into his palm, crying, "Da-amn! I thought that was gonna be a *bread stick*!"

I was still standing in stunned silence, contemplating the end of our clandestine whatever it was—a bread stick, dude? a fucking bread stick?!—when Mark approached the table, filling the space Arkansas had vacated when he left to find a trash can. Although there were platters of veggies and dips and tiny sausages, Mark, too, reached first for my cheese twists, bringing it to his lips much more slowly, breathing in the aroma, taking a small bite (more like a discerning food critic than a hungry dog). "Mmmm," he said, chewing and swallowing completely before opening his mouth to say, "Wow. Someone made puff pastry. Did *you*?"

Imagine my pleasure.

THE FINAL STEP in our coming together involved margaritas and darts, something our crew did every Tuesday night, and again, I can't pinpoint exactly how many days after Gerald Stern this Tuesday rolled around, but I know it wasn't more than a week or two. I was single and Mark was single and I knew this was a window that wouldn't be open for long. On the night in question, there was talk of Britney Spears and Gwen Stefani that hasn't, frankly, aged well, as Britney has gotten so much cooler since the nineties, and Gwen? Well. Not so much. In any case, suffice to say that despite the heat, smoke, and tequila, the choice between Mark and Arkansas became clear that night. There was, well, no doubt. That night, Mark and I moved our bodies near to each other at every opportunity. Our force was magnetic. When we stood side by side at the bar waiting for our drinks, our hips touched. On the bar, Mark tapped his credit card gently, waiting to start a tab, pay for our drinks, and he let his pinkie float over and touch mine. When I pulled out a cigarette, he reached into his jacket for a lighter and I nodded. Hips, hands, eyes. When I came within a certain number of feet from Mark, a switch flipped in my body. My pelvis pulsed with his nearness. I wanted to swallow him.

For me, Arkansas disappeared—but unfortunately, Arkansas didn't notice his own disappearance, and after last call, as the barkeep started hitting lights and showing us the door, Arkansas, who thought he was being sneaky, asked loudly if I could give him a lift home, and walked to the passenger side of my Honda. Fuck.

Mark lived only a few blocks from the bar. He didn't need a ride home, but at the moment Arkansas was settling himself into my car, he'd been walking toward me, and even in the multicolored glow of the beer signs, I saw the shock, and then the disappointment in his eyes. Mark doesn't miss a lot. I wanted to start explaining, "Oh no! No, no, no, no. This isn't what you think! I mean, yeah, it is what you think, or it *was* what you're thinking, but it's nothing, less than nothing. Arkansas! Get out of my car! Mark, get in. Please, get in. I want to take you home with me. I want *you*."

Despite the tequila and the darkness, everything was so *clear* to me. But also, everything was such a mess. I didn't want to start this next thing from the ashes of a stinking dumpster fire.

"Goodnight," I called to Mark with as much subtext as I could squeeze into two syllables. For the first time that night, he didn't meet my eyes. He said goodnight politely and headed down the road. I stood by my car, with Arkansas inside, and lit my own last cigarette. Well shit.

Pulling into the lot behind Arkansas's apartment, I turned off the ignition and told him, clearly and gently, that whatever it was we'd been doing, we wouldn't be doing that anymore. I wanted to give it a shot with Mark. Arkansas didn't seem to care one way or another. He'd done something similar with me a couple weeks before, a temporary breaking off of our purely sexual relationship. I remember this non-breakup breakup only because as I walked to the door of his apartment that morning, he'd followed me and said, with regret in his voice, "You do have really nice lips." As if the only thing he'd miss about me was my lips? Or as if my lips were my only truly distinguishing feature against the backdrop of a pretty regular everything else? Arkansas could be like that. Anyway, on this, our last night, I kissed him chastely on the cheek with my excellent lips and he got out of the car.

I considered driving directly to Mark's apartment, but Tango was at my house and needed to be let out to pee. And if what I was feeling with Mark was at all real, it would wait until morning.

NINE IN THE MORNING seemed like the right time to call. Banker's hours. Rising as we were from the smoky, beery mire of margarita night, the pursuit of fresh possibility and a lifetime of passion, joy, and commitment was no doubt a lot to ask. "Can I come over?" I asked. "I want to talk to you."

Mark sounded wary. "Okay," he said. "Come on over."

He lived in a crappy apartment in a crappy part of town. As I climbed the water-stained, stinking stairs, my heart sped ahead of me. Did I know I was climbing the stairs to the rest of my life? I think I did. I really do. Mark opened the door, led me through the living room and galley kitchen in about four steps, and out onto a worn, gray deck jutting out over the overgrown, postage-stamp yard. The concrete walls were lost in a tangle of kudzu and the insect drone buzzed like a live wire. "I'm sorry," I said. "I didn't know what to do." Then I told him why I was there at 9:00 a.m. on a Wednesday like some sort of crazy person—but not as crazy as a 2:00 a.m. crazy person—but of course he already knew. And he forgave me for the night before. He understood. Marriage is an arrangement of perpetual forgiveness and we began the cycle that morning.

At about 4:00 p.m. that first day, as we sat on the dingy gray carpet (there was not yet a couch) nearing the end of the world's worst first-date movie, *American History X*, Mark leaned closer and closer, occluding Ed Norton and his swastika tattoo, and said, finally, "I think I'm going to have to kiss you now."

I didn't leave for three days.

A FEW WEEKS LATER, we lay together on his twin mattress like naked spoons under a sheet and Mark said in my ear: *Would you like me to say a poem for you?*

Yes.

Since feeling is first, he began, stroking my naked hip with his warm fingers—my skin, his skin, the soft sheet—and I thought... no, I didn't think. I simply was there, fully present, in Mark's bed, our giant dogs on their respective beds, also loving each other from their first day, and I was wholly happy. I didn't think: This is too soon, this will not last, this cannot be real. I listened to Mark saying the poem, cummings, my body an instrument to this happiness, filled. In the warm curve of my neck, the tiniest hairs there blown by the breath of his words, he finished

> *lady i swear by all flowers. Don't cry*
> *—the best gesture of my brain is less than*
> *your eyelids' flutter which says*
>
> *we are for each other; then*
> *laugh, leaning back in my arms*
> *for life's not a paragraph*
>
> *And death i think is no parenthesis*

I LOVE that our origin story has poetry. I mean, yes, tequila and cigarettes—but also poetry.

HOW MANY YEARS had it taken me to get it right? And with my truckload of trauma bound with a tarp and strapped down with duct tape, could Mark and I make it through the landscape of fears we now navigated together?

A couple months after I told Arkansas we were done with our Tuesday night trysts, he caught me in a dark hallway by the bathrooms in the bar where we all went to play pool. Tall and olive-skinned, he was downright swarthy, especially when he wore a particular white shirt that made him look a bit like a pirate, and even more so when he was in one of his bearded phases—a good look for him as he wasn't in possession of the strongest of chins. I can't remember whether he was with or without beard on this night, but I can say it wouldn't have made a difference.

"So," he said, shifting his hips toward me the way tipsy people do in dark hallways by bathrooms in bars. "So, I've been thinking, maybe we could try again? I'm ready to give it another shot."

I almost laughed out loud. Such confidence. *I'm ready to give it another shot.* At this point, Mark and I had been dating a couple of months. We were crazy in love. The Arkansan pirate and I would not be trying again. How he'd failed to note this transition I wasn't sure. "Umm," I said as gently as I knew how, shifting my own hips back and away. "It's too late. Mark and I are . . . a thing."

"Right," he said. "Right." He smiled down at me, just a bit sadly, beaten but not bitter. Apparently he *had* noticed what was going on, but on that night he felt good, his daring stoked by clanking bottles of beer, the satisfying knock of the cue ball against its target, and the delicious, descending thunk of the ball into the corner pocket. Or maybe he figured any shot was a good shot. He trailed his eyes down my body, and up again, lingering on my lips and then settling at last on my eyes. Clearing his throat with a noise as soft as the felt on the table, he said finally, "Okay then. Good good. You and Mark. You two are like tongue and groove. Tongue and groove."

"Tongue" and "groove," both, are sexy words, but I don't think our friend meant anything dirty, even if his intentions were rarely pure. He was talking in lumber, finding his metaphor in joinery.

When I made my way back to the pool table, I could see we had entered one of those late nights when Mark's eyes took on a mischievous sparkle of light, and nothing short of last call would push him away from the games and the drinks and the fun. He liked it when I stayed these final few hours, but he understood when I made the choice for sleep. Still understands when I make the choice for sleep. That night, he walked me out to my car, kissed me long and hard—tongue, groove, tongue, groove—and I drove home thinking about what our friend had said.

My mother had used tongue and groove on the floors and walls of the mountain house she designed and built with her own hands, lining up edges like a puzzle and pressing them into place without nails or glue. Laid properly, the wood's natural shrinkage would bind the joints together to make a sturdy floor—a foundation, I thought, hands carefully at ten and two on the wheel, on which a family of children could take their earliest steps.

The year Mark and I started dating, I was twenty-nine, just finishing my first book—*in a world like this, can I really have a baby?*—and actively, unashamedly scouting out a father for those unborn children. "Tongue and groove," I said aloud into the dark, a lick and a kiss of a phrase, and I said it a few times into the warm, spring Alabama air, tasting the magnolia blossoms, so sweet and fresh. "Tongue and groove."

I didn't think we needed to go male/female like with plumbing or electrical parts. Maybe I would be the tongue and Mark would be my groove. Maybe we could switch off. Maybe we were coming closer to making that safe family I wanted.

6   Feminist Fury
An Interlude

I need to interrupt this love story to say some things about reproductive rights, the endless ways men exercise the power granted them by the patriarchy while women are denied basic bodily autonomy—and my rage. We could start at the Miami Baby Hospital in August 1969 where my mother, attended by a team of male doctors, is incapacitated by the birth cocktail they called Twilight Sleep. She misses everything. Later, we're living on an island in Massachusetts, and my mother—supported by neither my absent father nor any kind of social services that would have provided childcare she could afford—works long hours as a waitress at a bar on the mainland. A predatory neighbor, a teenager when it all begins, sees I am vulnerable. The sexual abuse continues for nearly six years, until I am twelve, I get my period, and I am made brave by my terror of pregnancy.

Think of the twelve-year-olds you know. Now think of a twelve-year-old who hasn't felt like a kid in years, a twelve-year-old who knows it's on her to make sure she doesn't become a thirteen-year-old mother because what does she know of abortion? And what would that pregnancy reveal about her? That she is a slut. That's what. She can't let that happen.

So she threatens the neighbor boy, who at six years her senior is now a nineteen-year-old man. She will tell her mother, she whispers through a crack in the locked door. She will tell and he will be *arrested*. This last part she has only just learned from a girl at school who was telling a story about her cousin, so she tries saying it out loud. It works. The neighbor boy has enjoyed taking her body risk-free, using her body to get off whenever he wanted to get off, but she isn't worth this kind of trouble. Statutory rape is not a charge he wants any part of.

This might not seem like the happy part of this story about the girl who was me, but listen to what I am saying: In desperation, I mustered all my courage, and instead of receiving *his* threats, I threatened *him*. And my threat worked. When I fought, I won. Please don't hear this as victim blaming.

Over four decades have passed since I was that girl, and the world has given me ample opportunities to continue fighting back. I am safe now, or saf*er*, and I can let the memory of my preadolescent years sink under the surface of the water like a free diver plunging down alongside her rope, enough air sipped into her damaged lungs to keep swimming for four minutes if she's lucky, and if she's not? If she goes too deep into the sea's darkness and thus doesn't return to air soon enough?

Well. Maybe that's too dramatic a metaphor.

Maybe my memory of carrying on a full-on sexual relationship *as a child* is more like Virginia Woolf, her pockets full of rocks, making the well-considered choice to walk into the river and be done with the pain.

I tried to push the pain under by submerging memory, but we all know repression doesn't work forever. Holding onto secrets makes us vulnerable, and there is always someone waiting to exploit that vulnerability. This is one of the ways the patriarchy does its work. The patriarchy teaches us to capitulate, smooth over, hide. Most damaging, the patriarchy teaches us to stay silent. The patriarchy discourages real healing because healed humans want bodily autonomy. Healed humans want their power back. Wounded, hiding humans are easier to manipulate. When we're at our most vulnerable, there's usually someone waiting to use our subterranean pain to get what they want out of you. Above ground.

For me, that someone is my high school boyfriend, a guy who is already out of school when we start dating. I am fourteen and this boyfriend is nearly six years older, but ours is a relationship I choose—not a secret—consensual if such a thing is possible within the context of our age difference (spoiler: it's not). He works at the lumber mill and has his own apartment, a black metal lunchbox, a soft-top Jeep he loves—wax on, wax off. Let's call him J. During our time together, I don't ever doubt that J loves me. If he didn't love me, why would he cry when he confesses that he fucked my friend in that very Jeep while I was off visiting my father in the summer? He was drunk, he told me, sobbing, so drunk. He didn't know what he was doing. Again and again, J professes his love for me. He buys me gifts—a Black Hills gold heart flopped sideways on a slippery chain, a Gund stuffed rhinoceros he names Horny, all the California Coolers a girl can drink.

On Fridays, when he can clock out early from the mill, he's waiting for me outside the high school, leaning against the gleaming Jeep, holding a bouquet of grocery store flowers. This doesn't feel like a John Hughesian cinematic romantic gesture to me, even in the moment; even at sixteen, I recognize J's performance as the equivalent of spraying my backpack with urine. I don't know how to talk to him about this, but I do begin to recognize the value of my body in the marketplace called life in rural Washington state. I flirt with what feels like a growing power. I practice cruelty with J. "Don't bring me carnations," I tell him, tossing the hideous fake pink things into the back of the Jeep with a crinkle of cellophane that sounds like a burst of flame. "They're like fake flowers. They remind me of cheerleaders. I want sunflowers, or red roses."

Again and again, we have sex—in the Jeep, of course, but also on the waterbed in his apartment, on the couch in his apartment, on the weight bench in his apartment basement, even in the woods on the way to my grandfather's funeral—and the only thing I can remember is the way my hand got stuck between the rubber bladder and the wooden frame of the waterbed or the stick that scraped my back in the woods. I remember worrying that my uncle Mark would notice my bleeding back at the funeral, that he would smell the sex on me. Uncle Mark would know, I believed, why we were late to the funeral. I don't remember anything else. It's wild what the brain can do to protect us.

Everyone thinks I will marry him, J, this boy-man I've been dating for three whole years by the time I graduate from high school, but I know I won't. I always know I won't. I'm getting out of this hick town and going to college and no way am I taking him with me. No way in hell.

When my mom and my grandmother have to sell our house and move away a few months before I'm finished with school and my summer job running a camp for preschoolers in the town park, we all decide the best solution is for me to move in with J. I'm already enrolled at the University of Oregon, so this temporary cohabitation plan feels okay enough, until the first night I spend in his cramped, skunky house in the shadow of the Safeway: He wakes me up at dark-thirty and tells me I need to get up, make him biscuits and gravy, and pack a lunch for him. I think this is a joke. I laugh and roll toward the wall to go back to sleep. *Pack your lunch?! No way.* J doesn't find my refusal funny. He tells me this is part of the deal: If I'm living under his roof, there are rules to follow. I don't give in, but his rage scares me. Without eating breakfast, J leaves for the mill, the wheels of his Jeep spinning furiously in the gravel outside the bedroom window. I get up, pack up the single cardboard box I'd brought in the night before, and head to the park for morning circle with my preschoolers. *Little Bunny Foo Foo went hopping through the forest . . .* At lunchtime, with nowhere else to go, I drive to the place that's most familiar to me—my high school.

Grace herself is waiting to receive me in the form of my English teacher, Miss Chase. She listens to my story and looks at me with level-headed clarity. She seems neither surprised nor alarmed by what I consider to be a humiliating reluctant child-bride story. From her, on that afternoon, I feel no judgment. "Well," she says when I finish telling her about the empty lunchbox and the spinning tires. "I have a spare room. Come live with me."

"What?"

"It's nothing fancy, but it has a bed and a closet." She says this casually, as if the invitation is nothing to her, as if she takes in wayward teenagers all the time.

"Really?"

"Sure," she says. "Of course." Miss Chase doesn't make it into some big, dramatic moment. She has a spare room. She isn't using it, and I can live there for the summer until I head off to college. No rent. No strings. No big deal.

This kindness alters the course of my life.

What Miss Chase gives me that afternoon in the summer of 1987 is the capacity to consent—or to withhold my consent. She gives me the gift of choice. By providing a safe, secure, no-strings-attached place to live, she offers me safety, and with this security, the power of true consent. Before Miss Chase opens the door to her home, the option to get out, I can't say no to J. Not really. I need what he has to offer me, so I can *only* say yes. Yes to everything. Yes to sex, yes to silence, yes to obedience. But that afternoon, she hands me an actual key, and with that key, the option of *no*—and my god, do I ever run with it.

I AM SEVENTEEN when I drive alone along the banks of the mighty Columbia, heading south when I get near the coast and landing on the University of Oregon's campus in Eugene. I have never driven on a freeway before, but I don't have a choice, so that's what I do. There's a first time for everything. I buckle up, grip the wheel, and pay close attention. I am afraid, of course, but I also feel powerful.

Here I go. I am leaving. I am driving down the freeway to the rest of my life.

YOU, KIND READER, have no doubt already recognized the alarming parallel, but I am in my forties before it fully dawns on me that J was exactly the age of my abuser. This late-coming recognition takes my breath away.

Also, acting mostly alone, I escaped. Twice.

Now I try so hard to see dangerous patterns. I am ever vigilant. Trust me when I tell you: My amygdala is on the job.

7 Testing Begets Testing

Individual experience matters. For every human who came into this world with a basket of eggs to drop one by one or two by two month by month in a bloody river, the past matters. For every human who has stood upon the bank of that dry bed, waiting for the flow, and then, searching for answers in the drought, has made her way to the CVS on the corner—or, you know, the Walgreens directly across the street from that CVS—and selected a pink box or maybe a blue box from the dizzying array of pastel choices in the aisle with the tampons and pads and adult diapers because y'all are making some kind of mess up in here—because she needed to know: pregnant or not pregnant? The past matters.

For all of us who test, there is the life that came before—perhaps only barely recalled—and the life we can see or maybe only hope for stretching out in front of us, and in both directions are infinite possibilities of roads both taken and turned away from, so many possibilities and questions the mind is set to spinning, but this I know for sure: For each of us, the answer we get from that stick will mean something totally different.

For each of us, so much has gone down. For each of us, before that moment when we find our perch on a toilet, peeling the stick from its foil pouch, flexing our toes to elevate our knees and make as much room between our legs as possible so that when we aim our stream, our stick-holding hand gets only a small spray as we pee on the wick, counting *one Mississippi, two Mississippi, three*

Mississippi . . . thinking *shouldn't the guys with the actual nozzles be the ones to get pregnant?!*

Before this moment, so much has gone down. As the Indigo Girls point out in "Ghost": even the mighty Mississippi starts as a trickle. Roll up your pants and walk right across.

Sing it, sisters.

Four Mississippi, five Mississippi.

Yes or no?

One line or two?

Hold it up to the light.

Shit.

Are you sure?

FOUR YEARS AFTER our first date, Mark and I are not sure, not *totally* sure, but we've both graduated and rounded the bend on thirty, (miraculously) we're both employed, so we decide we want to have a baby, and oh baby, this baby's conception is the conception of dreams, right out of a storybook: February 2003, Valentine's Day, sushi and champagne. All of which is to say, in my personal ob-gyn journey, it was a simpler time. A time of innocence. If you're the kid in question, no story of conception is a pretty one, but from a mother's perspective, hers was the golden ring grabbed from the edge of the merry-go-round.

After cooling off with fresh ginger and champagne and heating up with the scalp-tingling wasabi and a warm bath, bubbles and all, the details are softened by steam and suds, but if there was lubricant, it was no doubt the wrong kind, the sperm-killing kind. If I stayed on my back afterward, it was because I wanted to be there. Maybe there was pillow talk. If we were interrupted in our shenanigans, it was by the cold nose of a big dog.

Actually, it might have been that day, or the day after. I wasn't really keeping track. There were no basal thermometers, no pinpointing graphs in the ovulation software, no "secondary" signs—

the stretching mucus, the ferning saliva, and the rest of it. Maybe I'd been tuned into my mittelschmerz, but that would have been because I've always loved the word for that tiny, sharp, ovulatory cramp, German for "middle pain."

Fifteen days later, although I wasn't even counting back then, on the day *after* I missed my period, I got up in the morning and read the directions on the home pregnancy test I'd gotten at the drugstore the day before. There was only one test in the box, which seemed exactly right to me. At the store, I'd seen tests that came in packs of two, and I'd thought, *Huh. That's weird. Why would I pay more for two tests?* My reasoning was this: I'm either pregnant or I'm not. So I peed on the stick in the dim light of the early morning bathroom, and as my urine seeped cheerfully into the testing window, two equally dark blue lines appeared on the stick in the shape of a cross. There was no waiting. I unfolded the directions, and sure enough: two lines = pregnant. I grinned and carried my pee stick back to the warm bed, kissed Mark on the ear, and said, "Good morning, Daddy."

His eyes popped open. Wide open. "Really?" he said, and then he smiled and kissed me back, warm with sleep. That afternoon we got on a plane to Baltimore, for a writing conference where I was going to get to read to a big audience from my first book, packing my prenatal vitamins and our secret along with us.

I was thirty-three years old and that's how I thought conception worked. I thought it was that simple. For heteros such as myself—*First, find a father*—you waited until you wanted a baby, getting your life together in all the ways you could manage to pull it together, stopped the diligent precautions (for me, seventeen years on the pill), and then: You had sex, got pregnant, grew a large belly (just the belly, as round and cute as a Halloween pumpkin), and had a healthy baby. Just like that.

I can't even remember being afraid, for once. It's a good story, but now I shake my head. What was that? Denial? Foolishness? *Hopefulness?*

Sometimes, is it better to just not know?

IN THE BEGINNING, in utero, Mark and I called our first baby "Filbert," or "Fil" for short.

I was thirty-three when Fil was conceived, oh-so-prettily, but I soon learned that in the ob-gyn universe, the maternal age that mattered—the one in the chart, circled in red—was my age at delivery. With my own birthday in August, and my baby's slated for waning October, I was thirty-four to the men with the speculums and Dopplers. Although I hadn't yet heard the phrase "geriatric mother"—that was still coming—I learned this essential obstetrical rule from the friendly nurse practitioner who did my intake appointment at the most highly recommended group practice in my newly adopted small Midwestern city.

The doctors I would be seeing for the next seven and a half months were all men (prior to this moment, I'd never spread my legs for any gynecologist with a Y-chromosome), but on this first day I didn't meet any of them. The nice nurse asked me some simple questions about diet (vegetarian) and vitamins (yes), drinking (not now) and drugs (of course not! what could you be *thinking*?!), and she taught me how to use the plastic dial-a-baby chart. Turns out, I was seven weeks along. Bonus! I would have said five weeks, but what I learned just that day—despite my minor in women's and gender studies from the University of Oregon—is that we pregnant folks get to start the count from the last menstrual period, and so I was two weeks pregnant before we even had sex. What a magical world. I don't mean to rain into the baby shower here, and I suspect I'm talking to the wrong crowd, but I'd like to propose to the states who have or are trying to implement a six-week abortion ban that they add this tidbit to their required sex education course, and you know, maybe send any voters who missed this day in school a special memo: By the time you recognize you've missed a period—rather than just being a little late as part of the totally normal vicissitudes of living in a female body—test, confirm pregnancy, and find a provider within driving (or busing? *walking?*) distance, it will be too late. The window is too small.

But back in 2003 I wasn't thinking about any of this, and there's a part of me that's grateful that I lived the first thirty years of my life in relative ignorance, measuring other women's pregnancies in months, not weeks—and starting at the sex. But after my first obstetrical appointment, I was hip to the week-by-week countdown.

Five years later, creeping through pregnancy number five, I would count in days—two hundred eighty for a full forty weeks—and the turning of the calendar pages in my head, so desperately slow, would click to the five beats of the word vi-a-bil-i-ty. I wonder if fear requires us to live in smaller and smaller increments. Does counting—those woolly, high-stepping sheep of our nighttime wakefulness—give us comfort? Do we perceive a greater measure of control in manageable slices? Day by day, hour by hour, kick by kick, we count and pray.

But I'm jumping ahead here, skipping time. For now I'm still an innocent. I believe that pregnancy equals baby, and I'm in a pretty green room explaining to this nice nurse how I crave spinach, pineapple, and juicy, seedless clementines, which I carry to my bed, tiny moons of comfort, one in each palm. I fill my sheets with scraps of their peels, tossed in with the cracker crumbs, a veritable hair shirt of food refuse, because on some days I can barely lift my head from the pillow. I am that sick. I am the kind of exhausted that makes me feel as if someone has poured molasses over my face.

The nurse tells me she has something that might help, and she smears some gel on my wrist and straps on a flashing bracelet. It zaps me, this personal, portable lightning bolt. I yelp, and then I get used to it. The idea is that the electrical impulses in the nerves of my wrist will interrupt the message to my brain that I am being attacked from within, that I really, really need to vomit. I can turn it up so high that my middle finger spasms with the force of the current. This is freaky. With this machine I can observe my body acting independently of my will, my own twitching finger flipping me the bird.

This is just the beginning. There is the nausea, yes, but I haven't yet touched the myriad other ways my body will turn against me in favor of my baby before all this is over. My baby is a glob of cells. She's the size and substance of something I could scrape out from under my fingernails and wipe off on the leg of my ever-tightening jeans, and already my body chooses her over me. The rest of me won't be far behind. I would lay down my life.

I dub the crazy thing "my Zapper" and I wear it everywhere for the next couple months. I still feel sick most of the time, but I vomit less. We schedule a long series of appointments, including the one for something called a triple screen, and that's that.

"Aren't you going to give me a pregnancy test?" I want to know.

"You're pregnant, aren't you?" she asks back.

"Well, yes..."

"Okay, then. I believe you." And she smiles and walks out the door.

AT THIS POINT I knew that for all practical purposes, I was thirty-four years old. Isn't "thirty-five" the magic number by which we measure and track our lives? Don't we all imagine that as long as we get all things gestational wrapped up by age thirty-five we'll be a-okay? Even in my after-Colin plan, my two beautiful children were conceived, gestated, and birthed safely before the clock struck midnight at age thirty-five. But here I was running down the stairs, skirts held up in my sweaty fists, slippers flying, the first chimes resounding in the midnight chill, imagining what could become of my fine carriage and eager horses before I could reach them.

I never meant to cut it so close. As I've said, despite a persistent lack of evidence that it does me any good, I've responded to this chaotic, dangerous world by trying to control it. I'm a planner. And in my plan I needed to finish school, publish a book, get healthy (physically, emotionally, and spiritually), land a job, buy a house, *and find a father*.

Early on—too early?—I chose well, got it right, but he died, leaving those children unconceived, unborn, forever imagined. After Colin, as we've already reviewed, there were other paternal possibilities, I suppose, but they were all wrong in one way or another having to do with too much or too little—smarts, responsibility, ambition, talent, heart, love, loyalty—not to mention willingness to procreate.

I was pregnant seven months into my first tenure-track job, married seven months before the birth of my first child. The numbers say plenty about my life, especially when I tell you that I may have made some mistakes, but there were no accidents.

Enter the decision to test unborn baby in the womb. I feared my lateness, my failed planning, the time lost to the frivolity of the ball with all that lovely dancing and drinking and whirling freedom. Oh silly, stupid me. What if I was left with nothing? I saw what could happen before I even made it out of sight of the castle, my sparkling carriage collapsing into an unkempt pile of pumpkin rind and unsprouted seeds, of scampering mice and lizards.

I thought the doctors were offering a glimpse at the end of the story, a page flip ahead to the happily ever after, no risk involved. Of course I got the triple screen. Hell, I got the *quad* screen. We were in it for the reassurance.

They weren't supposed to find anything.

By the eighth week, my pregnancy books told me, this little person, no bigger than an eyelash, had all her parts: brain in two hemispheres, heart with four chambers, fingers, toes, tightly sealed eyes. My own progesterone-flooded brain whirled around this fact like cells looping around the track of their centrifugal petri dish. *Hello in there, Baby. How's it going? Are you warm? And the food? Are you getting enough?*

ON THE DAY after that morning in May when the lab tech filled her white pocket with clicking vials of my blood, Mark and I hit the road for a cross-country drive from Indiana to Washington state. We'd rented an SUV and equipped it with a rubberized doggie ramp so that Tango and Walt—who were both now a sobering eleven years old—could take up a comfortable residence in the back without straining their hips with the jump. We loved those dogs like, well, children. My girl, Tango, was the smart one, a Rhodesian Ridgeback with attitude and wits to spare. (She was also a scaredy-cat, and easily chilled, preferring to sleep under a blanket.) Mark's boy, Walt, was the whiskered mutt who brought pure, foolish love into our lives. That good boy was all heart, tucking his giant head between my cheek and the door and blowing hot, hellfire breath in my face for thousands of miles. I turned up the Zapper, and played with the silky tips of his ears. With dogs that big, and that old, Mark and I had started to wrestle with their mortality, and we were bringing them along on this journey because my mother's place in Washington was doggie heaven on earth: forty acres of hills and aspens, deep grasses and Ponderosa pines, all of it fairly jumping with witless chipmunks and flag-tailed rabbits.

The only dark clouds on the South Dakotan horizon were those vials of blood I'd left behind. Where were they now? What did they know? How was the story going to end? I'd programmed the ob-gyn number into my cell phone, and by South Dakota we figured it was time for the test results to be in. I called and got a nurse who checked the file and reported that, no, there were no results, but when did I come in for the test? Oh, well, it should be at least two more days then.

"How'd she sound?" Mark wanted to know.

I didn't want to tell him, but I couldn't hold back. "Evasive," I said. I thought she sounded like she knew something she wasn't telling.

The next day we distracted ourselves by driving through Mount Rushmore, a side-trip down to see Crazy Horse in progress, and a stop for greasy burgers at a roadside stand in the middle of Wyoming nowhere. While Mark went for the burgers, I held down the SUV fort with the dogs, and watched a man pull up in a pickup truck with four children clinging to the flatbed. Okay, they weren't clinging, they were scrambling around like puppies, and they were all under seven, and of course I thought: *Outrageous! Criminal!* And as I waited for my burger, I watched. The driver—the father?—slammed his door, ordered the kids to stay put in the truck, and ambled toward the back of the shack.

Here were four seemingly perfect children: towheaded, lively, and smiling. Then I started making up stories to make myself feel better. These children had probably never been anywhere near a Snugride Graco infant seat (top-rated that year by Consumer Reports, I just happened to know). These children had probably not had their chromosomes tested prior to birth. Would a mother who would flout basic safety rules bother to keep track of her intake of essential Omega-3s and folic acid? Would she avoid the other vipers of pregnancy? Stinky cheeses, Jacuzzi soaks, and sushi? Maybe. Beer, cigarettes? I had no idea, but I was skeptical, and sitting smugly in my giant vehicle, addled by hormones, to my deep shame, I was only vaguely aware of the glare of my class consciousness through the nicely tinted windows. And I had *been* the kid in the back of the pickup truck. Those kids were *me*. Perhaps that was part of my problem.

Of course I knew nothing about these particular children or their mother (mothers?), really, except what I could observe from where I sat with my bare feet on the dashboard, peeking undetected through my dark window and making up stories: When the father (okay, the lanky man in the cowboy hat who was driving the truck) came out of the back of the hamburger shack, he was accompanied by a stout woman in a stained apron (maker of my much-desired burger? mother of these children?). She ruffled the hair of one, kissed a second, and shared a laugh with three and four, while the man in the hat handed out paper cups of soda (water? milk?) from a cardboard drink holder. As the woman waved goodbye, the truck went bumping out of the gravel lot with the children, two sitting with their backs to the cab, straws thrust into their mouths (dangerously near the soft tissue at the back of the throat?), one leaning on a wheel well, and the fourth (the oldest?) standing wide-legged in the middle of the truck bed like a California surfer as the truck spun the last of the gravel out of its wheels and picked up some speed on the country highway.

Holy shit.

Nevertheless, *those* children were alive. And when Mark came out with the burgers, I—the erstwhile vegetarian, fallen in the third month of pregnancy because of a fierce craving for steak—unwrapped the greasy paper, took a ravenous bite, and chewed as if I were feeding some kind of prenatal bloodlust. "Did you see them?" I asked Mark. "Those four kids? They were riding in the back of that truck. Geez!"

"Yup," he said. He was chewing too—the hamburgers were absurdly good. "That's the way they do it around here."

And I didn't know how to explain to him how comforted I felt. That if those four kids (all four of them!) could survive speeding down the highway with straws in their throats, then our baby should be okay too—the blood tests should come back and reassure us that everything looks good, the baby's going to be fine. It was only fair, right?

But I kept it to myself. He might have said *Well, honey, the world's not fair* (which is true), or *The world doesn't work that way* (which may also be true), and besides, he was enjoying his burger and I hadn't brought up the blood tests in over three hours. Couldn't I give the man a break? Before Mark met me, he was a person who believed in the basic premise that things he loved would live, and just a week before I'd spent too much time in the Walgreens a couple of blocks away from our house because I went astray in the lipstick aisle, torn between a wintery plum and a summery bronze, and when I emerged half an hour later, there he was on the corner with the dogs, looking for me, afraid he would find me and our unborn babe crushed in the street.

Crashing vehicles had been *my* species of fear, and already I had given it to Mark.

Fear, I have learned, is transferable.

A QUAD SCREEN is just that—a screen. Because it's not diagnostic, the results are used to make decisions regarding further testing, thus confirming my midwife friend of a friend's premise that *testing begets testing*. Knowing this, knowing the high rate of false positives, and having witnessed the way in which noninvasive screens can so quickly morph into invasive diagnostic tests, this woman who ushers babies into this world every day refused all testing: No ultrasounds, no bloodwork, no nothing. She chose against fear from the beginning. She and her partner decided to have faith in the odds. Can I tell you how much I wanted to be like her, even way back then? Can I tell you also how desperately far I was from that possibility?

A quad screen measures the level of four biochemical markers in the mother's blood: alpha-fetoprotein (AFP), human chorionic gonadotropin (hCG), unconjugated estriol (uE$_3$), and inhibin-A. Many, many factors can affect the levels of these four chemicals to varying degrees, but the two early on biggies are multiple fetuses and a misdated pregnancy. I'd already prepared myself mentally for some too-high results by honing my supposed gut-sense that I was carrying twins. After all, my body's production of enough placental material to accommodate *two* babies was the only rational explanation for a weight gain that was about four times what the books and doctors predict for the first trimester. (Note to pregnant women everywhere: The books and doctors are wrong on this point. Many, many, many women I've talked to tell me that they too gained the most weight in the first trimester, despite the fact that one of *my* doctors looked down at my chart and then up at me and said snidely, "You know, it's not unusual for mommies in their first trimester to actually *lose* a few pounds." The man was looking at my chart. He could *see* I'd gained seventeen pounds by week fifteen, despite a meager diet of crackers and clementines. *Screw you, buddy*, I thought maturely. *And I'm not your fucking mommy*.)

Two days after we arrived in Washington, I called again and got yet another nurse who said she'd check my file and see if the results had come in.

"Everything looks fine," she said casually when she returned to the phone.

"Fine?" I asked. "What does that mean, 'fine'? Fine, fine?" (Go ahead and say "fine" three times. How quickly it loses meaning.)

"Everything looks fine," she repeated, sounding annoyed. She must get this a lot, mustn't she? "All of your numbers are in the normal range."

"Okay," I said, relenting. "Great. Okay. Thank you very much."

I hung up. Four pregnancies later, in another lifetime, I would demand the numbers. I would already know what defined "normal range" in each case, and exactly where my numbers fell, but three months into my first pregnancy, the abbreviated report of the overworked nurse was enough for me.

"Hooray!" I shouted, kissing my husband and hugging my mother. "Hooray! Fil's okay! If I could, I'd drink to that!" I felt unreasonably relieved, deliciously good, even though we'd told ourselves that bad news wouldn't be the end of the world, and that good news wasn't the end of worry.

FOR THE MOST PART, I consider fear—even mine—to be adaptive, protective, and sometimes even funny. I've been known to jump on a kitchen chair at the sight of a dashing mouse. I've frozen in fear at the sight of a black bear on the trail. These are primitive, short-lived responses. I laugh at my media-stimulated response, climb down from the chair, and write "mouse traps" on my shopping list. I stand quietly on the trail, fear making an easy transition into naturalist thrill as I admire the bear's glossy fur (is that red mixed in with the black?) and the curl of his lips as he pulls berries from the bush. He sees me, too, of course, and runs away through the woods. He flees, my fear retracts, my heartbeat slows, my breathing returns to normal and I continue on my way, watching the path of my feet for fresh bear scat.

This pregnancy, thank goodness, was sticking around longer than a bear. I needed to understand my shifting fear, and I needed to learn how to manage my response, or it was going to be a very long nine months.

There are two related, and opposite, fear response effects: sensitization and habituation. Sensitization makes us more afraid. Habituation raises our threshold for fear. Imagine driving on a rainy road, too fast for conditions, and coming upon the scene of a recent accident. We see a car like ours upside down on the median and wonder if someone, like us, had been trapped inside. Even after we navigate around the remaining emergency vehicles, we maintain a much slower speed, hands gripping the wheel at ten and two o'clock. Having witnessed the consequences of what we assume to have been excessive speed and carelessness, we employ the control we feel behind the wheel to prevent our own tires from leaving the road. That's sensitization.

On the other end of the spectrum, in the habituation realm, we become accustomed to dangers we see every day and therefore lose some of our natural fear and caution. During the regular bombings of World War II, Londoners acclimated to the falling bombs, the noise, the smoke. They were able to adapt.

Think about the state of the world. You can get used to almost anything.

AS WE WERE LEAVING Washington that summer in the midst of a summer storm, the windshield wipers broke. We needed to get back for my sonography appointment, and there was no place to switch out our vehicle or get it repaired for over forty-eight hours, so we hit the road, in the rain, wiperless. Stupid.

This is what the broken wipers would do: swish upward at whatever speed was requested and then ... stop. Right in the middle of the windshield. Essentially, the driver—Mark—was granted half a cleared windshield per switch-flick and then the vehicle had to be stopped and one of us had to manually pull the wiper back into starting position. The rain was steady and progress was slow. We tried to drive sans wipers, but there's a reason for them.

This was my solution: I pulled the cord from the generous black sweatpants I was wearing, secure in the knowledge that I didn't need a string in my pants to keep them snug. I tied the cord around the tip of the wiper on the passenger's side and climbed back in, wrapping the extra cord a couple of times around my puffy hand. "Okay," I commanded, "turn them on." Swish. Here, timing was crucial. Just at the millisecond the wiper reached the apex of its rain-swiping assent, I raised my elbow high in the air and gave a Herculean yank. It worked: Both wipers returned to their starting positions in time for whatever was still functioning in the wiper mechanism to send them skyward again. Swish. Yank. Swish. Yank.

Somewhere in South Dakota, the tornado warnings kicked in, and Mark kept saying, unhelpfully, "Does that cloud look to you like it's funneling?" I would have done anything to stay ahead of that storm. The driving rain, magnified by our own highway speeds, drilled the freezing rain into my arm like needles, so I scrabbled around in the suitcase for a tube sock and pulled it over my hand and arm to ease the sting. This helped, and we drove like this for hours, my tube-socked arm curling out the window, already acclimated to our manually operated wipers.

WE ARRIVED BACK in Indiana just in time for Ultrasound Day, looking forward to finding out if we were waiting for Filbert or Filbertina. Mark and I sat together in the waiting room. I scribbled notes in my pregnancy journal above a pen-and-ink drawing of a hobby horse and next to the publisher's note that the nineteenth-century Loango of Africa permitted no one to approach a newborn (not even the father) until the umbilical stump fell off "for fear that the child would fall into evil ways." I focused on whatever I could to take my mind off the thirty-two ounces of water I'd dutifully ingested prior to the appointment.

The technician came out to get me alone first: "Don't worry," she said to Mark. "I'll just get her started and take some preliminary measurements. I won't tell her anything until you're in the room."

Truer words have never been spoken.

I lay back on the table and she lubed up my bare belly with jelly, flipped some switches, and started sliding the wand through the goop. I tried to distract myself with muscle-flexing Kegels, determined not to pee on the table, but the air in the room had shifted. The sense of the celebratory in the routine had been broken—the acrobat's foot slips on the wire and the audience gasps as she grips her bar, trying to regain balance. Something wasn't right. The screen was turned away from me, but I could see the technician's poor attempt at a poker face, and I could tell there was something wrong. The corners of her mouth twitched, and she kept twisting her wand over the same three-square inches of jellied flesh.

"What is it?" I asked. "Is something wrong? What's wrong?" But she didn't answer. She said something about how if she said anything Mark would never trust her again. And then she let me get up and pee and Mark came in.

And then: "It's a girl!"

I was so sure the baby was a boy—Fil or Bert... either one—but she's not! She's a girl! And she was so cute in there—wriggling her little fingers and kicking her feet. And then she sucked her thumb and sort of floated back into a recline position, looking as if she was already kicking it on the couch with her dad, catching a game. And from here, while Mark and I watched in awe, clutching our own hands together, she kicked out her legs and crossed them at the ankles, all casual like. And this from a child just six inches long. Absolutely mind-blowingly amazing. By the time the sonographer sent us out to wait for our appointment with the doctor, I'd forgotten her expression, and I scrawled happily in a large, blank area of the book, "June 6—ultrasound appointment—It's a GIRL!"

But Dr. S's face was grim when we entered the examining room. I don't remember sitting down. In my memory, the whole consultation occurred while all three of us remained standing, in a kind of diagnostic limbo. I also can't remember the exact words he used, but it was one of those reassuring comments with an immediate segue into disclaimer, "Well, everything looks great on the ultrasound, but..." The doctor's "but" was a sharp bone in my own throat. I felt airless, dizzy, the fear flooding over my body like a violent wave of morning sickness. That "but" hunkered there in the room like another person, like a man behind the door with a knife. In self-defense, I reached out with both hands—one landed on the tissue paper stretched across the empty exam table and the other caught Mark's sleeve. The paper crinkled. Mark's breathing turned raspy and fast.

"But," Dr. S continued, "we do see something that concerns us."

I have trouble recording this now because I know so much more about what he was about to say. When he was saying what I'm about to tell you, I had no idea what he was talking about. None.

He held a picture of the top of our baby's head and pointed with a pencil tip to two black circles, saying, "These are bilateral choroid plexus cysts." Even as he called to the nurse and had her schedule the next possible appointment with the high-risk obstetricians for a Level II ultrasound, he tried to reassure us. I stared at the dark circles under Dr. S's pencil. If our baby's imaged brain was a creamy moonscape, the problem, these two dark holes, were the moon's craters. The sun cast our baby girl into shadow.

THIS WAS THE BEGINNING of something I called "Googling my greatest fear." We've all done it. You have a sore throat. You're hoarse but you don't seem to have a cold. You don't type in "symptom sore throat," no, that would give you plenty to worry about, no doubt, but you go for the jugular, you type in "throat cancer symptoms." This is not a healthy habit. Reeling, and with three days to wait before our appointment with the specialist, I spent long hours hunched over a glowing search screen, one hand on my belly, honing the blade of my fear as the search progressed:

Choroid plexus cyst
Choroid plexus cyst rate
Choroid plexus cyst soft marker
Choroid plexus cyst soft marker Trisomy 18
Trisomy 18 symptoms
Trisomy 18 survival
Ohmygodohmygodohmygod

If you Google your greatest fear, you will receive confirmation. You can go from zero to dead in seconds. That's the way the game works. It's a great big cyberworld, and here's something about human nature in the modern world: When disaster strikes, we turn to the internet. You can Google your greatest fear and get immediate confirmation of whatever terror you've concocted in your mind—and this wretched and debilitating practice can seem like actual science.

Here's what I learned on that first afternoon: Choroid plexus cysts are a "soft marker" for a terrifying chromosomal disorder called Trisomy 18. Eighteen weeks into pregnancy number one—hard to believe as this may be—I'd had to be reminded that Down syndrome (wasn't *that* my real boogey man, gestational grandmother that I was?) was Trisomy 21. So I kept typing and reading. Trisomy 18 is also called "Edwards' syndrome," and it's devastating. Ninety-five percent of these poor babies die before their first birthdays, if indeed they make it into the world. They suffer from profound retardation, heart defects, deformed hands and feet, and on and on. In the interminable days between those tiny craters on the ultrasound printout and our appointment with the specialist, I sweated and prayed and swiveled in the pointless orbit of my groaning office chair, the computer screen glowing like another world, the evil planet. *Please, please, please, please let my baby be okay. Don't let her be doomed. Don't let her die. I am begging.*

WE DROVE to the appointment doubled over with fear, but in that cold room, the paper crinkling against my back and the perinatologist's wand slipping over the globe of my belly, we saw our baby swimming and stretching on an overhead screen. She was putting on a show.

This was the summer of 2003 and this perinatologist was keen on the new research coming out at the time about nasal bones—he had a buddy perinatologist who had recently published an important study citing a high association between the presence of a nasal bone and normal chromosomes. He spun the wand across the slippery globe of my belly and we watched on the monitor as our girl swiveled her perfect chin to display her perfect profile. This was 4D, the fancy stuff, and so instead of the ghostly white-and-black haze of our first ultrasound, this was more of a sepia portrait, the tone akin to one of those old-timey pics you might get with your family on the boardwalk after gartering the ace of hearts to your thigh. I mean, my god, we could see our girl's *face*. And her face had a *nose*. The doctor reached back with his left hand, hovered his finger above the monitor, and booped her tiny, but obviously nasal-boned nose. Then he swirled the wand away from her face and in a cheerful voice listed off the other markers of Trisomy 18: club feet, abnormal kidneys, fisted hands. As if she'd been listening for her cue, the baby lifted her right hand and waved to us, stretching all five fingers, and wriggling them—*hello, hello, just me in here, you can turn off the lights now*—giving even the tense laypeople in the room a chance to count those spectacular, well-differentiated, unfisted digits.

Was it the peri, or the baby herself, who assuaged our fears, and allowed us to make what seemed to us the best and safest decision? Is "best and safest" a thing? Ever? The doctor clicked and measured, swooping his slicked-up wand with his flicking wrist, citing cheerful data about nasal bones, as insouciant as the smiling majorette at the front of the Fourth of July parade. No, of course he couldn't *guarantee* our baby was free of that extra chromosome that would shorten her life to a month, two, a year at the most, but it was clear to see that it sure looked that way to him as he printed out still photos for our baby book and pulled up some numbers from his computer. Based on my age, the cysts, various blood levels, and that day's measurements, the chance our baby had Trisomy 18 was: "One in eight hundred. The only diagnostic test is the amnio," the doctor finished up, handing me a towel to mop the lubricant of my belly, "but the risk of miscarriage with an amnio is about one in three hundred."

This was easy math. We'd seen that fine nose and those wiggling fingers. Our decision to forgo the amnio was set. We chose to move forward into the remaining twenty weeks of the pregnancy with faith, believing in our excellent odds.

8   Becoming the Mother I Am

Over and over again, I hear the echoing advice of our first obstetrician who had asked us to consider this when making decisions regarding testing: "Think about what you would do if you got a bad result. If you know you wouldn't terminate the pregnancy, then what's the point of testing?"

I am afraid of the implications of writing the truth about the way it felt to hold my daughter in the cradle of my hips, still largely invisible to the world, my secret of secrets. I remember, still and forever, the stunned look that Mark and I shared ten weeks in when we first heard the tiny staccato heartbeat on the Doppler, the submarine sounds of our baby beginning her ascent to the surface of our world, making her way.

We want all this technology to be a tool for *controlling* fear, but in fact, prenatal diagnosis magnifies fear—and tests our politics and our hearts. Technology presents us with decisions we didn't have before, and the scope of what we can now see and know has far outstripped our capacity to understand what all these new pictures are showing us.

Twenty weeks in, the longest twenty weeks of my life to that point, Mark and I thought we knew we would continue the pregnancy no matter what. I believed our window for terminating the pregnancy had closed for me when I first felt her move, quickening. A tickle, a whisper, and I was hers, even if that meant the best I could hope for would be to hold her in my arms for a week or a month and love her until she died. If that was our only choice, we said to ourselves, we would grieve, but we would take it. What else could we do?

But, also, we didn't really think anything was wrong. Science had given us every reason to hope.

BUT BACK THEN, five months pregnant with our first baby, I'm ashamed to say that despite that minor in women's studies from a flagship institution, I was still woefully ignorant of much of the history of abortion. I didn't know that quickening had anything to do with it. Had I missed that day of class? Or had I let the information slip from my brain like an egg from its shell because, coming up through my twenties, I guess I *thought* about abortion, but I never *worried* about abortion? I was four years old when Roe v. Wade became the law of the land in 1974. I had never dropped an egg down a fallopian tube and toward the possibility of swimming sperm—fertilization, implantation, pregnancy!—during a month when my right to make a choice about that pregnancy was not protected. It would be too easy to say I took that right for granted, but certainly true to say that I felt confident that if I needed an abortion, I could find a doctor somewhere to give me a safe one. So, no, I didn't know that in the days before male doctors wrested control of obstetrics from midwives and birthing mothers that women themselves determined the point after which they would not have an abortion—the quickening. And if you're reading *this* book, it will disgust but not shock you to learn that a core argument levied by male doctors against midwives and the pregnant women with whom they partnered was this: What if the woman doesn't feel the quickening? What if she confuses quickening with indigestion, or hunger? How can we trust a woman to both feel the quickening and report that information faithfully? I mean, really, how could a woman know her own body from the inside better than a male doctor with a gleaming tray of metal instruments rather than a uterus? It really is fucking enraging, isn't it?

And also? All of this? Driven by capitalism. The guys with the medical degrees saw that there was money to be made in controlling the means of production—in this case, women's bodies—and they wanted a piece of that. The language persists even in our broken post-Roe laws, doesn't it? When is an abortion "medically necessary" to "save the life" or "preserve the health" of the pregnant person—only a doctor can decide and those decisions are fraught. How close to death do I need to be?

Years later, I would co-coach an all-girl, multiple-title-winning team of future problem solvers and one thing we taught them to consider in the analysis of any problem—be it antibiotic resistance or food waste, terraforming or cyber security: Follow the money. Where is there money to be made or lost? Therein lies the problem—and possibly a solution.

SETTLING BACK into my body after the choroid plexus cyst trauma, and now five months pregnant, I became determined to make the most of my final baby-free months. I decided I needed to get out of my own way. I needed to work, to travel, to "enjoy freedom"—that oft-repeated advice—before I was housebound with an autumn-born babe. With all this in mind, I accepted a grant to do research in Ithaca, New York, deep in Cornell's archives where I would learn more about a weirdly forgotten time in our nation's higher education history: *real* infants—newborns—surrendered in hospitals or borrowed from orphanages to be raised by the book in "homemaking apartments" by undergraduate home economics majors who were also practicing cake baking, household budgeting, and stain removal. Why weren't we all talking about *this* in our history classes?

Real babies! Granted, this was strange timing on my part, but I'd been thinking about these borrowed babies for years, and this was my opportunity to flip through their baby books and examine the meticulously recorded logs of their care. I mean, I wasn't going to take an *infant* down into the archives, was I? It was now or not for a very long time. Off to New York I flew.

At first, I'd been excited to turn my attention toward something, anything, outside the growing contours of my pregnant body, but I soon realized I'd neglected the fear factor. By the time I slid between the scratchy sheets in the borrowed artist's loft in downtown Ithaca where I would live—alone—for three weeks, I'd already been afraid to (1) pass my belly through airport security's X-ray (the TSA women, mothers all, seemed both disgusted and offended when I insisted on a hand search), (2) drive the boat-like rental car with the ridiculous number of satellite radio stations on the long and winding roads, and (3) step outside the loft after dark to buy food.

Here was the crux: I felt unprepared to be this baby's mother. I felt unprepared to be *any* baby's mother. I didn't know what to *do*—and I'm not the kind of person who can exist comfortably in that feeling. And now here I was off on a journey too far from home, too risky for the baby. What if I messed up?

I lacked my own mother's spirit of adventure. When we were kids, she took us everywhere. *Babies are easy!* she assured me. *Portable! You just take them with you.* And it's true: We got to do fantastic things. When my mother was a hand and cook on a tuna fishing boat in the Atlantic, sometimes went out with her, swinging from ropes, using big knives to shuck scallops, going up on deck when the sky and sea were as dark as squid's ink to kick the jellyfish bucket and watch them glow crazy colors under the brightest stars we'd ever seen. Once, she took us on a trip across the country on Amtrak and we ate crackers and hard cheese in the observation car, drawing endless scenes in our sketchbooks: I still remember one rainbow we saw over the Rockies, more storybook than storybook. And there were the more daily things of our lives, like prayer-meetings and potlucks for the cult-like followers of the Maharaji—which, I have to say, while I was never a fan of the mushroom-bulgur wheat pie, offered a mind-expanding place to people watch.

I was never hurt indulging my mother's spirit of adventure; instead, I was hurt when she had to leave us to go make money. I was hurt when she went to her waitressing job and left me unsupervised—the lone girl in a wild pack of teenaged boys. The wide world didn't harm me, but being home alone did. Lying in bed that first night in Ithaca, ears pricked to every voice and bang from the street below, each fan clank and refrigerator hum from within, I thought about how fear morphs and expands. I had so wanted to be *done* with the abuse from my childhood—I mean, *look at me*, for fuck's sake! I was a professor, married to a good man who loved me, rich with friends I adored. Hadn't I made it through? Hadn't I made it out? How damaged could I be, right?

Pretty fucking damaged. I was only just beginning to let down my guard enough to recognize that there are some things we carry with us all our lives, always, no matter what. Sure, we learn the weight of them, we know which shoulder best bears them up, and when to shift the burden to our hips, but we bear them nonetheless. Colin's death was a tragedy I would never put down, and the loss of my childhood—not all of it, but the too-early theft of my belief that the world could be a safe place, a *just* place—was another. Just because I'd built what looked like and could even *feel* like a well-functioning life held up by real and healthy relationships didn't mean I could trumpet a squeaky-clean bill of emotional and psychological health earned through the power of the written word. That's exactly what I'd *been* doing—"Writing *Darkroom* saved my life," I'd told whole auditoriums full of people. Maybe it had, maybe even literally—here I was, after all, and pregnant *on purpose*—but I was a fool to think the specter of my abuser with his sharp, dirty fingernails in that dark garage would ever vanish. I could crawl away from the futon jammed in that creepy corner—the sign posted on the ceiling that read *Are you stoned or stupid?* I could leave behind my fear of *him* and the intrusive memories that had haunted me in my twenties. Yes, I could do that. But I'd built my defenses up too high and too strong to ever lay them down. In other words, I realized, I was going to have to learn to live, and to mother, inside all that I'd constructed in *response* to that abuse.

WHEN I WAS A CHILD, between the ages of four and thirteen, we lived for nine years on a long strip of sand separated from the Massachusetts mainland by the Merrimac River and her marshes. Because my mother likes to live in wildly beautiful and beautifully wild places, she had chosen the last house on Plum Island before the nature reserve. The teenager who abused me lived across the empty lot that backed up to our house, spiked with prickly beach grass. I could see the boarded-up windows of his garage lair from my bedroom window.

On the island, we were joined for a time by my mother's fisherman boyfriend, Captain Billy Packer, and his teenage son, Jeff. Jeff was a good kid with a floppy mop of sandy blond hair and twinkling blue eyes. We all loved him. One day, Jeff came home from his job on his dad's boat with a giant tarantula in a small, square, wire cage. Because a deckhand from another boat had bestowed the hairy beast, we were all forced to imagine a foreign port, a skulking castaway tucking into a crate of green bananas—no defanged, pet-store spider for us.

Why did Jeff accept the cage when it was offered? Because my brother had called him a cream puff? Because he could? Whatever the reason, he had taken the spider in hand and brought him into our house. Maybe Jeff figured that having a full-grown tarantula of indeterminate sex would be *wicked cool*. Maybe he thought owning something dangerous would give him street cred, make him look tougher than he felt.

I was all of seven years old and the image of that barred cube, maybe nine-by-nine, is vivid in my mind, burned there, the way things that scare us can burn. There were gaps between the stiff wire bars, about a quarter of an inch wide, and you know the way you feel when Jodie Foster's Agent Starling comes too close to the cage holding Dr. Hannibal Lecter in the first *Silence of the Lambs*? The way Hannibal reaches his hand through the bars, and it just doesn't seem safe for Jodie? *Get away! Step back!* And then Hannibal's sucking his scary teeth and delivering that famous line about fava beans and a nice Chianti? It's the creepiest.

Well, that's how it was with this huge tarantula—its body alone must have been at least five inches long, maybe six, and his abdomen was eerily fat, like the pod of a giant poppy, ready to pop. And we were all hoping he was a boy tarantula, not a girl, ripe with eggs, bursting with babies who could find their way out through those too-wide spaces and find a nice windowsill to settle on, feasting on unwary flies, until their own legs grew long, hairy, reaching. Because of this collective wish, someone gave him a boy name—Spike.

SO MUCH of our lives are buffered by Virginia Woolf's "cotton wool" of memory, but those weeks in Ithaca, in the loft, left sharp indentations on my progesterone-addled brain. With a precision that rivals Woolf's childhood moment in her bed at St. Ives with the acorn of the blind scraping back and forth on the gentle breath of the seaside breeze, I remember moment after moment from those last weeks I spent alone. If there is no real danger, if no real harm comes to pass, the kind of harm that sends memory packing to a dark dungeon of the brain, then is it possible that memory is jazzed by the electricity of fear? The terrible stress brought on by fear even—or *especially*?—when there's nothing to actually hurt us?

What if we think of my child-brain as another species of caretaking parent? When my real mother was away and the neighbor took me into that dark, smoke-filled garage, Led Zeppelin and Pink Floyd pumping through mounted speakers, peppermint schnapps sweetening my terror, his hands so big, blackened in the cracks by the work he did with grease and metal, candles and incense, everything smoldering and dark, my mother-brain protected my heart somehow, packing up those memories, neat as you please, and storing them in the closet under the stairs until Colin came along and helped me pull them out, open each one, dump them on the floor, sort it out.

In my early twenties, before Colin died, when I finally told my *actual* mother what I'd remembered—less of a remembering and more of a regaining of access—she helped too. She believed me from the instant I told her, loved me harder than ever, felt sorry and sorrow with her own open heart.

For me, there was no second betrayal. My disclosure of the years of abuse was met with belief and love, and that has made all the difference. But no matter how hard we tried, working together—as we always had—we couldn't take the abuse away. "Oh," my mother moaned. "I want to go back and *get* that little girl." But she can't. None of us can. That little girl is back there in the garage and it's not good. She's scared and hurting and ashamed of things she's too young to understand. We can help the woman I became, but for the girl there's no rescue. It will always be too late.

Or at least that's how it felt during the long, scary nights in Ithaca. *What have I done?* I thought, keeping one wary eye on the loft door from my huddled spot on the couch where one night I binged, staying up until one o'clock, watching four episodes of *Six Feet Under* in a row, eating Swedish fish scooped into a plastic bag in bulk foods, wishing I would stop, but I didn't want to lie down in somebody else's bed and listen to the sounds of the street.

The girl I was had loved Swedish fish—in the seventies, they only came in red. I used to ride my bicycle to get them at the island store, a penny apiece, and eat them on Friday nights with my favorite shows—*The Love Boat* and *Fantasy Island*—hoping he would leave me alone to work the sugar from my teeth with my own tongue while I dreamed about being Julie with her clipboard, so adorable, so put together, so on top of it all.

THE FIRST NIGHT with Spike did not go well for Jeff. He'd set the tarantula in his cage up on his dresser by the window. There was a full moon that night and the spider danced in the light of the moon. Jeff said Spike never stopped moving. All day long, he'd just sat there, legs pulled in tight, still as a rock. But at night, Jeff said, Spike came alive. He looked as if he were trying to escape, and I'm sure he was: long legs feeling the air, testing, testing. At one point, Jeff says, Spike hooked four legs through one vertical gap, and it looked to Jeff as if he were going to be able to propel himself right out of that flimsy cage. *Bloop.*

Jeff couldn't take it. He got up and put the cage in a paper grocery bag. He rolled down the top. Then he put the cage in the bag in a box, and closed it up, tucking all the edges. Maybe he tied it with string. Maybe there was even duct tape involved, and at last, Jeff could sleep.

I don't think I could have slept. Not being able to see a gargantuan spider I *knew* was there would have made it worse. Where was he? Was he still in there? What if he wasn't? What if he'd managed to suck in his pod body, the way a mouse flattens itself for a trip through a crack in the kitchen floor and into the bounty of the pantry? Or maybe he could gnaw his way out. I'm just making this up now, but maybe Spike was of a rare species of vicious Himalayan gnawing tarantula, who, given time enough and reason, could work his way through the trunk of a tree. For a spider like that, a paper bag, a box, some string, and some tape would be nothing. If that were the case—and this is the way my mind works, in a looping series of eventualities and possibilities—then that tickle I felt on my ankle might not have been the harmless sliding of the sheet, but . . . Spike himself, moving in for the inevitable kill.

    That's how I roll in my brain. I am Queen of the Worst Possible Thing.

UNLIKE THE MEMORIES of the abuse, which came back one at a time, unbidden and choking, as if I were pulling a knotted scarf from my own throat, my memories of that loft in Ithaca are crystalline. The gritty hardwood floor, the coffee filter I fashioned from a metal pie tin, the morning voices from the flower shop below, the slam of the delivery truck door, the well-thumbed IKEA catalog by the toilet: My brain holds onto the tiniest details of the cavernous loft. Across from the kitchen counter where I made my coffee, careful not to splash my belly with boiling water, the door of an antique armoire gaped open, and every morning I marveled at the strange maternal creature in the snug maternity dress peering back at me from the old mirror.

    How are you doing, kid? I would sometimes say out loud, not sure whether I was talking to myself or the baby, but anxious to hear a human voice. Already, I was somebody's *mother* and I remembered something my own mother seemed fond of saying in that first year after my brother went to college and she and I moved all the way across the country, from Massachusetts to Washington, where we first lived in a cabin with her pot-growing, Vietnam vet, mountain man boyfriend, and then—when that didn't work out—into a house made of cut poles stretched with thick plastic and blankets on our own twenty acres of mountainside. My mother would say, repeatedly, as if she needed to remind herself: *Just you and me, Jill! We're in this together. What an adventure!*

    My mother had crazy ideas, but this time, taking me away from the island—even if it was to a mountain with god knows what kind of new dangers—she was saving me from that dark garage. Her rescue was unwitting—or maybe something in her knew?—but it was salvation nonetheless. I was packed up in a pickup truck with all our remaining worldly belongings and saved. *We're a team*, she would say. And we were.

AFTER HIS FIRST, restless, fearful night with Spike, Jeff bequeathed the tarantula—packaging and all—to my brother, who was not afraid.

Jeff graduated high school, moved out, got married—and Spike became our family pet. In time, Ian upgraded Spike's living quarters to an aquarium suited up with a small log, grass, and leaves. Mostly, Spike hid under the log, but we'd get a good look at him on feeding day when my brother lifted the screen top and slid in an unlucky cricket. First, a couple tentative hairy legs would emerge from beneath the log, and then the lightning-fast leap of the cricket kill. Chilling. Consuming the cricket, Spike's vertical mouth would move in a mechanical, rotating motion, like a gear turning, catching the leg of the cricket and grinding the creature in.

On feeding day, I could not look away, cringing as I watched the shiny black cricket fall from my brother's uncurling fingers. Even then, I was horrified by the vulnerability of small things. The way the doomed cricket stood so still in Spike's aquarium, antennae quivering, taking stock while Spike bided his arachnid time under the shadow of his log. I tried not to think too hard. I didn't want to think about Jiminy with his tiny blue top hat. I didn't want to anthropomorphize or try to get into the trembling cricket's head: What did he know about what was about to happen? If he could remember the songs he played in the corner of my room at night, could he remember anything that would help him now? I knew Spike had to eat and I was obviously never going to reach my hand into that aquarium, but my immobility felt more like fear than choice. Frozen, I stood by my brother and watched Spike leap onto the cricket. I watched, barely breathing, until Spike had drawn the last spindly leg into his creepy sideways grinding mouthparts and the little leg stopped kicking and disappeared.

WHILE THE GIRL I WAS navigated dangers both real and imagined, my mother seemed fearless. I have only one memory of seeing my mother really scared. When I was eight or nine, mad at a sharp-toothed girl from the other side of the island who had humiliated me in some way I cannot now remember, I decided to punish everybody by hiding my bike in the sand under our house, erasing the tire tracks with my sneaker, and crawling in after it with enough supplies to last me until midnight. My anger at the mean girl fed my determination, and I stayed in my hiding place beneath the floorboards long after darkness fell. I could hear my panicked mother calling my name in a voice that sounded increasingly like a howl, an animal. By the time I emerged, the police were searching the island and my mother's face was contorted into a mask of fear and horror. When she saw me, alive, she hugged me, pushed me away, and slapped me. Hard. Then she hugged me again, sent me to my room, and came in not ten minutes later with a plate of fried chicken. This was also the only time my mother ever struck me. It was confusing for both of us.

In the loft, I thought about that slap, a solitary act I could point back to from over twenty years in the future. And I thought about the hundreds of decisions, from the unnoticed to the life-altering, a mother might make in any given day—and then, in my exhausted head, I tried to multiply that by 365 days in a year, and then . . . by what? By eighteen? By a lifetime?

And I thought about mothers. My mother. Myself as mother. Mother mistakes and mother triumphs (was that even a *thing*?) and mother love. Makeshift mothers like those who took care of the infants they borrowed to practice on in the home economics apartments. I wondered if I could figure out the *right* way to mother if I could pick out what was wrong. As usual, I thought if there were a way to really think through the details, I could control what was happening to my body, what was about to happen to my life, and ultimately, whether we would all be okay—me, Mark, and this new human we had decided to make together who was, even as I rolled around on the hard mattress, right there with me, submerged in a temperature-controlled plunge pool I'd somehow constructed *inside my body, where our daughter was, in that very month, working on developing her own minuscule uterus.* We were like Russian nesting dolls of uteri. Abso-friggin-lutely mind-blowing. But I was going to figure this out. I was going to do my research, think it through, make a plan.

"It's okay, baby. We've got this. We're going to be okay."

Ridiculous, I know, but the world had tuned me to believe that vigilance and preparation might keep me safe. And now there were two of us. In the same body.

It was a lot to take in.

I had closed the blinds, but the light of the moon pushed through the cracks. She was so bright that night.

THE LOFT'S OWNER nurtured a rooftop garden in big clay pots on the black tarmac of a large patio twelve feet above the parking lot. On the other side of the alley, a motley collection of men would crowd onto their tiny fire escape and yell at each other in a language I could never seem to understand (although I think it was English).

I had been charged with caring for the plants in the clay pots—cherry tomatoes, parsley, and geraniums with blossoms bigger and redder than a man's fist—and between the leering, jeering men on the fire escape, the hooligans in the parking lot, and the sun baking that tarmac into a giant briquette, I had to choose my moment well. When the sun was low, but the coast was clear, I cracked the kitchen window, snaked the end of the hose through, and attached the adapter to the faucet in the sink.

I love watering plants, always have. One moment, the leaves are drooping, sad, considering permanent wilt, tilting toward desiccation, and then you come along with your trickling hose, aiming all that gushing life at their dusty feet, and voilà, they are saved, resurrected.

Thank god, I would think on those hot Ithaca evenings. *I have cared for something.*

This is good. I have kept something alive. This is goodness.

WHEN I WAS SIX or so, my mother got me started in our little patch of black soil she had trucked in and dumped in a hole she'd dug in the sand in front of our island house. It's hard to grow a garden on a beach. Together, we chose hardy, sand-tolerant plants that could hold up their heads in the strong winds. Even back then, I couldn't stand *waiting*, and so my favorites were radishes. My mother brought me home colorful packets of the Easter Egg variety, and after folding the tiny seeds into soggy paper towels overnight to jumpstart germination, I'd draw careful lines into the sandy soil with a knife and sprinkle my seeds in neat rows. I'd water and wait, water and wait, but I didn't have to wait long. Within days, I'd see a push of bright green, and then two sweet leaves, round and reaching, and every day from then forward, bigger and bigger.

I was terrible about thinning the rows because I wanted to give *everyone* a chance. Water and wait, water and wait. And then, late in the spring, before my mother shipped us off to my father's house in Connecticut for the summer, I'd begin my harvest. Sometimes, my impatience getting the best of me, I'd venture a test-pull too early and a pallid, skinny radish would slide from the soil looking like a fetal carrot.

Water and wait. And then, when I'd give a little tug and meet real resistance, I'd really pull, and—pop! Out of the soil would emerge a perfect globe—dusty purple or fire-engine red, popsicle yellow or snowball white—and I would run inside to the sink, rinse off the dirt, and hold the pretty, shining thing in the palm of my hand.

Look, Mom. Look what I did. Mom, I grew a moon!

IN ITHACA, BY day I caught a bus to campus and went down into the archives. In the dark, windowless depths of the library, silent, wearing the white cotton gloves of an archival researcher, or a lady, I turned the pages of baby books put together by the teenaged surrogate mothers in Cornell's practice apartments. I examined the feeding charts, reviewing the measured ounces of orange juice, cod liver oil, and fortified cereals. I looked at photos of the babies napping in the brisk Ithaca air and being weighed in the apartment laboratory. Miniature models of mothercraft—the *science* of mothering! Turning the pages, I watched as the babies gained weight and new color in their once sallow cheeks. A flipbook of human development.

Take little Bobbie, Cornell's second baby, who arrived at the homemaking lodge in the fall of 1921: "six weeks old, malnourished, pitiful looking mite weighing only six pounds as compared with seven and a half at birth." A year later, in his baby book, Bobbie's student caretakers assessed their bright, chubby, "pink and white" 22-pound charge and declared him "an excellent example of what proper food and care can do to develop a healthy normal child and firm, understanding, kind and sensible treatment to make him a happy, sweet-tempered, good dispositioned little lad . . ." The photos were black and white, so I had to take his pinkness at their word, but the chub and the grin? That I could see.

And still, I felt so sad. Not only were the answers I might have found in those brittle pages still evading me, even the right questions seemed beyond my grasp. How was I going to take care of my own baby? How would I know what to do?

Mother. Mothering. To mother. In the summer heat, the word seemed to melt, stretching in all directions, like newsprint on Silly Putty—almost funny at first, then weird, and finally losing meaning altogether.

Mothermothermothermother.

There were days in the archives when I was astounded and invigorated by the bold experiment these women in higher education had pulled off in the middle of the twentieth century, making a place for themselves and their work in the male world of higher education. They proposed courses, received grants, and established the Home Economics Department. I mean, what a coup!

There were other days when my swollen ankles hanging under the archive table were throbbing with all that extra blood and I came across a shabby entry in a baby book and realized that these apartments with their actual human babies and handful of rotating undergrads were essentially group projects. Anyone who's ever been part of a group project—everyone, right?—knows how annoyed Sue got with Betty on the night Betty was supposed to prepare the baby's night bottle, but instead stayed out late with Joe on their dinner date, tiptoeing in with rum on her breath at 10:00 p.m. after Sue had already fed Bobbie herself and gotten the baby into his crib where he was screaming bloody murder and Sue was collapsed against his closed bedroom door with a stopwatch on her lap timing the duration of Bobbie's screams so she could log those minutes—hours?!—in the damn log for the night.

Bitch, Sue might have whispered as Betty stepped over her legs to get to the bathroom.

And then there were the days I turned a page and found myself looking into the eyes of a baby who looked so gentle, so wounded, and so wise, and I thought, *What do you know, little guy? What have you seen? What do you need?*

After three weeks I needed to go home.

9   Ways of Seeing

After all this talk of fear, will you believe I was not afraid of labor and delivery? Of course, I was terrified of the baby dying before, during, or immediately after birth, and while such possible tragedies entered my mind, unbidden and intrusive, I was not afraid of the pain of birth and I was not afraid for my own safety. In this arena, my ferocity rose up, roaring. Birth, I reasoned, was the stage of this journey when I might wrest back some control. Sort of. At least, I thought, there would be something for me to *do*. Sort of.

It never occurred to me to be afraid for my own life.

From the beginning, I was chomping at the bit to compose and deliver my—I mean, *our*—birth plan to the Midwestern gentlemen at the clinic, but I waited obediently until the seventh month. I had many early, unread drafts. The writer in me wanted to take some time to elaborate on my newly acquired theories on childbirth and what I considered to be the calamity of the birthing mother entrenched in a male medical paradigm, but since nobody was going to wade through twenty-five pages of *that*, and because this was no time to alienate the guys on the rubber-glove side of the instruments of modern birth, I decided it would be best to begin with a generic online plan in list form. Of course, there were revisions to be made, personal touches to be employed.

Mark reined me in.

We began with a letter to the doctors telling them how happy we were to be working with them and how, *of course*, we were flexible and would respect their vast experience and resulting medical counsel. This was a lie—particularly the first part. Before we moved to Muncie, I'd never even spread my legs for a male gynecologist. It just hadn't made sense to me—like taking your shiny, temperamental Mercedes convertible in for a tune-up with a mechanic who had never even driven a car. Or going to eat at a restaurant where the chef didn't possess, well, a mouth. Then, in the midst of the most significant gynecological event of my life, I found myself with not one, not two, but *five* male gynecologists, and I'll confess, I resisted them with every residual scrap of Women's Studies 101 that remained in my brain fiber. Phrases like *power over* and the *male medicalization of birth* sounded in my brain when one of these men patted my knee through the lap napkin and told me a little something about pregnancy. *Yeah, right, fucker*, I'd grumble internally. *And how many times have you felt a baby's head smash a nerve onto your pelvic bone?* But Mark insisted that a little kissing of the asses of the men who would have their fingers on the epidural button and their hands wrapped around the episiotomy scissors seemed wise. I relented and puckered up. Grudgingly.

We ended our letter with something true: Everything in the plan hinged upon the well-being of the baby (and, here, Mark made me add "and mother") and if the baby ("or mother") was threatened in any way, then I'd let them do whatever they wanted to me. Thus, effectively, we rendered the entire plan void; if the doctors in the birthing room expressed any doubt or fear about the baby's stress level, we'd be headed for the operating room.

Women have been giving birth without Pitocin and epidurals and narcotics and prostaglandin gels and crochet needle-like amniotic sack breakers (not the technical term) for a lot of years. As I prepared for my first delivery, I understood there would be risks, but I also knew *most* births were perfectly normal, so I saw no reason to approach our baby's arrival with the opposite assumption. (The question, perhaps, is why I couldn't approach such routine undertakings, such as Mark's drive to Illinois to visit his parents, on the list of events he would most likely survive.) The doctors talked about the pain, the ripping, and the risk to the baby with a prolonged labor. I knew an epidural costs between $1,500 and $3,000, a tear takes longer to repair than the clean slice of a man-made episiotomy, and Pitocin can get a doctor home to his own bed sooner than waiting out a woman who insists on doing things naturally.

In those prenatal visits, I did the opposite of what I do in most of my life. Instead of taking on the fears these doctors held out for me to take, I resisted them. I *defied* them. Now I wonder if I brought on what happened next through hubris and overconfidence, but there I go again with the magical thinking.

On the day we presented the birth plan, my appointment was with my favorite doctor in the practice, which is to say the one who'd never called me either "mommy" or fat, the one who'd never once patted my bare knee. He shook his head a little superstitiously when I handed him the stack of collated and stapled birth plans and said something I'd hear again before my years in obstetrical stirrups was over: "A birth plan is the best way to make sure that everything doesn't go as planned."

But I held firm. I requested that he hear me out now so that when it came down to the nitty-gritty, and I was too focused on laboring (oh, how I loved the sound of that word as a verb: so productive, so proactive, so pain for a *reason*), he'd know what I wanted—and here was the response:

"With no episiotomy," Dr. P said, "as a first-time mom, you'll rip in five places instead of one clean cut."

"But couldn't the clean cut start a larger rip? Like if I cut this piece of paper with a pair of scissors . . ."—having no actual scissors for my demonstration, I used my fingers—"and then I pull on either side of the paper, that's where the paper has been weakened, and it will rip farther, right?" (What I was thinking was: *I don't want to rip all the way up—down?—to my anus!* But I don't think I could have so boldly referenced my anus in front of Dr. P and Mark. Now, "vagina" I would have said all day: *vagina, vagina, vagina.* But *anus*? Probably not.)

Dr. P shrugged and shook his head, gently agreeing to disagree. He was a good and kind man, I'll give him that. "Okay then," he said. "No episiotomy unless absolutely indicated." On the issue of using the Pitocin injection to contract the uterus after the delivery of the placenta, he was more passionate: "If I tell medical students one thing, it's this. This is what kills women in third-world countries, and this is what I worry about in birthing centers: Hemorrhage is the leading cause of maternal death and we have something we can use to prevent it."

Basically he tried to tell me that without it I'd bleed out on the delivery table, my helpless babe in my arms. Again, I thought he was just trying to scare me. What were the chances?

Dr. P persisted. "Pitocin is completely natural. There's no reason not to have it."

I told him about a friend of mine who had warned me away from the post-birth Pitocin, which she claimed had caused terrible swelling, slowing her recovery.

Again, he shrugged, looking me in the eyes with a kind of sad resignation. "That sounds anecdotal to me."

MUST I SAY HERE, in print, that Dr. P was right? Or can we agree, in this isolated case, he just got lucky with his predictions? (Or, rather, *I* got unlucky?)

Or, maybe, in thinking about fear, can I distract us all from our finger-pointing to celebrate this anomaly pushing out like—well, you know—from everything I knew myself to be: I was not afraid, I was not afraid, I was not afraid. I looked forward to labor and delivery. Here was something I could do. Here was something I could control. (I thought.)

I was excited. I wanted to be finished with pregnancy and get on to baby. *Bring it on.* I felt invincible.

IS IT TRUE for all of us that death and food, grief and hunger—or its opposite, the impossibility of swallowing—cannot be pulled apart? Pregnant with my first baby, I thought about what I was holding in my body and how much I had to lose, how—if I was lucky, so very, very lucky—I would live with the possibility of this loss every day until I died. In the first days after Colin's accident, I couldn't eat and I couldn't stop vomiting. I maintain only flickers of memory from those early weeks, but I remember the ginger snaps. With Colin's sisters and brothers and parents all around me, numb or wailing or rocking in the lava flow of deep grief—of seven children, Colin had been the youngest, their baby brother, their *baby*—I know I wasn't the only one who needed something I could swallow, but my recollection is that the ginger snaps were brought home for me.

Why can't I remember any faces? Why can I better remember the yellow box of dry, round cookies than the decimated family who tried to feed me? The psychiatrist at my university had called in a prescription for suppositories to calm me down, stop the vomiting, and put me to sleep. But I wasn't using them faithfully. I wanted to be awake if Colin visited me in the night. I was a shattered body waiting for one that had been burned to dust. I wanted to follow him, but someone (my mother? Colin's mother? my friend Diane?) broke off a piece of ginger snap and made me stick out my tongue. The fragment of wafer stuck there. I remember the dry bit of cookie adhering to the barely moist surface of my useless tongue more vividly than any other physical sensation in those first days after the accident. I think I held my tongue out for too long, not really knowing what to do, and then, like a toad, I pulled both tongue and that fragment of ginger snap back inside my mouth and swallowed hard, hoping they could now let me die.

WE DROVE with Colin's ashes to the ranch in Northern California where he'd played with his dogs and learned to catch calves. We made a mound of him on a hill, almost a sandcastle. When the rest of the family stumbled back to the barn for a pancake breakfast, they let me stay with Colin on my knees, my mind frantic. What could I do? What now?

Here is what I did: I sprinkled some ashes into my palm, thick, grainy, pieces of bone, and I kissed them. I licked him from my lips, felt him crunch between my teeth. I told him to stay with me. I explained my sudden plan, an inspiration: *I am taking you into me. Stay with me. Don't go.*

IT DIDN'T HELP that the hormones of pregnancy were spinning my dreams out of control. The first-trimester dreams (when I was still sleeping heavily and often) had been nightmarish: a kind of Nazi Germany for pregnant women where armed members of the Gestapo would stop us in the street, check our temperatures, and make us sit down and eat entire sleeves of Saltines; or the baby would arrive and she would be so small that she would fit into the palm of my hand and so I had to keep her moist so she wouldn't dry out, but she began to shrink anyway, smaller and smaller, and about the time my new baby was the size of a hazelnut, my fingers slipped and she dropped down into the grass, and right before I awoke I was on my knees, separating the grass blade by blade, looking for my lost baby.

And so it went.

In the second trimester, the crazy dreams had gone the way of frequent urination, but nearing the end now, the dreams had returned with a vengeance, typically reaching a kind of crescendo at about two in the morning, a climax of such emotional intensity—and typically tragedy—that I was up drinking orange juice and doing kick counts for the rest of the night. By this stage, I had over seven months of pregnancy-book reading under my belt (okay, don't be mean, "belt" here is a *metaphor*), and there was no need to dream about cracker-toting Nazis or disappearing babies—anybody could have those dreams—no, no, I was dreaming about ruptured placentas, compressed umbilical cords, seeping amniotic fluid, anything related to late-term stillbirth. These dreams were horrible and gory and completely incompatible with any kind of sleep. By the eighth month, mentally I was so ready to hold Ella in my arms, out in the air in the light, out where I could see with my own eyes and feel with my own fingers whether she was breathing, wiggling, getting enough to eat, *breathing*.

THROUGHOUT MY PREGNANCY, I had trouble hanging onto even the idea of an actual baby. With my eyes, I had seen the two blue lines in the pregnancy test window. In the dim room of my sleeplessness, I could see my taut mountain of a belly. Technology had even allowed me a glimpse of my swimming baby projected in all her ultrasonographic glory, stretching her tiny fingers wide and wonderful, but still, pregnancy was a hard concept for me to fully wrap my mind around: *In your body, Jill, you are growing a person. She began with the meeting of sperm and egg, a microscopic possibility, moved on from zygote to embryo to full-on fetus, and now she is seven or eight pounds, and she is a she, or so they say, and soon she will emerge from your body. Somehow in the next two weeks, she will be born—you will open up and push her out, or something will go wrong and they will cut her out, but one way or another she will be made separate from you and she will be your daughter. She will have a name and live in your house. And you will love her more than you have ever loved anyone before.* These are some of the things I'd been told to expect from the biological endeavor in which I was presently engaged, and I was naive enough to believe them. I had never had so much to lose, and yet, I didn't even know, really, what such a loss would mean, what I would be losing.

EVEN THOUGH I didn't know the half of what I had to fear in the approaching years and subsequent pregnancies, still, there was too much I didn't know, couldn't control, couldn't see. Lygophobia is the scientific name for fear of the dark, but it's also a fear of this inability to *see*, a fear of the way things look in gloomy light—the way the chair with the jeans thrown over the back looks for all the world like a hooded man, watching you from the shadows. Is that a knife in his hand? No, it must be the corner of a book. But, here, in the dark, alone, the book is a knife. What about the moaning box fan? No matter how many times you blink and tell yourself the fan is a fan, the fan is *not* a fan. The fan has a snout and fangs. The fan breathes like something hungry.

Children, imaginations whirling, know this fear, and I wonder if sometimes fears are a celebration of possibility. If the stack of laundry on the dresser can be a crouching troll, maybe it can also be a magic carpetbag. Maybe that's Mary Poppins waiting by the door with Jane and Michael in tow; perhaps that's not the table with the radio on top, but a perambulator with the Banks twins tucked inside and the whole group is waiting for you to join them for a romp in the park. *Find your hat! Get the kite!*

Think of the books we read to our children: Frances of bread and jam fame sees a tiger where her bathrobe hangs and hums a little tune in which she rhymes "tiger" with "dryer." And, of course, Max sails into his world of Wild Things only after his room grows thick with vines and a boat arrives on the shore. To know darkness, we need light. To live in the light, and know we are there, we are required to walk through the dark.

I wanted to shine a light into the dark and step into it together, a family, unafraid. I wanted the lists I made in the weeks before our baby's birth to shield her from disease, the well-researched birth plans to weave a hammock for her no harm could touch. I wanted my careful preparation to make a difference.

But the world doesn't work that way, does it?

TWO SUMMERS AFTER COLIN DIED, I attended a five-day "Life, Death, & Transition" workshop hosted by the mother of going gently into death, Elisabeth Kübler-Ross—although, alas, she couldn't be there in person. How I would have loved to meet Dr. Kübler-Ross, to say thank you, but also to look into the eyes of someone who was so clear and so *unafraid*. Grief, for me, had become a kind of shape-shifter—sometimes indistinguishable from fear itself, and sometimes making me numb in a way that felt more like the absence of fear.

The retreat was at a monastery in San Luis Obispo, and driving south—and alone—to California on Highway 1 in the old Subaru station wagon my mother had loaned me for the journey, I kept having flashbacks (joyful, piercing) of a spring break road trip Colin and I had made. I'd flown down to San Diego, where Colin was going to school, and we'd driven north to San Francisco together via Highway 1, a breathtaking stretch of road if ever there was one, partially because of the green cliffs and the blue, blue crashing Pacific, and partially because this two-lane highway winds along the edge of all that and every turn and pass feels as if it might be your last. We were both tanned golden from the California sun. I splayed my painted toes across the dashboard of Colin's BMW and his hand strayed from the wheel to my calf, then my thigh, and I stretched my hands through the open sunroof and felt the warm wind we made with our speed. The cassette in the stereo was Simon & Garfunkel, and we sang along, flashing our eyes at each other with the lines we loved, *I said, "Be careful, his bowtie is really a camera!"*

I had never felt so beautiful, so free, so adored. I remember thinking how happiness, finally, seemed like something I could have, something I deserved. I would stop throwing up completely, I vowed. I would *be* the strong, gorgeous woman Colin believed me to be. His love would believe me back into myself.

Of course Colin had loved my body, as I loved his, but he also loved *me*. I'd been having sex since my mid-teens and before that, when I was a child—that bedrock violation, my body the property of the neighbor across the field long before I knew it was mine. Before Colin, I'd held all that down, buried deep, not knowing how much work I had to do before my body was mine—bones and flesh, skin and hair, hard parts and soft parts—a body I could share if I wanted, without giving anything away.

It makes sense, then, that the sex I had before Colin was like something I watched on TV—not all bad, sometimes comical, never better than a book, but always from a distance, always from the other side of a screen. Before Colin, I didn't stay in my body for sex. I slipped out, a curl of steam, a wisp of vapor, and no one seemed to notice she was gone.

Not even me.

But Colin loved me enough to know this and we practiced. He'd watch for my departure, and if something pulled me away, he would stop whatever he was doing and lie next to me holding my hand. Together we were safe and together we could burn.

In the single year we had together, Colin had beckoned me down from the walls, back from the edges, to inhabit my body, a grown woman's body. With his fingers, his tongue, the firm pressure of all of him, he walked the ledge of my collarbone, fed the curved lines of my ribs, and kissed—again and again—the freckled birthmark spreading across the top third of my left thigh. In the middle school dressing room, the mean girls had pointed, calling out my *dirty spot*, heckling me to *wash off the mud*, but Colin saw something else. "Look," he said, turning my hip with his palm. "A lion. She's running, looking over her shoulder." And I could see her there. *Yes*. Together, we roared, and then Colin took his own body and went away.

Three years after our spring break journey, I was alone—on the same highway, but chugging along now in my mother's ancient station wagon. Something about the sunshine, the quality of the light, brought back that golden day, and in my grief—not deep

grief now, but moving, in Kübler-Ross speak, between acceptance and depression on a daily and sometimes hourly pendulum—the yellow, happy glow we had known together seemed unattainable.
Not for me. Not with anyone. Not anymore.
How could I love that way again when I knew how much could be lost?

THE MONASTERY was at the end of a winding dirt road, and after I parked, I sat for a few minutes, recovering, and watching my fellow transitioners carry bags from trunks. There was a striking blond man with chiseled cheekbones in purple running shorts and a matching boa. He would become my best buddy at the workshop—he'd lost his partner to AIDS, and now he was dying himself. The workshop was by application only, and to qualify we all had to demonstrate that we knew something of death and grief. That we needed to be there.

In the workshop, we sang songs together—*You are my sunshine, my only sunshine*—we wept, we told our stories, we made pictures, and when one of the therapists saw we were ready, we'd be led to a small room, empty but for a few pillows, thick phone books, and a stretch of black, pliable rubber house. "Go ahead," the therapist would say. "Hit it." The first few whacks of the hose on the phone book felt awkward, but then something happened, something cracked open. I thought I had let myself grieve, but what happened over those five days in that little room, lifted the hatch on an aquifer of black sorrow I didn't know I was holding. The sound that came from my mouth didn't even sound human—I was cognizant enough to think that even as I was, somehow, producing that sound. *What if I'd kept that sound swallowed? My god.* I howled like an animal, I moaned and rocked, I cursed, and I fell to my knees and wailed on that phone book with my hose until the muscles in my shoulders gave out and fell limp. How long did I stay my first time in the room? Minutes? Hours? At least an hour. I moved in and out of my body with the force of my keening, dissociating and reconnecting, the blows of the hose on the phone book both time portal and a fulcrum between my physical body and—I don't know what to say here: the spiritual world? my psyche? A connection between my physical body and everything else.

I screamed until all I could manage was a quiet *thank you*. What had felt like depression and fear, I realized, was mired grief, and in mourning Colin I mined the layers, using the power of that rubber hose to unearth the collapsed entrance to the mine shaft and let loose the sealed agony of that girl neither my mother nor I could go back and rescue—but maybe I had found her and helped her, in a way. Maybe I could continue, on my own, the work Colin and I had begun together. Maybe the strategies that had once kept me alive and functioning—denial, perfectionism, the careful mortaring of protective walls—weren't helping me anymore. It's a snarled emotional landscape we spend our lives weaving, and in California that summer we mourners all grabbed onto the yarn and tugged, hand over hand, following Kübler-Ross's tenet that compassion for ourselves leads us to greater compassion for others. When I hugged my new friends, many of whom would soon die—we all knew that—and climbed into my mother's car to make the journey home, I did so with a new sense of peace and the unshakable belief that Colin's love had saved my life—and I owed him something for that. He had been my greatest teacher and I knew he wasn't really gone. When I needed to pray, I would pray to him, and he would hear me.

Now, in the final countdown to Ella's birth, I checked in with Colin regularly. *Pay attention*, I'd say in the night, my hand following the baby's heel as she traced an orbit across the top of my giant belly. *Keep her safe. Please let her stay with us and be our dear one.*

10   Nothing's Going to Change My World

Approaching, and then passing, the due date, everybody had a theory to share about when the baby would come and what would inspire her to make the journey. The woman working in Customer Service at Target when I waddled in to exchange a nursery monitor asked the requisite question: *When are you due?* When I answered, she smiled (these are the rules and the pattern of this particular social dance) and said: "I went bowling. It really worked." Mark came home to report that another professor had stopped him in the hall and said: "Tell her when she can't stand being pregnant for another minute . . . it'll be two more weeks." The woman in the fabric store, with a three-week-old bundle in her arms, said: "Walking. You have to walk. I walked fourteen blocks and then I went into labor."

At this point, my mother was in Indiana playing the waiting game with us. We'd scheduled her arrival a full week before the due date—because I was so absurdly, ridiculously sure the baby would come early—and because the whole point was to have her present in the delivery room to make up for her having been deprived of the birth of her own children by Twilight Sleep. *My greatest regret is that I wasn't awake to see you kids born.* I wanted to give my mom a childbirth do-over.

In retrospect, this was an error. For everybody and in all the ways.

While my mom was as domestically helpful as ever, we were all a little tense, on-edge expectant. To get out of the house, and because the walking suggestion seemed like actual science, she and I took the dogs on a long walk, way more than fourteen blocks, me feeling like some kind of carnival float rolling through the neighborhood.

I didn't go into labor.

By night, Mark dutifully attempted his homework. *Homework*—that's the euphemism the obstetrician used when he winked at Mark at the end of our last appointment and explained that sperm contains natural prostaglandins that bring on labor. I'd hazard to say he even gave Mark a little punch on the shoulder at this point, but I might be making that part up. Either way, Mark must have shuddered inside. *Homework.* Wink.

On Halloween night, the actual due date, Mark and I kissed and fondled a bit, and I delivered what is possibly the least sexy thing any human has uttered to another human during foreplay for sex they were hoping to have: "Oh, you know what? Maybe you could just knock the mucus plug out while you're in there."

Mark pulled away.

"Oh, c'mon," I said. "I'm kidding. I mean, I'm sort of kidding? What's wrong?"

"Well, honey, the bloody show is not exactly the kind of thought that gets me fired up."

"Right. True. Sorry."

So the sex didn't work. And the walking didn't work. Neither did the raking, the jalapeño potato chips, the hot water on the nipples in the shower, the raspberry leaf tea, the deep knee bends, the pleas directed at this comfortable child in my womb: *Okay, baby, we're ready for you. Come out, come out, wherever you are.*

I SPEND A GREAT DEAL of emotional energy wrestling with the essential balance between safety and freedom, and this struggle is made manifest through a fundamental philosophical disagreement with my mother (naturally) that first emerged—like the dark, wet head of an infant—in that week before I gave birth to Ella. I'd written a whole book about my unsupervised childhood, for heaven sakes, and somehow I managed not to see this one coming.

My mother had been browsing my shelves, stuffed with babycare texts, and she said, "In the books, they have some strange things on the lists of things to remember to take to the hospital. Like a car seat. For a little baby?!?!" I didn't know where she was going with this. I truly didn't. "You don't put *little* babies in car seats! You just hold them."

"Well," I said, starting to catch on. "Mom. I mean, yes, you need to have a car seat. You don't want to serve as a missile launcher for your newborn."

"That's why the mother holds the baby in her arms. You just *hold onto* the baby!"

"Well, what if you got rear-ended or something?"

"Oh, what if, what if..." She looked stricken. "Well, it sure is a lot more complicated to have a baby these days. I'm just glad *you* survived."

Thinking myself a saint—an enormously pregnant, past-date, hormonally supercharged saint—I said nothing. What my mom meant was that given her own apparently lax and irresponsible parenting methods for which she now felt acutely judged, beginning with that first ride home from the hospital in Miami when she held me in her own two arms, it was either a miracle my brother and I had survived—*or* I was hysterical and overcautious because *of course* we had survived.

My mother had her last word. "I mean, in what kind of world can a mother not hold her baby on the way home from the hospital?" She shook her head and repeated, "I'm just glad *you* kids survived."

This became my mother's mantra as a grandmother. *It's a miracle you kids survived.*

AFTER THE DUE DATE came and went—*tomorrow, and tomorrow, and tomorrow, creeps in this petty pace from day to day*—we'd begin every day with either Mark or my mom saying, "Today might be the day!"

In my weary resignation, I'd decided that every single labor augmentation trick is a matter of pure coincidence. On the fifth day or so of acupressure and walking and swinging and sex (not unpleasant activities in themselves, except for that surprisingly painful Spleen 6 acupressure point), I'd come to an all-too-obvious conclusion, delayed by my persistent hope: Because every woman in the world has to have done *something* on the day she went into labor, that *something* simply becomes the trick of the day. That's all. There is no there there.

Moving into November, I decided the baby would never be born. I would be pregnant forever. Nary a contraction. No bloody show. No leaking of water. Nada, nada, nada. Then one night I dreamed I was thin again. In the dream, only two days had passed since the birth of the baby and we were all marveling at the rapidity with which I'd regained my waist. I knew this wasn't going to happen, but how luscious to feel—even if only in my sleeping head and only for a moment—lithe.

When my mom came downstairs at seven thirty in the morning, toting camera equipment, she reported that she'd been taking pictures of the sky because the sunrise had been such a stunning shade of pink. "Perhaps today is the day," she said again, and in the interest of posterity I consented to have my photo taken. My mom focused her lens on my great baby belly, emerging taut and round and glowing from my fuchsia pajamas that were by then much too small. "Just the belly, Mom. I swear, if you get my thighs . . ."

My mother, an artist, described the triptych of photos she envisioned: pink sunrise, pink belly, pink baby. A birthday gift.

A FEW DAYS before I finally went into labor, I fell. Mark pinpointed this moment as my "first act of motherly sacrifice." The *first*? Shit. Oh, for men to experience pregnancy.

We were walking Walt and Tango back from the park. I was holding Tango's leash and she was meandering along the way an eleven-year-old dog will. My stumble was not her fault. In fact, when I fell, I dropped her leash, and she stopped also, touching her wet nose to my cheek. What a good girl. On my feet I was wearing Dansko clogs, because with my puffy feet they were comfortable. But I'm graceless, and even the best clog in the world is also a little graceless. There must have been one of those break-your-mother's-back cracks, because I stumbled and began my inexorable journey down toward the asphalt. It was one of those falls that lasts forever. It seemed there was time for everything except preventing the inevitable. Did I scream? I don't think so. But still there was time for Mark to notice I was falling and turn to look into my face in abject horror. And so there was time to register this look on his face and still more time to look down and see the ground coming up to meet my own face, not *rushing* up, but just moving, and time still to think about how vulnerable our baby was hanging down there between my body and this hard ground, and since *not* falling was no longer an option, I braced my arms and legs like a cartoon cat, and I landed with a thud on the pavement. If Pregnant Cat were a yoga pose, that was me.

"Honey!" Mark screamed.

"I fell," I said, reporting the obvious, still on my hands and knees, tail bone tucked, core tight, hanging belly mere centimeters from the asphalt. "It's okay. It's okay. Don't worry. I saved the baby."

THAT EVENING, I was lying on the couch counting kicks when my mom came in from the kitchen looking frustrated. We were all at a breaking point.

Mom: "Where are your containers for putting away food?"
Me: "Oh, I'll get up with you." (Me, getting up. Allow two full minutes for this exercise.) "We have all kinds of mismatched tops and bottoms."

Mom: "I was surprised when I saw you put that guacamole container away with just that little bit of guacamole in it. I could have used that for the enchiladas. That would have been perfect."

Me: "Well, Mom, maybe I'm going to eat that tomorrow. I didn't want any more."

Mom: "But it was just a little scrap."

Me (cracking, falling): "Fine. Put it down on the floor and the dogs will lick it out for you, I'm sure. Then you can put away the leftover enchiladas."

Mark (entering kitchen, right): "What's the problem?"

Me (keeping it light, keeping it light): "Mom wants me to get the guacamole container out of the fridge and tape it over her mouth."

TWO NIGHTS BEFORE I finally, finally went into labor, I had a dream in which the birth was a kind of physical amoeba-like separation. A splitting in two. Ella was one half and I was the other. After our division, we floated in the water, circled by exactly eight species of sharks with menacing, flashing fins.

In my real-life womb, Ella was more restless than she'd ever been before. Could she see the sharks? She squirmed and punched and kicked—twice, I swear, her kicks were accompanied by *sound*: a popping noise. Like the one some people can make with their fingers and cheeks. I couldn't see her yet, but by god now I could *hear* her.

LIKE STORIES about sleeping babies or really big fish, I'm guessing that most stories we hear about labor are, if not patently false, at least greatly exaggerated in one direction or another.

The less common, but perhaps still damaging in the way of raising false hopes, narrative is the I-didn't-even-know-I-was-in-labor story. You've heard these. She stays home and whips up an extra batch of Toll House cookies and when she goes in at 4:00 p.m. for her weekly checkup—oops!—already six centimeters dilated. Better get to the hospital. Whoa! Already crowning! Two pushes and there he was! Everybody was all freshened up with a good appetite by the time the dinner trays came around.

The most common birth story should be cataloged under horror. If you've ever been pregnant, you heard these stories from the moment you shared your news. It's bizarre. You think your officemate is your *friend*, and then she invites you out for coffee in the fourth month of your pregnancy and regales you, in bloody detail, with a story of five hours of pushing, the botched epidural, a compressed umbilical cord, the resulting deceleration of the baby's heart rate, an emergency C-section: the pain, the panic, the pain, the panic, the pain.

I suspect that baby showers are a thinly veiled excuse to gather en masse and tell these stories, each woman trying to outdo the next. Forget about prizes for the identify-the-brown-smear-on-the-Pampers contest—let's earn our scented votive candles and Starbucks gift cards by telling the story that most effectively scares the stuffing out of the expectant mother. Is the circus-themed crib bumper in her hands trembling a bit? Was that a tear I saw drop into the pee-pee teepee?

Seriously. I shouldn't even be writing this chapter. Shame on me.

What's the parallel? If you've recently been diagnosed with some illness, do mere acquaintances tell you about how their own treatment went terribly wrong and not only they but their precious children all knocked together on death's door? Does this seem like a nice thing to do?

Or in a parallel time of great joy and expectation, do we say, "Oh, that's great that you're getting married—congratulations! Let me tell you some details about *my* first marriage! Well! Turns out he was already sleeping with my cousin when he proposed. While I was planning the wedding, he got my account number under the ruse of ordering flowers, and he withdrew money—for a casino trip!" Etcetera. No. We wouldn't do that. But with birth stories it's no holds barred. And it's sick and weird.

SOMEHOW, I STOOD STRONG against the hype. The scaredy-cat to beat all scaredy-cats, and I wasn't going to be afraid of this one. I was going to be in control. I was going to have an experience like no other. *If there's pain, it will be pain for a purpose*, I explained to Mark, *good pain*, who in his typical style gave me the you're-nuts-but-if-that-makes-you-feel-better look and went on with whatever he was doing while I drew stick people in labor positions on note cards, assembled the ingredients for the lemony calcium-enriched Labor Aid, and bounced my ever-widening bottom on a wheezing exercise ball.

I had a plan—and I *love* a plan. It certainly hadn't occurred to me—to any of us, except maybe Dr. P—that I might be risking actual death.

The day I had been *sure* the baby would be born came and went, and on my last regular ob-gyn visit, I drew an unlucky straw and ended up propped up on my elbows, heels tucked into the oven-mitted stirrups, waiting for one Dr. H.

This was the guy who, alarmed by what he considered to be excessive weight gain, had suggested I try to take a walk once in a while. *Oh, yeah, buddy? Do you want to come over to my house in your stretchy pants for the cardio portion of my Fit Mama DVD?* While I had never forgiven him for this insult, I wanted what the other ob-gyn had offered, and I'd refused, at my previous appointment. I couldn't *stand* to be pregnant for another week—and was ready to have those membranes stripped.

I'd been reading up, and the books warned that stripping could be a painful procedure. The nurse checking my blood pressure had told me that the pain level seemed to vary from doc to doc, adding, *I haven't seen how rough Dr. H is . . .*

Rough? Mercy. Alright then.

When Dr. H came in, I flipped up my paper lap pad and encouraged him to do what needed to be done. "Give it your best shot," I said. I could take it. Mark winced and scooted back in his plastic chair.

I don't remember Dr. H saying anything at all as he plucked a couple of gloves from the dispenser, pulled them on with a snap, and leaned in. I felt his hand go up, all the way up, and then there was some circling of his fingers—stripping, I suppose?—and then his hand came out the same way it went in, not at all roughly, he rolled off both gloves, flicked them into the trash, and that, it appeared, was that.

"That's it?" I asked. After all the lead up? There was no way what had just happened in my vagina was going to inspire *anything*. I'd had more action from a super-plus tampon.

"That's it." His face was expressionless. Who is it in the Lorrie Moore story with "a face as blank as a donut"? The donut image came to mind as I watched Dr. H pick up his clipboard and check off a couple boxes before reminding me to give the office a call if contractions started coming in a regular pattern.

Oh. Right. Good idea. I'll for sure do that.

BUT PERHAPS I'd underestimated Dr. H. That evening there was big excitement: the Bloody Show! I had Vicki Iovine's *Girlfriend's Guide* to thank for the scoop on the show, and perhaps that's why I was neither scared nor grossed out. How could things get any grosser? Seriously, earlier in the day, my husband had sat dutifully by the examination table and watched as an ultraconservative thirty-something ob-gyn with a face as placid as a dumpling had thrust his gloved hand into my most private of places, halfway up to the elbow, and rotated like a man trying to remove a clog from a drain. Ugh. So when I peed for the forty-sixth time that day and the toilet paper came up with a gob of bloody mucus, I didn't cringe—I grinned. I swear, it took all the remaining self-respect I could muster to flush that toilet before I heaved myself off it and waddled ecstatically out to the living room: "It came! It came! The bloody show!"

We thought the main attraction was about to begin. We waited. Contractions came and went. I was so tuned into my body I felt like a transistor radio. Even the dogs seemed bored with the waiting. Tango rested her chin on her paws and let out a zombie-worthy groan. "I know," I told her from my post on the couch. "I know."

The next day, with contractions coming pretty regularly, I decided to take a shower and gauge the usefulness of a directed flow of water on my contracting uterus. The water was stone cold. When I asked my mother to go down in the basement to check the dial on the hot water heater, she didn't return. When I myself ventured down the steps, I found my poor mother standing ankle-deep in the flooded basement.

"The hot water heater is broken," she said mournfully. *Of course it is*, I thought. *Of fucking course. Perfect.* But here's the amazing thing: When I called the plumber, I told the receptionist I was in labor (perhaps saying so would make it true, and I *was* contracting). I told her I *needed* that hot water. She had a serviceman at our house within the hour, and within two hours I was taking a hot shower. Remarkable. And while I'm praising the goodness of humankind, let me tell you this: With neither a drain nor a wet-vac at her disposal, my dear mother *bailed out* that basement with a bucket and a sawed-off milk jug. By evening, she had the fans blowing out the last of the dampness. The email joke to my anxious extended family was handed to me: *My water broke!* And maybe that was the distraction I needed, because that night the contractions intensified and established the longed-for pattern.

Let the wild rumpus begin.

WHEN DAWN BROKE on November 6, 2003, I knew it was the real deal. First, I emailed the dog sitter and put her on notice. Then, in the interest of staying home as long as possible, I hung out in the living room watching—weirdly—*The Water Is Wide* on some high-number movie channel (remember, these were the days of cable, not streaming) and bouncing on my exercise ball. Occasionally, Mark would come in and stand with me while I had a particularly intense contraction.

The contractions felt like tightenings, cramps, and thus my hubris grew. I was so well prepared. So ready and calm. This was going to be easy. I called my doctors expecting instructions to get to the hospital. Nope. They said I should come over to the office instead. Whatever.

Dr. H again. He took another run at the membrane stripping (this time, I have to hand it to him, with a little more oomph) and told me I was *not* in labor, something, something, false contractions. What?!? I've been *timing* my contractions! There's a *pattern*, Mister!

But when the nurse hooked me up to the contraction-measuring machine, the scratching needle arced all the way up to the top. "Wow," the nurse said, "that's as big as they get."

"But Dr. H said I wasn't even in labor!"

You're in labor, she mouthed, with a dismissive smirk on her face.

My cockiness, now, was unconcealed. I practically skipped out through the waiting room, rattling the magazines in their metal racks. "Did you hear that?" I said to Mark. "That's as bad as it gets!"

I DON'T KNOW what kind of fucked up machinery they have in that office.

A couple hours later, when we got to the hospital, the brand-new Jacuzzi room was occupied by another laboring woman (who, it turned out, had no interest in using the tub). A nurse named Sheila, whom I would come to love in the way that those sharing captivity become devoted, got me settled, cleaned up my vomit, and checked my cervix: c'mon, c'mon, c'mon. I had labored so long and well at home, I was thinking, *She's going to say seven centimeters! I'm almost through transition! I'll be ready to push within the hour! I'm there!*

But that is not what Sheila said. "Three centimeters, *maybe* four," Sheila said, rolling off her glove.

Well shit.

I brushed off these disappointments and asked to get in the shower. Mark and my mom waited outside while I rocked myself, the warm stream focused on my belly, fingers spread and braced against the slick tile. I began humming. As the pain increased, I traveled into myself where my baby was waiting to be born. Together we would find the passageway out. Although I'd imagined swaying and dancing and walking with Mark, we did none of these things. I didn't want to be touched, and this time that was my choice. My birthing partners bore silent witness to a dance I danced alone in the final hours that Ella and I were the same body.

Mark's role became that of ice-chip feeder, and from the glider chair that became my post, I would give him a slight nod—we rarely spoke—and he would scoop two ice chips out of the Styrofoam cup he held at the ready and slip the plastic spoon between my dry lips. My mother, as close as she would ever come to making up for those moments she missed in her twilight sleep when her own children were removed from her body, sat directly across from me with her hands held up, doing a kind of short-distance Reiki to help ease the pain. Maybe she was the one who hit play again and again on the *I Am Sam* soundtrack. (Why did I choose Beatles *covers* to welcome our baby into the world? How tacky am I?)

We had a whole case of CDs, of course, and my plan had involved changing the music as labor changed and progressed, but that was beyond my capacity to adapt. I didn't want anything in that room to change except the position of my cervix, and ultimately my baby.

Not the lights, not the smells, not the angle of my chair, and for god's sake not the music. The consistency of that room tied me to the earth in a way I required to travel where I needed to go to find Ella. Since *I Am Sam* was the first CD to go in, that became our soundtrack. *Nothing's going to change my world.*

At sunset, my labor stalled around six centimeters and so my doctor, the red-haired Dr. S on this evening, appeared with the crochet hook to break my water. When he snagged the bag, he leaped back out of his stool as a tremendous gush splashed out. "Whoa!" Then he said, "Okay, there's a little meconium."

As Sheila whisked away the soaked bedding and scooted me into a giant diaper, I was only partly cognizant of Mark's question to Dr. S about the meconium and what that meant for the baby's safety. Dr. S was reassuring. "Oh, that just means there'll be four more people in the room when she gets here."

AFTER THE CUSHION of water between Ella's head and my cervix was drained away, I descended deeper into pain. When my mom worried that Mark needed something to eat and peeled open a package of turkey jerky, I thought the smell would send me over the edge. Eyes only half open, between contractions, I whispered viciously, "Get that out of here. Get it *out*."

The image I hold in my mind from these last couple hours is the view from my chair, with no people in it, across the labor room: on the ledge by the window, a propped picture frame, a close-up of the dogs' faces, Tango's smooth and Walt's shaggy, and past them, the pink of the setting sun, the last glimmering rays illuminating the clouds like something out of a Maxfield Parrish painting. I focused on this glowing patch of sky with the intensity of a tiger with a gazelle in her sights. No. Not that fierce, more meditative, but still, excluding everything else. Nothing but pink. All that muted, musky, glowing pink. I was in those clouds, in that light, with my baby girl, and from here, I knew, I would carry her down to join her family on earth. I never doubted I was in control of our future, and our safety.

Rocking and moaning, I went so deep, I would actually fall asleep (or what appeared to be sleep) in the mere seconds between contractions. I remember mumbling what I hoped would play as a kind of joke in a quick second where the pain released her grip—"Twilight sleep is looking pretty good right now..."—but I don't think anybody thought that was funny, and before anyone dared respond, I went back down.

When I got the word to "push past that last centimeter," after seven hours of *I Am Sam*, I pushed. Hard. Here was something I could *do*, and apparently Ella was as ready as I was, because after only twenty minutes, Sheila cried *Stop* and ran into the hall for Dr. S.

Sheila set up a mirror for me, Dr. S took up his post between my legs, I pushed again, and my god, there was a great shaggy crown of black hair, soaked and shining. One more push and Ella's whole head emerged, turned to the side. My mom reported she could see an ear. An ear! Dr. S told me to stop again, and while he suctioned Ella's nose and mouth, we three who already loved her so much watched that wet head: *Oh my god. There she is.*

"OKAY." Dr. S gave me a nod.

When I bore down for one last, determined push, I met no resistance—the rest of Ella slid out as smoothly as an egg slips from it cracked shell. There was no pain, only this amazing slipperiness, this fast feeling of someone being *born*. The doctor deflected her up onto my stomach, a kind of half-caught toss, and I pulled her to my chest, grateful and loving her already, yes, and her eyes were open, and she looked into mine, and I thought, *You're here, you're here!* and *You're okay! Look at you! You're whole and you're breathing—a little blue, but you're breathing, and you're okay!*

In seconds, this moment was over and the neonatal team swooped her onto the glowing infant bed and put a tube down into her lungs. Dr. S and those four extra people in the room did all the right things and I never had to research "meconium aspiration syndrome"—because although there was meconium in the amniotic fluid and here was a horror that would appear on the list of terrible things that can happen, this one did not. Mark stuck close to Ella, and even though there couldn't have been more than ten feet between the foot of my bed and the baby station, they seemed an ocean away. I called across that gap: "Is she okay? Is she okay? Is she okay?"

"Yes," Mark called back, "yes! She's at a hundred percent." Even though he looked a little terrified, he was on the job, I could see that, so I dropped back into the pillows and pulled my attention to the man in the long gloves hard at work between my still spread thighs, sewing up the evening's damage, which was neither as bad as Dr. P had predicted nor as good as I had hoped. Three tears, one of them fairly serious.

The baby I'd been waiting for all my life lay on a glowing table within the range of my sight, but somehow she seemed far, far away.

I wanted her back.

I WAS NURSING Ella for the first time when things started to go black.

At first I thought my dizziness was a by-product of all that newly expressed maternal love. Maybe this was the breastfeeding hormone I'd read about, some kind of love-juice. Maybe initially there's so much, your blood is so awash in the stuff, you almost feel as if you're going to throw up. *Maybe this isn't wooziness I'm feeling*, I thought, *but motherly devotion.*

The room undulated. I was looking down at Ella as she suckled, and the little pink cap on her head moved in and out of focus. I turned my eyes up, Mark on my right and my mother on my left. Their images lurched and went gray.

This was not about love.

"Mark," I said. "Mark. Take the baby. I don't want to drop her. I think I'm going to faint."

That did it.

Mark took the baby, and Sheila rushed over with the blood pressure cuff. Sheila, of course, knew what was happening and called for help. I needed an IV immediately, but I was hemorrhaging, and my veins were already collapsing. Neither Sheila nor the other nurse who ran in could find a vein. The space around my bed was buzzing with uniforms. I remember feeling as if I were watching all the commotion from the ceiling and thinking—*Oh man. I should have gotten the hep-lock. Shit.* And then looking over to Mark, rocking our new baby girl, and thinking, *Awwwww* . . . I didn't feel scared, but I did feel tired. So tired. All I wanted to do was sleep.

Sheila called in a nurse from another floor. *She's the best*, I heard someone say. *Get her.* And then the best was there by my side and she found a vein. They got the Pitocin started, and lots of it. But already I'd lost too much blood. When poor Sheila pushed on my stomach to help my uterus contract, I could feel blood clots flopping out like more babies. The pain was so sudden, so extreme, that I took a swing at her, caught her arm, tried to hold her back, all the while muttering, "I'm sorry, I'm sorry," but not loosening my grip. Mark tells me that's when *he* almost fainted.

Dr. S had gone home, but the nurses called him back to the hospital. Postpartum hemorrhage. There were some follow-up hairy moments, but after the IV was in place, the room cleared out again and the tension eased. I wasn't going to die, and my poor mother, who looked stricken and kept muttering things about *her* baby, and how horrible it was to see me in such pain and then the bleeding and those awful clots, went back home to check on the dogs and get some sleep. Through the whole ordeal, I was pretty calm—actually, really calm, likely the chemical result of a cocktail of painkillers and blood loss shaken up with the mama endorphins I oozed every time Mark carried Ella to my bed and tucked her to my breast, an avid sucker from the first, so impossibly beautiful. *Our baby.* I was woozy with love and relief—and blood loss.

By morning my bleeding was finally under control, but I'd lost too much and Dr. S told me they were going to have to do a transfusion. That was the first time I felt afraid. In the starkly lucid light of the day, I watched the nurse agitate the first quivering bag of blood and hang it from the pole, suddenly terrified by the thought of a stranger's blood mixing with mine. I started to cry, and then I felt ungrateful—here, this woman (I was so hoping she was a she) had given so selflessly, given her *bodily fluids*, and I was judging her, questioning her, hoping she'd led a good life, a clean life. What an ingrate. I cried the whole time her blood flowed in with mine, thinking way too hard about whether the currents mixed right away, or whether our bloods ran side by side through my filling veins. I imagined rivers of blood.

Transfusion is not really something you want to overthink on a day when your progesterone levels are plummeting. Plus, I felt like a fool. *Oh*, I thought, *how those ob-gyn guys must have been shaking their heads at the uppity hippie chick insisting on no hep-lock and no Pitocin*. Now I would be the cautionary tale they'd tell the medical students—anecdotal or no.

Still, if I hadn't been "a bleeder," everything would have been fine. *Usually* everything is fine, I want to record here in these pages—but I can also hear Mark's voice. *Can you just say it? Can you just say that the doctors were right and you were wrong?*

Okay, yes, but can I say also that I was not afraid? Can I say that I had once been a kid so full of fear that I flushed the toilet with my toe in order to be in a good position to outrun the crocodile I was sure would someday emerge from the depths, snapping? I had once been the kid who protected the real thing that was hurting me, the teenager who took big, swinging steps across the field to come see me when my mother wasn't home. Back then I had been too afraid to speak. But now I had done this hard thing. I had made it through a natural labor and delivery without fear. I felt... triumphant. And grateful to be alive. Grateful our baby was alive.

I've read that sometimes women who have been abused are retraumatized by childbirth, and that makes sense—the pain, exposure, vulnerability, and intensity of the birth experience dig deep, but I was okay. To use a metaphor from my kayaking days: I'd scouted the rapid and made the choice to paddle right down the tongue, leaning hard into the rock, swooping around and through the waves and obstacles to emerge triumphant—with our baby. Maybe I'd been empowered by making so many of my own decisions about the birth, maybe I'd truly done the work of excavating what needed to be excavated before stepping across the open space and into motherhood, but again, I was okay. Maybe even better than okay.

I was clear-eyed and awestruck, present in all the right ways, when Dr. S swept my naked, wet, breathing babe up onto my own naked body in the seconds after her birth. I was there to love Ella from the start—with nothing in between us.

The bleeding had come later, so yes, a hep-lock would have been a good idea, but other than that I had no regrets. *Next time*, I thought—*if there is a next time, I will ask for the hep-lock and enough* IV *Pitocin to clot the flowing blood of Napoleon's army on its march to Moscow.*

11 Moona's Story

In September 2005, I had my first miscarriage. Ella was almost two and must have been at our university's infant-toddler lab, a daycare where she spent her mornings, because the house was quiet and I was working in the guest room, under a quilt my mother made us for our wedding, writing.

I was pregnant again and I felt a rush of something between my legs. Here was a feeling I would spend the next four years fearing, waiting for, but this first time is so distinct in my memory. I was unprepared. I didn't know what was going on. I set my laptop on the bedside table, swung my feet off the bed and onto the floor, and walked across the hall to the bathroom. This distance across the cool hardwood floor, no rug, to the even cooler bathroom tile is no more than ten feet and likely I could have traveled the distance in five strides, but it's that walk I remember.

While I was making that journey, I was still a woman who'd never had a miscarriage. *How am I going to feel?* I wondered. *If this is blood between my legs, if this is blood and if that blood means miscarriage, how will I feel?* I wasn't sure. Here was a species of loss I didn't know. I hadn't yet made it to the bathroom where I would pull my underwear down to my knees, sit on the toilet, and see this new fear spreading down my thighs.

The blood was bright red. I was just seven weeks pregnant, too early even to have had my first doctor's appointment, so early. (I am looking at you, six-week bans.) I sat on the toilet, staring at the blood, and then I kicked my bloody underwear off my toes. I tossed them into the bathtub, pulled a maxi-pad left over from my postpartum months out of the bathroom closet, peeled off the paper, and having no strength to go downstairs to my dresser for fresh underwear, stuck the adhesive directly to the crotch of my sweatpants. Then I returned to my laptop in the guest room. I Googled "bleeding first trimester." I Googled "bleeding first trimester bright red." I called the ob-gyn and made an appointment for tests.

A day later, when the nurse called back with the results, I didn't need them. By then, the flow was heavy and there was no doubt. Not even the fiercest cognitive dissonance could interpret what was happening as "spotting." The nurse told me my hCG levels were dropping. She was sorry. Not unusual. Up to one-quarter of early pregnancies end in miscarriage. "Many women have miscarriages and don't even know," she said by way of comfort.

I knew. If I hadn't known, would I have felt nothing? Is knowledge the source of grief? Is *hope*? With the phone in my hand, I returned to the guest room, pulled back my mother's quilt, and climbed into the guest bed. (Again, Ella must have been at the Child Study Center. What granted me the luxury of this curled sadness? When the nurse called, I was alone.)

We had been trying for another pregnancy, but not aggressively. I hadn't resorted to thermometers and charts, mucus stretching and five minutes of feet in the air. A second pregnancy would happen or it wouldn't. We couldn't decide, so we would let nature take her course. Now I wonder if I really believed this, or whether I just pretended to believe this—for Mark? To avoid attracting bad luck? Or to tamp down hope and protect my heart?

Whatever the reason, we'd told ourselves we would leave it to chance. Chance made a choice, and I was pregnant. And then she made another, and I was not.

Pregnancy doesn't always equal baby.

WHEN MY MOM and I arrived on our mountain in Washington state in 1983, Moona became my horse, my very own horse—*and she was pregnant*. Imagine my delight—a horse-crazy fourteen-year-old girl with her first horse. Not just one horse, but a *pregnant* horse. Fueled by years of reading every horsey series I could get my hands on, from *The Black Stallion* to *Misty of Chincoteague*, my mind galloped through the possibilities of my future life with mare and foal. In a way, my girlhood was getting a second chance, a dream come true.

Granted, my delight was tempered by the harder realities of my situation: I didn't ride Moona just for fun. She and I didn't win blue ribbons for barrel racing at the county fair as we surely had in my preteen fantasies. I needed Moona. Every morning, I angled a sharp, crescent pick, pulled the ice from her hooves, and saddled her up for the frigid ride to the one-room schoolhouse. There, I tied her out with the other girls' horses (the boys rode snowmobiles) and tossed her a flake of alfalfa from the communal schoolyard stack.

Moona's was the first pregnancy I had a hand in nurturing. Horses gestate for nearly a year, and I understood that in the final months, I wouldn't be able to ride Moona to school. Instead of saddling her up on those snowy, early mornings, I would bring her a can of her special maternity grain, a sticky mixture of oats and honey. She was crazy for the stuff and when she saw me coming, she'd toss up her tail like a flag and trot around her paddock in a one-horse grain parade. I'd rub her tightening belly, scratch her dusty forelock, and head down the snowy path to school on foot.

How many times had I worked through the details of the May morning I would walk up to Moona's paddock and see the new foal trying out her wobbly knees? Afterward, in my imaginings, our fuzzy filly would trot along behind her mama when we road to school in the final days of that year, the bright yellow balsa root flowers blooming on the hillsides and the tiny hooves clicking in the hardening mud. She would be a chestnut, like her mother, with a fringe of a black mane, with a dark nose that would fit into the palm of my hand like a chestnut, cool and soft.

Here was a creature of my imagination and dreams. Here was a creature I would love like no other.

WANTING A SECOND CHILD, it turns out, isn't like wanting a second car or a new dog. I didn't get to simply *decide* to have a baby and then do it. That's not the way it works.

I knew that, and early on, in my naivete, I also didn't know that. Because I am a second baby, the breathing result of just such a decision, I thought of my mother. When my older brother, Ian, was thirteen months old, he was burned in the bathtub of their apartment in Providence, Rhode Island—almost to death, with only a one in ten chance of survival at first, and then he endured months and months of terrible pain and surgeries and skin grafts. A couple months into this horror, my father left for graduate school in Syracuse without his family. I don't understand the choice to separate during a time of such struggle, so soon after the accident that came so close to killing their firstborn, but I wasn't there, was I? My father insisted this was a decision he and my mother made together—the choice to split.

For her part, my mother tells me about those dark days she and her burned but breathing baby rented a single, bare room near the hospital where the baby needed to go daily for treatments: They had barely enough money for food and so she would buy a package of hot dogs—the cheapest meat—and she would peel off the casing for her meal, and chop up the soft inside for my brother. In this way, they survived.

"Why didn't you ask Grammy and Grandfather to help?" I want to know. My grandparents weren't rich, but they were middle class, a high school principal and a librarian; surely, they would have welcomed the chance to help their daughter after such a tragedy.

"I don't know," my mother says sadly. "It was such a terrible time. I don't know. Why wouldn't I have asked for help? I can't remember."

Around this time, my mother decided to sell her wedding ring to get money to make payments on the astronomical hospital bills, and my father's aunt and uncle bought the ring. When I was young, I found this part of the story horrifying, but now I understand that what I had once interpreted as a callous move to keep the family jewels in the family was way more likely to have been a strategy to help my struggling mother in a way she could accept. A kindness.

"But then I went back to him when your brother was three," my mother tells me. "It was Christmas! Maybe I was in the holiday spirit, maybe it seemed like your brother should be with his father at Christmas. I wanted to have another baby so that Ian would have a little brother or sister. I wanted to have another baby that *matched*." Chalk one up for the holiday spirit, but I arrived in the world the following August—exactly nine months later—on the same day that Janice Joplin took the stage at Woodstock.

My mother had decided she wanted a "baby that matched," and lo I was delivered. My mother was twenty-five when I was born; still a young mother, after all she'd been through.

WHEN I WAS A TEENAGER on the mountain, my biggest fears—beyond, you know, not being good enough to deserve love—were Bigfoot and cougars. There was a dark stretch of road on our mile-long driveway just before the aspen grove and the final approach to our house. At dusk, it was like something straight out of a Tim Burton movie, silhouetted trees grew spindly fingers and leaned out over the road. Riding home, the world seemed to tilt toward Moona and me, pressing on us as we clip-clopped through, trying to look cool, trying to look like a girl and a horse that were not afraid. I don't know how I first came to associate this dark stretch with Bigfoot's lair, but once I'd folded my uncle's campfire stories onto this place, I couldn't shake the chill. I felt watched, sure I could be taken as a girl-bride of Bigfoot. Horses sense fear, and as soon as my body tensed, Moona's ears would start twitching and she'd dance a little under the tug of the reins until we both just gave into our nerves, and I loosened the reins and spurred her into an anxious canter with one cluck of my tongue and squeeze of my knees. We were both ready to get out of there.

At this time of night, there was still one more spook before home. The ridge above the final curve held a rock that, in falling light, looked exactly like a crouching mountain lion. *That rock is always there*, I'd tell myself. *That's not a mountain lion. It's a rock. A rock.* But the mind is powerful, and the mind said: *lion.* I didn't pull in the reins until we skidded to a stop in front of Moona's paddock, our hearts pounding together in the darkening silence of our imaginary fear.

I mean, there *were* lions on our mountain.

There are so many ways to be afraid.

IN THE SPAN of Ella's first year, both dogs died—first, Walt to bone cancer in April and then Tango, seemingly of a broken heart, a few months later. She just lay down and died. We were devastated, grieving, unsure of how we wanted to move forward in the building of our family. Maybe we could be a family of three. No more dogs, no more babies—just the three of us: Mama, Daddy, Baby. I don't remember consciously thinking, *Why push our luck?*

Also, I remember being practical, or pretending to be, justifying. Where had I heard the formula that a woman writer trades a book for every baby? If we had another baby, we would start over with everything—the nausea, the all-day nursing, the babycare negotiations, the diapers. Plus, I reasoned, as a family of three, we would be more portable. Fitting comfortably into the three seats on one side of the plane, we would travel together and often. College costs would be more manageable.

Opinions among our friends, siblinged and not, were varied.

My friend Libbie, an only child, had often told me of her triangulated childhood, the quiet dinner table with both sets of parental eyes fixed on her and only her. She alone was responsible for entertainment and disappointment. At the time of my first miscarriage, Libbie was also in her first trimester with her second child; her boy, almost two, hurt during his birth, could not yet walk. Libbie helped her son eat, took him to therapy of all kinds, held her breath for an unharmed child, this second child.

Colin's sister, Diane, one of seven and mother of two, pronounced the possibility that we would choose to have just one child, failing to provide a playmate and confidante for Ella, "unconscionable." Not one for a loosely held opinion, Diane scoffed and rolled her eyes and stomped her feet.

When I shared Diane's view with a friend I'll call Amy, one of three and childless by choice, presenting the picture of alone-in-the-world Ella, Amy countered with the example of her own brother and sister with whom she was locked in a well-worn pattern of dysfunction. "But you were the last born," I countered. "You were the last one." Without her, Amy's parents would be sunk; Amy's siblings were the opposite of what I imagined in Ella's nonexistent baby brother or sister. In times of family trouble, they were combatant or needy or simply not there. Amy loved Ella dearly, I knew, but I knew also her well-founded opinion that the value of siblings was overrated and the specter of onliness overwrought.

But I was most struck by the response I got from a friend who is the mother of a single unspoiled boy whom I adored. Hers was the model of one-child family to me, but I knew she had suffered from years of secondary infertility. One day as we sweated side by side on the elliptical machines at the YMCA, I asked my friend—mother, teacher, researcher, feminist, fluent speaker of five languages: "When did you know you were ready to give up trying? That enough was enough?"

She looked at me grimly, and then away. "Never," she said. "I never gave up."

This stuck with me.

I never gave up.

BEFORE THE MISCARRIAGE, when I'd peed on the stick and got two lines, any vestige of uncertainty had evaporated. We *would* have another baby! We were thrilled. And now, without my having decided, without any consultation with me about what I wanted, my body had closed the door. In my mind, I'd sprinted past the nausea and the weight gain, the tests and the labor. In my mind, I'd moved us into our new reality as a family of four—all this in the short time I'd known about the pregnancy. And now all that was gone, wiped away, a sliding bar on an Etch-a-Sketch erasing the picture.

Alone in the spare bedroom, I cried. I remember one lucid thought. I remember thinking, *Now I am a woman who has had a miscarriage*, and forgive me, but I was surprised by the pain. I remember thinking this sentence, so clear in my mind: *A miscarriage is a death of hope.* I wanted to figure out *why* I felt so sad.

And then: *Oh, poor Ella, now she will have to carry my fear alone. She is all my eggs in one basket.* Instead of the usual image of the precariously stacked eggs, pulled warm and brown from beneath laying chickens, risking a bump that would break them all and set them to oozing, I saw the magnified textbook illustration of the twin fallopian tubes and ovaries. A single, monthly, dropping egg, and at the bottom, a colorful basket with Ella inside. I shook my head to clear the image. Poor Ella. What a mother she had to deal with.

ON THE DAY Moona gave birth, I was off the mountain on a school skiing trip. That morning, when I had delivered her breakfast, I'd seen no signs that delivery was imminent, but what did I know? Nothing. It was too early, way too early.

When I ask about it now, my mother cannot remember what brought her to Moona's paddock. Had she heard Moona's grief? Was she nickering pitifully, or was she agitated? Neighing and stomping? Pawing the ground?

My mother remembers approaching the paddock gate and seeing the dark, wet shapes of the foals, lying in the bright snow, steaming lightly, wrapped in the translucent gauze of their amniotic sacs. My imagined filly turned out to be two. Twins. Twins!

Born still.

When I got home from the slopes that night, and my mother was waiting for me with the news, grim-faced and sorry. "They looked like angels," she said. "Angel horses."

LATER, when I entered into the online support community for women who had lost pregnancies and infants, I would learn about the phrase "angel babies." From other women, women suffering unspeakable losses and pain, I would learn to imagine happy babies in the clouds—our angels. Through these women, I would be introduced to the spiritual concept that the soul of a baby lost in pregnancy might not mind that much. He might hang out with the other angels, cloud-hopping and playing.

Here, I couldn't let my mind linger. Even in fantasy, I was an overthinker: Who fed them? Cuddled them? Made sure they were warm enough? Did we have to age our helpless infants to outstandingly self-sufficient toddler-aged cherubs? Did they ride across the clouds clinging to the manes of stillborn foals, angels all?

In the angel baby stories of the online support groups, these not-yet-born babies would watch their original, lost moms for the next pregnancy and then, *zoop*, they would come home again, settle in, and wait to be born. In this way, the suffocating sadness of pregnancy loss, even repeated, could be reimagined into something temporary—a gentle, waffling ellipsis, not a chapter break. Not the end.

I NEVER SAW Moona's foals. Earlier in the day, before I got home, my mother's boyfriend had bagged them in black plastic, hauled them in a truck to the place in the woods where he took deer carcasses, and dropped them over the cliff. I remember an impulse to go there and find the foals, to see that they had been real and were really dead, gone, but that was impossible.

I asked my mother to tell me more. Born still, they had seemed perfect, she assured me. They were beautiful, she said, one white and one black—so far from my imagining of a miniature Moona in every way. The detail she returns to again and again is the eyelashes, a luxurious fringe curtaining the closed eyes of each foal. "They looked like angels."

Afterward, Moona seemed okay. When my mother found her there, standing beside her dead babies, she took pity and emptied the rest of that fancy horse granola into the feed trough. The grain seemed to do the trick, break her mourning, but who knows with horses? Who knows what they think?

Not long after the twins died, we learned that Moona had been bred many times before and never achieved a live birth. In horses, the successful gestation and birthing of twins is crushingly rare—a mare's body doesn't have the space and resources to nurture two foals—so if a twin pregnancy is revealed via ultrasound early enough, it's standard veterinary protocol to do a twin reduction to give one foal and the mama a fighting chance. I didn't know this when I was fourteen, and the fancy grain was the beginning and end of her prenatal care, so poor Moona's pregnancy was doomed from the start, but none of us knew.

We never tried again for Moona. For her, enough was enough.

What about for us? For me? Would we try one more time? Three times? Until we got our baby—or died trying?

12   The Secret of Secrets

My obstetrician, not the kind of guy I would call a lactivist, and likely working from some outdated research, suggested I'd up my chances of maintaining a pregnancy if I weaned Ella. With the ogre of "advanced maternal age" looking me in the face like a bad mirror in a department store dressing room on bathing suit day, I decided to go along with it—grudgingly, and with a breaking heart.

Ella was just over two on the morning of her last breastfeeding. She'd stumbled in from her own room around five o'clock, as usual, scrambled up into our bed, and latched on. Humming and suckling, she slipped into sweet sleep. Most mornings, this was the method by which my husband and I got to be those rare parents who slept until eight.

This morning was different because I would be catching a flight, without Ella, to interview job candidates for three days at the Modern Languages Association Conference in Washington DC. I'd never been away from Ella for a night. Not ever. I lay awake and watched Ella nurse, feeling sick with love and fear and the specter of our separation, touching the tiny droplets of sweat on her soft temple, watching her jaw pumping out the rhythm of our bodies together.

Mark and I had decided that this forced separation would be the perfect weaning window, and I knew chances were good that this would be the last time she and I would lie together like this: cuddled, content, sleepy and sleeping. I must have dozed off myself because the next thing I knew the morning news was mumbling in my ear and the clock glowed six thirty. In that alarm-clock moment I did what I had always done when I needed to get up without Ella: I slipped my finger between her lips and my nipple to break the suction, held a gentle pressure under her chin until her sucking wound down and her mouth relaxed. And then I got out of the bed.

In the dark, on the way across the room to the bathroom, I realized what I had done. I had failed to mark the last time as the *last time*. Standing frozen in the warm stream of the shower, I felt as if that moment should have been something more. What should she and I have done? Lit a candle? Whispered a prayer? Shared a promise?

My last morning with Colin had not been unlike this one with Ella, quiet and quotidian. I know there are dramatic endings: lovers pried apart by prison guards, babies snatched from their mothers' arms, sick children wheeled down long hallways to operating theaters from which they may never return, fingers slipping away—drowning or falling or stretching out a train car window like in the movies. The last morning I saw Colin was a Monday. We were living in Eugene, Oregon, where I was in college and he had to leave early for the two-hour drive to Tillamook on the coast where he was working for a blimp company: They were doing an inflation that week. That morning, I was only vaguely aware of Colin showering, dressing, and packing his duffel in the three-bedroom ranch we shared with his sister Diane and her two small girls. Before heading out to his car at 6:00 a.m., he got down on his knees next to our low bed and leaned into me, cool skin and minty shaving cream scent. He gave me a real kiss. He told me he loved me, how much he'd miss me. *I love you I love you I love you*, we said into each other's mouths. We thought he would be back on Friday evening. We thought we would be apart for four nights—which felt to us like quite a long time—so maybe we did mark this moment, our last goodbye, even as we had no idea what we were marking. By Wednesday Colin was gone.

On the morning of Ella's last nursing, standing under the warm stream of the shower, my heart breaking, tears mixing with soap mixing with water, I told myself firmly that no one was dying. I was only going away for a few days. No one was going to die. Everything was fine. We were all okay. Everyone was okay.

I needed to hurry or I was going to miss my plane.

THINK OF ALL your last times in love. Did you know they were endings? The end? This time, so rare, I had known, and I had let it slip away.

In nursing, Ella and I had located each other. Seconds after the doctor tossed her onto my belly, she'd rooted around and found what she needed. Knowing nothing but what I'd read in books, I had followed her lead. *Here you go, Baby. Here you go. Shhhh.* Since then, we had known no other way of being.

But motherhood is about letting go—first from our bodies, then our arms, then our sight, then our homes—and then? Always, I see my own mother gripping her pocketbook on the gangway when I looked back to wave my last goodbye when I flew off to Central America in dark winter after Colin's death. I needed to find my way, alone, and she let me go. Weaning fell hard on this spectrum and forced me to see the life I prayed she would live far beyond me, where she would learn to find her own sustenance, her own comfort.

I had never seen a child of mine grow up, but Ella's weaning gave me my first real glimpse. I was afraid and I was joyful, both.

THERE ARE SO MANY different kinds of fear. One morning, when Ella was two, she and I sat together at the kitchen table eating English muffins. She chewed slowly and turned her big blue-green eyes up to look into mine. She didn't make a sound, and she continued chewing, but her eyes filled with tears.

"Oh, honey," I said. "What's wrong?"

"Nobody knows me," she said.

"Nobody knows you? Of course we do!" Obtuse mama. False comfort. "Mommy and Daddy know you! Grammy knows you! All your teachers at school know you..."

Ella shook her head, eerily calm, tears on her cheeks. "No. Nobody *knows* me. You don't really *know* me."

"Okay," I said. "Okay, honey. I see. Okay. I will try to know you better. What can you tell me to help me know you?"

She shook her head again and took a bite of her muffin. She was done.

Later, when I told this story to Mark, part of me was proud—our young existentialist—but then I cried too. "She's right," I said. "She's right."

I wanted to know her, really know her, and for her to feel the comfort of that communion, but I knew what she said was true. Had we made her feel this way? Had I not been paying close enough attention?

I felt sad and helpless. We could not protect Ella from her new understanding, and we could not protect her gentle heart from all the wounds this world would bring.

I am glad I didn't know how close we were coming to her first close-up tragedy, the first loss she would need to grieve.

MARK AND I share a memory from an evening on our couch in the winter of 2006, a turning point. Ella is weaned and it's been over three months since the miscarriage, so we could try again, but we haven't. Flipping through the latest issue of *The Oxford American*, Mark comes across an essay by the poet Beth Ann Fennelly. He folds the page and hands me the magazine with his finger resting on a single paragraph. Fennelly and her husband, blessed with their perfect daughter, Claire, shared our second-child uncertainty, but in writing the essay, Fennelly imagines her own death: "I see [Claire] standing alone before a grave, and I want to paint in a brother or sister to put an arm around her."

Mark and I look at each other. *We* want to paint in a brother or sister. We want to paint in a brother or sister to put an arm around Ella, in the back seat of the station wagon or at our double grave. In the end, it comes down to this: We don't want to leave Ella alone. Our determination roots in our love for Ella and grows outward to the children we can't yet know.

By the end of that month, I am pregnant. Once again, my body holds "the secret of secrets." For months, despite myself, I am all hope.

13 The Eighteen-Week Ultrasound

By the middle of the second trimester with pregnancy number three, Mark and I were so done with numbers and needles, test tubes and horror stories, that we almost skipped the eighteen-week ultrasound. Despite the dramatically thickened nuchal fold in the first-trimester scan, the amnio results had come back clear just two weeks earlier. The fold must have been a fluke, a mismeasurement. In this game of prenatal fear, there was so much room for human error. Could we rest for one blessed moment in the seductive sparkle of hope the amnio had given us?

We certainly hadn't been prepared for anything good from the amnio. I'd taken that call on my way out the door on a cool spring morning, snatching my buzzing phone from my bag just as the storm door clicked closed behind me, my whole body braced for the hard news I was so sure the nurse was about to deliver. I will always remember her first words, the last words I'd expected to hear on that morning.

"Looks like a healthy baby boy," the nurse had said.

I started crying, sinking down onto the concrete front steps of our house with the phone to my cheek, the fear breaking loose, floating away like dandelion fluff. I made her say it two or three times—*Looks like a healthy baby boy healthy baby boy healthy baby boy.*

After the nuchal fold measurement, the doctors had brought our baby's chances of a chromosomal abnormality up to about one in five. Mark and I had prepared ourselves for the news that we had a Down's baby on the way. After all, I was thirty-seven. I was a "geriatric" mother. Here was a fear that was going to come true. We thought hard about how to get ready for this special baby. We had a lot of love we were ready to give. "Love is not finite," I had explained to Ella, knowing this to be true. "That's the wonderful thing about love. You can't use it up."

We were so sure the news was going to be bad, and we thought we knew what species of bad it would be. I hadn't even permitted myself the luxury of imagining a phone call like the one I had just received. *Looks like a healthy baby boy.*

"Thank you," I said. "Thank you." And then the nurse scheduled the standard eighteen-week ultrasound.

I sat on my front step in the afterglow of that call, out in the fresh spring air, bright yellow daffodils poking through the dark soil, the whole world smelling sweet and loamy. I dialed Mark from there. "Oh my god," I said when he picked up. "You're not going to believe it! They just called with the amnio results. He's healthy! He's a he and he's okay!"

For days, my heart felt so light I thought it might float right out of my chest. For months, my worry had crowded out the good stuff in my brain, every day a struggle to be present for Ella over games of pretend (never easy for me—I have a ludicrous sense of plot and am easily bored) or living room picnic lunches with everything cut into tiny wands—carrots, toast, apples. These were precious days and there had been too many when I'd had to fake it, my body down on the picnic blanket with Ella while my mind was sifting through data about blood tests and nuchal measurements. After months of feeling as if I were only just hanging on, now, finally, I had returned to my body.

"Really?" Mark asked a couple of times. "Are you sure?" And I repeated what the nurse had said until we were both satisfied.

So it makes sense that we were losing faith in the value of prenatal testing. There had been so much scary stuff, so much tense waiting—and for what? Our baby boy was fine! We were on the verge of cutting out on this next scheduled test, the level-two ultrasound, and taking the rest of this pregnancy on faith, made justifiably hopeful by the amnio's good news. We had to plan early summer travel to see our families and we wanted to think about something fun for a change. "They'll just give us something else to worry about while we're at your mom's," Mark had said. "I think we should skip it." Plus, there was Mark's sister's wedding at the lake in Champaign on Saturday—maybe we could head to Illinois a day early, leave Ella with Mark's mom, and spend a relaxing afternoon browsing bookstores.

What could an ultrasound tell us that the amnio had not?

I was a woman brought low by three months of nausea and we were both worn ragged from worry. But then I decided we should go. Tempting every god who ever swirled around this green, green earth, I claimed this one would be fun, a chance to get a good look at our baby boy—we'd bring a video tape. For posterity! Maybe Baby #2 wouldn't get a baby book like his sister, but Ella didn't have a womb video.

I convinced Mark to keep the appointment and we brought Ella along. She was in the room with us when it all came down. We'd promised her a late breakfast at Biscuits, the Mexican breakfast place across the street—hashbrowns and guacamole. Her favorites.

The waiting room was empty, although now I imagine Conrad's two women, sitting in the corner, knitting black wool. Why didn't I see them there? Why hadn't I heard their needles clicking? We didn't have to wait long. Five minutes tops. Now I wish I could go back and buy half an hour more.

THE ULTRASOUND ROOM was dim, high tech, level two. Ella got the chair by the door, some paper and markers. I climbed onto the tilted table facing the monitor, folded down my pants, and poked my belly up and out. Mark took a seat by my head.

The ultrasound technician was Julie, the same one we'd had all along. Two kids. Emma, so close to Ella, and a little boy . . . Sam? Maybe. Something classic. We were springing into the future, talking about boy names. I remember that she said *I go for the classic names*. I liked Julie, a few years younger than me, sweet-faced with wavy brown hair and quick hands that could slide the ultrasound wand through the warm goo on my tight belly to find the baby, line up cursors, click keys, and take measurements, while still managing to track the screen, my face, and the keyboard with her eyes and seem attentive to us all.

She'd been there for the amnio, too, making sure the needle stayed clear of our baby's little body (I couldn't look). After the amnio, after the stone-faced doctor had pulled off his gloves and left the room, Julie had been comforting. Her son had made a poor showing on the nuchal measurement too—3.0 to our 3.4—and he was just fine. Perfectly normal.

We had talked some about the ways in which technology had outstripped our medical capacity to understand the information we gathered. Months earlier, when Mark and I had entered the world of prenatal testing with this baby, this treasured baby we all called Baby Brother, one of our pro-life-leaning obstetricians had said, "Well, if you know you wouldn't terminate the pregnancy, then what's the point of testing?" Perched uncomfortably on an exam table that day, naked from the waist down, feet dangling from beneath my paper lap napkin, vulnerable to pretty much everything, including ideology masquerading as logic, I remember initially thinking *Oh. Okay*. I remember the temptation to accept what the doctor was offering up as medical counsel: *If you know you wouldn't terminate the pregnancy, then what's the point of testing?*

These words sound almost reasonable when you first encounter them, don't they? I can imagine he began—and ended—hundreds of that same conversation every year. *Oh. Okay. No testing.* And I'm not saying that's terrible. I'm not saying that the decision to skirt the dark entrance of the prenatal testing rabbit hole is a bad thing. What I am saying is that not testing *because* "you know you wouldn't terminate the pregnancy" is false logic. There are *many* reasons—to know, to be prepared, to be ready to intervene. And there's the biggest reason of all: because we never know *what* we'll choose in a situation until we're standing with our noses pressed up against it. We think we know, but we don't. Until you're the one making the decision in that moment—and you're making a decision no matter what you do, even if you do nothing at all—you do not know.

On the day of the eighteen-week routine ultrasound, Mark and I did not know. We had no idea what this day had yet to extract from us.

The universe has taught me this lesson again and again, and still I don't learn. I want to believe I can anticipate threats. Even as it's terrifying, my brain wants me to believe that these threats can be managed, mitigated even, with careful attention and a well-organized task list—but the worst thing is always something we don't see coming. The thing that takes us down is the thing we cannot even imagine.

IN MY LIFE as a writing teacher, I counsel my students to approach the present tense with caution because of the way the choice locks us into time. "We *think* the present tense is somehow more 'immediate,'" I say—"but well-written prose in the simple past can feel equally immediate." Then I demonstrate. I tell my students: "The English language is designed to navigate time: the simple past, the past perfect, future perfect. We can go anywhere! The present tense locks us in. The question is: Do you want to be locked in?" Or I'll say: "There's no reflection here because the present tense precludes reflection." Finally, when I want to blow their minds as my mind was blown when I was a young writer and laboring under the heavy influence of early Lorrie Moore, Jo Ann Beard, and Aimee Bender—all of whom, let me be clear, are geniuses—I share with my students something a wise professor said to me as he passed one of my stuck-in-time manuscripts back into my hands. "Present tense," he said, "is *less* immediate than past tense because present tense is an *obvious* construct. It's not *possible* for the events to be unfolding in the present tense, right? This artifice can throw a reader right out of the story."

And I heard what he was saying and knew it was true. And yet.

I recognize I'm stalling. I have to return in memory to something so hard and horrible I've been avoiding that return for nearly twenty years. Apparently I would rather offer a writing lesson than go there. This day is far in the past. Ella is in college, for heaven sakes, and yet, when I try to write that day, here comes the present tense. It's always present tense—and I know enough about the way the human brain deals with trauma to know this: I have some processing to do. My memories of that day and the days and weeks afterward appear in fragments and flashes. I haven't corralled those flashes into a story.

I will try.

I will try to tell the story. The whole. The whole story.

IN THE DARKENED ROOM with Julie, Ella draws a car wash with green marker on a white sheet of paper. Ella is afraid of car washes—the way the foam sprays the windows, blocking the view of the world. "There are lots of soapy bubbles," Ella tells us, swirling the marker in looping circles, seemingly okay with the fact that we are distracted.

We are watching you on the screen. Julie narrates, the tape rolls. Together, we count and measure: your one big brain, ten fingers, ten toes. You are still measuring big. A week ahead, but your sister was big too. In the beginning, they told us you would be born in the second week of October, the twelfth, the day our one body will become two and I don't change the date in my head. You will be our Halloween baby. Of course I'll dress you like a little pumpkin. Maybe your sister can be a farmer.

I am giddy with the planning. I am launching into the future with you in your little green hat, a crocheted brown stem tilting sideways in a jaunty way.

Julie swishes her wand around like a majorette, talking and laughing, clicking and measuring, pausing to take notes.

But now something changes in her face. Bad changes.

And now she isn't moving. She's pressing the wand into my belly like a slow punch, rotating the wand, holding still, leaning in to see the screen.

Julie is looking at your heart.

"What," I say. "What is it?"

Julie can't tell us, but she doesn't lie.

"It's not for me to say," she says quietly, "but his heart doesn't look quite right on the left side."

She lays the wand on the table. "I'll be right back," she says. "I'm going to get the doctor."

Mark and I must say something to each other in the short minutes—seconds?—Julie is gone, but I can't remember. That time has been wiped from my hard drive.

Now Julie is back and she has a doctor we have never met before at her elbow. The doctor is wearing a cute jean jacket and a stethoscope. She says hello gently—too gently—picks up the warmed tube of gel and squirts some onto my belly. She puts the gel down and picks up the transducer. *No,* I am already thinking. *No.* Whatever this is. *No.* Maybe if we stop now, stop looking more closely at whatever Julie is seeing on the left side that isn't good, well, maybe everything will be okay. I don't want to know.

Jean Jacket is merciful, really. She keeps it simple. She doesn't do a lot of explaining we're not ready to hear. I don't know that much about hearts. Not yet.

She zooms in and in and in and freezes the image on a close-up of our baby's heart. She explains we're looking down on his heart, points to two large black circles—"this is the right side"—and then at two dark dots, hardly circles at all.

And then she has the nerve to say, "Your baby has only half a heart. Just the right, not the left."

Mark and I are in shock. Of course we are in shock. We stare at the screen. It looks like a chalkboard, and someone has done some sloppy erasing. There are smears of white where the left side of our baby's heart should be.

Do we say, "Now what?" or "What do we do?" or do those questions hang from the ceiling like bats in a cave? Resting, but ready to drop and let gravity pull them into flapping? Ella pays attention to everything, so when I hear the page on her sketchbook flip to a clean sheet, a rustle of markers in the bag, I know this is a kind of message: *I am here. I am making pictures. I am listening.* She doesn't say a word, but I know she is drawing the thing that scares her. She is getting that car wash out where she can get a good look.

If you asked me to choose one word now, in this telling, for that room in those minutes, the word would be doom. The approaching storm had blotted out sun and sound, the birds had stopped singing to listen, and our bodies were tied to the tracks. The train was coming and we would watch the accident happen.

I had neither words nor tears. Not yet.

Jean Jacket knows exactly what she is seeing with her sound waves, that's clear, but there is protocol to follow and she is out of her league. She's sending us down to St. Vincent's Hospital in Indianapolis, to a center for maternal and fetal care, to the place where pregnant people go when things go wrong. She'll schedule an emergency appointment for this afternoon.

"Don't go home. Drive straight there."

HERE'S WHAT I DON'T REMEMBER.

    I don't remember saying goodbye to Julie. I don't remember what she said to us as we left. We must have gotten some lunch for Ella, but where? Did we go to Biscuits as we'd promised? I think we did, but our minds had switched into autopilot. Feed the three-year-old. Hashbrowns and guacamole. Drive to the next hospital. Don't try to think your way out of this one.

    All these years later, I ask Mark what he remembers. First he says, "Ella was *with us*?" And then he adds, "I remember remembering. On the day we found out, I remember remembering that the first guy, the doctor who did the nuchal fold measurement, said *We're going to have to keep an eye on his heart*. But we didn't really know what that meant, and then we all just kind of forgot about it. But then when it *was* his heart, I remembered."

    We're going to have to keep an eye on his heart.

    If I ever remembered this, I've forgotten now. My brain let that warning go completely.

MEMORY KICKS IN AGAIN when we're in the next darkened ultrasound room. Again, Ella is in a chair by the door with her coloring. The doctor is a pediatric cardiologist with a tough job to do, a ragged bedside manner, and a light Indian accent. He studies the ultrasound screen, sketches a heart on a piece of scrap paper, back and forth between the transducer and a pencil, and occasionally looks quickly at Mark. I don't think he ever looks me in the eyes, but I watch him over the gelled-up mound of my naked belly. Has he always been like this, I wonder, or has the role of delivering the worst news of having babies die under his hands worn him down? He wears his medical knowledge like a cloak of invisibility.

    We are here for a fetal echocardiogram, and I can't tell whether I'm too ignorant of heart anatomy to understand everything the cardiologist is telling us about right atriums and left ventricles—or if the shock is making it hard to think. *Is he okay? Is our baby okay?*

No. Our baby is not okay.

The part I understand is that we are looking at the right side of our baby's heart, lit up with pumping blood, and the part of the heart that is barely there, hiding in the dark, is the left side. Another part I understand is that without the left side, our baby's heart has no muscle to pump oxygenated blood out to the rest of his body. What I do understand is that a body needs oxygen to survive. What I do understand is that when our baby is no longer receiving oxygenated blood from *me*, from *my* four-chambered heart, then he will die.

What I do not understand is what we are supposed to do. What do we do? I ask if maybe our baby's heart could grow. Maybe his heart is merely a late bloomer. Is there any chance of growth? But the doctor tells me no, too late now, the left side can't grow, can never grow, because there's no blood flowing into that side.

"Half a heart," I say, as much to try out the words in my mouth as anything. "Half a heart? I've never heard of such a thing." My head is shaking. My hands are shaking.

Mark is a gentle man, but he gets mad at that cardiologist leaning into the ultrasound screen and then sketching our baby's heart on scratch paper (scratch paper!), crossing out, drawing again, jotting in percentages for survival along the way.

"When you say 'success,'" Mark says through a tight jaw, "you're not talking about his life, you're just saying he wakes up from the surgery, right?"

The cardiologist nods.

"So if everything works perfectly in every surgery," Mark continues, following the dark path none of us wants to walk, "he still has half a heart, right?"

The doctor nods again, and then reminds us: "This is a Catholic hospital."

We are silent. I hear the rustling of Ella choosing another marker from her bag.

Then the doctor leans into the screen, squinting. "Actually," he says, "I'm not seeing an aorta here. Nothing." He shrugs, as if, given the rest of the story, this anatomical fact barely matters.

Our baby has no aorta.

Mark and I shake our heads. Our hands shake. We shake and shake and the cardiologist offers neither solace nor hope. Our son, our gentle daughter's Baby Brother, our Sweet Prince. Here is what I want. I want the cardiologist to say, *Wait! There has been a mistake . . . Yes! A mistake! Look! See? Here. Here is the other side of your baby's heart. It was hiding in the shadow of your liver.*

But the doctor has nothing more to say. All our baby's miracles have come and gone. The darkened room is silent except for the humming of the machines, and the shared silence feels like waiting, a plasmapause, held in place until we are birthed together into whatever is next.

I lie on my back and stare at the white ceiling, the warm ultrasound gel thick and cooling on my exposed belly. Our baby safe inside.

You kick and turn. I can't breathe. "My god," I whisper. "Oh my god." I pull up onto my elbows to be closer to you. Your daddy touches my arm. Ella stands up from her chair by the door.

The cardiologist hands me a white towel. "You can clean yourself up."

14   Choice

The prenatal diagnosis of hypoplastic left heart syndrome is done in a second-trimester high-level ultrasound scan. Switching the color on the Doppler, a skilled perinatologist can diagnose the worst cases as early as seventeen weeks gestation. Of course, there will often be warning signs before that, most notably a thickened nuchal fold during the eleven-to-thirteen-week scan. This is precisely how our diagnosis had unfolded: A 3.4 nuchal measurement had raised the alarm in the eleven-week scan, an early thirteen-week amnio had allayed those fears (*Looks like a healthy baby boy!*), and an eighteen-and-a-half-week scan (repeated three times, by three different doctors in a nightmarish montage) revealed the horror that the left side of our baby's heart had stopped growing long before.

"The heart folds early," the genetics counselor told us, a phrase that wedged in my brain, its own category of terror held fast in the gray matter by the image of a crumpled origami heart.

At the end of a day that had started so hopefully when I smoothed the fresh label onto the blank tape for ultrasound video, I curled onto my bed, my knees and hands pulled in protectively around my shifting baby, my whole body unable to stop saying the word "No."

"No," my own pumping heart said.

"No," my frantic brain said.

"No," my weeping womb said.

"No," my lips said—in a whisper, then a scream into my pillow, and then in a mantra, sealing around my messy sobs like a capsule I could swallow back down to stop this thing from being true.

No blood was flowing into the left side of our baby's heart. Our son, his whole body no bigger than an apple, possessed a useless, two-chambered heart with no hope of growth.

My baby had only half a heart.

IN OUR COUNSELING session earlier that day with the pediatric cardiologist, we'd been given three options and intuited the third, unmentioned and unmentionable. Until we spoke it aloud ourselves—Did Mark do this? Did I?—no doctor offered the possibility of ending the pregnancy. All the doctors were grim-faced and hopeless, detailing the suffering our baby would endure—mostly without us. We would choose a hospital far from our home and I would move there early, just in case. Immediately after his birth, doctors would take him for his first surgery, and if he survived, they would take him again and again, cracking open his chest, playing god, but not as good as god. Playing god, but with the resulting heart still being one that would hold him back, keep him blue.

Every day, outcomes for babies like ours improve. Every day there's more hope. Not *enough* hope—but more hope.

There's someone reading these words who faced what we faced and chose differently, endured the kind of hall-pacing torture no parent should ever face, braver than brave, and now their kid is through the surgeries and loves hermit crabs and maybe even soccer. There are happy endings, or at least happy respites to love and be loved. In our shock and grief, our research was fast—our window of time for an abortion anywhere was sliding closed. We had only days, not weeks, to make a plan, and our options were scanty. In 2006, no one could show us an example of a child like ours who had lived beyond his teen years. In the end our decision to end the pregnancy took root in a single impulse: We did not want our son to suffer. We could choose against his suffering.

Years later, I talk to Mark about the last darkened ultrasound room of that day with the pediatric cardiologist whose name I must have known at the time but can't remember. As I said, he didn't have much of a bedside manner, leaning in toward the screen and rarely looking at my face, but what did I expect of him? What a job, to deliver such news. Who would want to look into a mother's eyes and say those words? I folded up the scrap paper he used that day and put it in my purse. I still have it in a file marked "Baby Brother" with other artifacts of his diagnosis and death—including that final ultrasound video. We have never watched the video.

All these years later, Mark and I remember the question of abortion counseling differently. We both remember the cardiologist's repetition—"This is a Catholic hospital"—but Mark remembers more; he remembers that the cardiologist said termination would be a *good* (surely he couldn't have used that word, could he?) option to consider. And now that Mark and I are talking, and he says that, my own memory is triggered.

Did I say, "What would *you* do?" And I think he said—without actually saying the words? with a nod and a gesture in case his employers had bugged the exam room?—that he would choose termination. I can't be sure of this.

Those early hours of the diagnosis felt like being in a car accident where the cars hadn't yet come to rest, a car accident from a nightmare, spinning across the asphalt toward the edge of the road, out of control, some part of you aware that you're dreaming and hoping to wake up before the end of this terrible story—the precipice, the fall, the impact.

There was no waking up. We went over. We hit the ground. Somebody died.

HYPOPLASTIC LEFT HEART SYNDROME (HLHS) is rare—according to the Centers for Disease Control, one out of every 3,841 babies born in the United States (although this does not account for the 79% of cases diagnosed in utero that ended in termination)—so in 2006, when there was 4,265,996 live births in the United States, this would have meant around 1,280 HLHS babies born that year and approximately 4,434 diagnosed and terminated in utero, so 5,714 pregnancies total(ish). So while I couldn't find this breakdown in any studies, I did the math (with great effort and the help of a teenager) and I can report that we're talking 5,714 out of 4,265,996—or right around a 0.1% chance of growing a baby with half a heart.

Rare, but as with all hard things on this planet, we were certainly not the first parents to face this impossible decision—not even on that day. Even on that day alone, even with such a rare condition, speaking in terms of probability, there would have been right around fifteen pregnant mothers in the United States alone getting the news that their babies were doomed.

So, no, we were not as alone as we felt. We were not the only ones. What I really wanted was a support group of other parents facing the same decision we faced.

What did other mothers do? How?

My own heart aches for every parent who has received this terrible news and committed to a decision. I don't want my own human need to believe our decision was the right one ring like a judgment on the mothers and fathers who chose differently. Even if they, in their turn, need to judge me.

We chose to let Baby Brother go. But these parents wake up ten times in a night to check monitors and leads, they know all the nurses on the pediatric floor on a first-name basis, their baby's cardiologist is practically a member of the family, they watch their children struggle—and grow, and celebrate—day after day, as they navigate a minimum of three major heart surgeries before their babies make it to four years old. There are good times with the bad times, there is gratitude for life, and the moments of every day, but there mustn't be a day without worry. These parents are fluent in a language my tongue, now, will always trip over—heart baby, NG tubes, oxygen sats, Norwood and Glenn and Fontan, Lasix and Loratab, and things I'll never know or get right. Their love, sacrifice, and courage is beyond imagining.

Our story for Baby Brother is about one choice, not thousands.

After our baby was already dead, I found a study of pediatric cardiologists; of the doctors who perform these surgeries, 50 percent would want to terminate if their own babies were diagnosed in utero with HLHS—which is a number *below* the 79 percent of parents who actually choose to terminate, but still pretty high for the very doctors who provide this super-specialized care. Of course, we can't know what these doctors would *really* choose—unless they've been there, unless they've actually chosen.

I keep coming back to this—choosing in theory is not really choosing. Choosing in the abstract is thinking, judging, maybe even imagining, and not terrible as a mind exercise, but that is all this if-I-were choosing can ever be: a mind exercise.

Unless you're a woman who has made this choice, yes or no, you cannot understand. I beg you to stop pretending you can.

HERE IS WHAT WE LEARNED on that first afternoon. Because I'm holding the evidence in my hand, I know the pediatric cardiologist explained the three essential stages of the palliative heart surgeries: the Norwood, the Glenn, and the Fontan. Next to each numbered surgery (all named after the doctors who developed them), our own doctor scribbled in percentages for our son's chances of survival as he moved (or not) through each stage of surgical repair—which, as Mark had him clarify, isn't really a repair, but a replumbing, a stopgap measure to reroute the body's blood so that the right side of the heart is doing the work of a whole heart.

The doctor's affect was flat, or maybe my hearing was somehow deadened by this feeling that I was underwater, drowning and muffled, but to me it sounded as if he were reading the odds of a racing card. Here is a super-simplified breakdown of the three surgeries laid out with a clarity I never could have grasped in those baffling early hours:

Stage I (the Norwood): Performed within a couple days of birth, the Norwood's job is to build a new aorta and insert an artificial shunt to allow blood to continue draining to the lungs. All babies are born with a natural shunt—the ductus arteriosus—which performs this same function, which is why HLHS babies can appear normal at birth. If this valve closes completely before the surgery, the baby will die. Seventy-five percent of babies survive Stage I.

Of course, in that dim, plasmatic room in 2006, we didn't know how to ask about the difference between *in-hospital survival* right after the surgery and survival one or three or twenty-four months down the road (much lower). These are details I can obsess over now, but none of it really matters. In 2006, we decided based on the information we could gather about hypoplastic left heart syndrome. We only had a few days to do our research. We were broken. Here is something a therapist once said to me—and I find it wildly comforting: "You made the best decision you could with the information you had at the time." We did. There was both too much information and not enough, and none of it was good.

Stage II (the Glenn): Performed between four and six months, this operation connects half of the veins carrying blue blood from the body directly to blood vessels heading to the lungs to get oxygen. This surgery begins the task of modifying half a heart to do the work of a whole.

Stage III (the Fontan): The final surgery in the series, performed when a surviving child is between eighteen months and three years of age, finishes the job the Glenn began by connecting the remaining blue-blood-carrying veins directly to the blood vessels going to the lungs. Essentially, at this point, the doctors have converted the right ventricle into the sole pumping chamber for the heart. The skilled surgeons have not *fixed* the heart, but they have modified that heart into a machine that can do the job, mostly, of getting oxygen out to the body. My mother calls this kind of work jury-rigging, or maybe she calls it jerry-rigging, and even here, in the language and the telling, I find no clarity. The first derives from a nautical term, when the "jury" mast was rigged to substitute for a broken mast at sea. This temporary mast, doing work it was never intended to do for a long journey, performed the essential task of keeping the ship moving, staying afloat, until the crew could sail her into the nearest friendly port and have the main mast replaced.

On the day of the diagnosis, the cardiologist had told us that our baby had no aorta, but then he'd shrugged it off. When the outcome was this bad, what was a little worse? Then he told us that the oldest living survivors of HLHS were teenagers. Teenagers.

Every day, new developments increased a baby's chance for a longer life—but still, in 2006, the news we got was that the longest lived, even with years of surgeries and daily cautions and never enough air, were teenaged. The goal, we gathered, was to stay alive long enough for a heart transplant.

BEFORE THAT MAY 2006 morning, I had never heard of HLHS, and these years afterward I struggle to pull apart what I knew then from what I know now. Every day, the science changes. Every day, hope grows for these babies.

On the day of the diagnosis, I was eighteen and a half weeks pregnant. If I'd needed help finding a hospital to deliver a cardio baby to be ready for the first surgery, I would have been assigned a counselor with lists and phone numbers and connections to hospitals all across the country, but in the decision to terminate the pregnancy, to let Baby Brother go, I had no one to counsel me. No one was offering guidance. No one even wanted to speak the word.

Abortion.

I had to make my own list.

I am an English professor, which means I spent many years learning to research, read, synthesize, understand, and communicate; in other words, by training, I should have been well equipped to access the resources I needed—and quickly. Never mind the obvious advantage of solid health insurance. And yet, in those two blurred days, I almost gave up. I was weak and shattered. In phone call after phone call, I had to say, "I've got a complicated situation. I am eighteen and a half weeks pregnant, but the baby has only half a heart." I was grateful to the receptionists who allowed themselves a small sigh, maybe an "oh, sweetie, I'm sorry," something human, something to recognize that I was not a mother who wanted to kill her baby—and then these kind receptionists would apologize again—*so sorry so sorry*—and let me know they could not help me.

No mother *wants* her baby to die. No decisions are uncomplicated.

Phone call after phone call, I heard some version of: "I'm sorry. It's too late."

With each click, every disconnected line, I felt myself waiting to breathe.

I slid my shaking finger down the list of names I'd culled from the internet, picked up the phone, and dialed again. *I've got a complicated situation*, I would begin—and then I heard myself apologizing. Over and over. *I'm sorry, but it's a horrible story.*

I told our story at least ten times that first day to ten different strangers. Between calls, I gasped for air and cried. Mark was keeping Ella in the back bedroom where she could play and not bear witness to my dissolution. He stuck his head in to check on me.

THINK OF THE FOURTEEN-YEAR-OLD raped by her father. Think of the single mother in the tiny town with three kids under five and no car. Think of the broke college student without health insurance or parental support or a partner. Think of the diabetic who just got her first job as a lawyer and made a payment on her student loans. Think of the woman whose boyfriend punched her in the stomach when he learned she was pregnant with a baby he didn't want. Think of all of these women and then keep thinking. The permutations are infinite. You will never reach the end.

EARLY ON I was told that in Indiana the law says no abortions can be performed past twenty weeks, and I didn't have time to question this information. I know now this isn't technically true: In 2006, abortion was legal in Indiana up to twenty-two weeks. I was at eighteen and a half, so we should have had options, but nobody was willing to take the risk. The publicity was too bad, and it put hospitals and clinics in peril of both funding cuts and potentially violent protests. Roe was still in place, of course, but this was one of the years in Indiana with bills on the state floor to define the beginning of life as the instant sperm meets egg, as well as an outright abortion ban stipulating long prison terms for doctors performing abortions.

Most places I called stopped at thirteen weeks, and I hung up the phone feeling like the murderer those protestors considered me to be. Despite myself, I had heard their toxic messages. I seethed, hating all the pro-life slogans that had seeped into my head after years of exposure. *Abortion stops a beating heart* I would hear in my head and talk back to this billboard of brain-stored propaganda: *Yes, or half of one.* I think I answered this echo aloud. I was losing my mind.

We wanted this baby. Desperately. Here was one of those tragedies I had always feared would come, and I prayed, as I'd promised myself I would, to be able to see the difference between protecting my baby and saving him. We needed to save him. We could not let him suffer. We would not let him suffer.

Mark, Ella, and I were in love with this baby already, and now my job in those two days was to find someone who was willing to remove him from my womb so he would die without pain.

WAS I AFRAID? Where is the place past fear? What is the name of that country? The place where we live when that which lurks beyond our worst imaginings comes to pass?

That's not true. I was still afraid. Baby Brother was going to die, we knew that, but even in his death we wanted to protect him. And Ella still needed watching over, guarding. I felt divided into multiple women, many mothers, splitting off to cope and survive and safeguard. The pregnant woman who had fretted over the early poor test results, scouring research for possible outcomes from an enlarged nuchal fold measurement, and then had felt such melting relief when all those ill-focused fears were assuaged, blown away, by the good amnio results. The new pregnant woman I was now, who had to pull herself together to find a surgeon, couldn't bear to look at the pregnant woman I had been. I sent her away. What good was she? She'd done it again, hadn't she? She'd had the hubris to think she could make predictions about life, about our baby, and she'd been wrong again. She'd been looking the wrong way when the worst thing was happening. Once again, she'd gotten it wrong and the pregnant woman dialing numbers from her couch couldn't find it in her heart to forgive.

Fear had not made us safer.

ANOTHER OPTION the cardiologist floated that day was heart transplant, but getting hearts was difficult, probably too difficult, the chances for a walnut-sized infant heart so remote, so dependent on another family's unthinkable loss, so likely to be rejected by a baby's immature system, that the doctor posited the idea that the staged surgeries might keep our baby alive long enough to make it to teen-size and get on the transplant list for a fully functioning heart. Most hypoplastic left heart kids rely on their altered half-hearts to grow large enough for an adult transplant list. Their jury-rigged hearts are not strong enough to carry them all the way across the ocean.

This was also the day I learned the phrase "compassionate care." We could let the baby be born and die, just as he would have if there were no high-level ultrasounds, no prenatal diagnosis, no surgeries or NICUs. Of all the options—termination, surgeries, transplant—this was the only one that didn't involve some level of playing god. Choosing "compassionate care," and depending on the severity of his condition, I might get four more months with my baby safely growing in my body. Connected by cord, in that beforebirth bubble with my body doing the breathing and circulating, there would be enough oxygen for both of us. As long as I held my baby inside, he would likely be okay. (What if I could have held my baby inside forever? What if we could have lived that way? A new kind of creature, breathing together? Permanently joined?)

With "compassionate care," Mark and I would share his birth. We would hold him in our arms, even for a few hours—but how compassionate is compassionate care? Would the morphine be enough to soothe his air hunger? I worried, too, that I might panic. We might panic. How impossible to hold our baby in our arms and watch him stagger his breaths, less and less frequent, and then stop altogether and slip away. How perfectly impossible. What if we couldn't bear it? What if we changed our minds, begged the doctors to try to save him, and so it would begin with the first cut to his chest, and then the horror of a brief lifetime of medical interventions would begin because we couldn't say goodbye and let him go.

And what about Ella? How would we explain to her that her baby brother would be born and die in the same day? How could we ask her to stand by and be part of such a loss? If we had been childless, part of me wonders if I would have chosen to carry him to term and let him die. But I will never know the answer to that question because we *weren't* childless, we had Ella, and I can know nothing beyond what we decided in that heart-tearing week with exactly who and what we were and knew and loved in May 2006.

In the cardiologist's office, my round belly slick with goo and pressed hard by the transducer, Mark asked the question:

When you say "success," you're not talking about his life, you're just saying he wakes up from the surgery, right?

And the cardiologist nodded.

So if everything works perfectly in every surgery, he still has half a heart, right?

And the cardiologist nodded again.

With this news, in the sucking, dark undertow of the next couple of days, we made our decision.

THIS BABY did not have what he needed to survive our separation. When he was no longer part of me, when he could no longer receive oxygenated blood from my pumping heart, he would begin fighting for every breath. He would turn blue and die on that day, or maybe the next. I now know a woman who watched her son die this way. If our baby was born, if the cord connecting him to my blood was cut, we could give him morphine and hope he died gently, or we could surrender him to the doctors to open his chest and begin a lifetime of radical medical intervention.

We could not choose either kind of life for our son.

Finally, finally, I found a doctor in Indianapolis willing to do a dilation and extraction (D&E) up to nineteen weeks. I would be at nineteen weeks and one day on the day of the actual procedure. *That's okay, honey,* the nurse told me, as long as I could bring $100 cash on the morning of the required consultation as a down payment.

"How much does the whole procedure cost?" I asked.

"Only $1,300."

"Whoa. The hospital in Chicago had told me the total cost would range between $6,000 and $7,000. How could it be so different?"

"They're charging you $7,000?!"

I asked what kind of anesthesia he would use for my surgery and was told a local, a pericervical block. The nurse said I should bring along some Tylenol for after the procedure. I might have some discomfort.

Tylenol?!?!? Are you *shitting* me? In the blur of my confusion, I couldn't muster the outrage this situation deserved. As someone who has been through the operation, I want to say that to perform a D&E without general anesthesia is both physically brutal and emotionally cruel. I told her how I had hemorrhaged after Ella's birth and she responded to this news with nothing I can record here— the equivalent of an over-the-phone shrug? Now, in retrospect, I am furious. What is that? Some kind of Draconian punishment? What I needed was real health care and what she was proposing did not sound like that.

We chose the hospital surgery in Chicago and made plans to leave the next day, which meant we would travel three hundred miles, pay over $200 per night for a hotel near the hospital, and find someone to take care of Ella while we were there for the two-day procedure. "If we weren't so privileged," I told Mark, "we would be having this baby and watching him die. That would be our only choice."

"If we weren't so privileged," Mark said, "we wouldn't know there was anything wrong with him."

THINK OF THE WOMAN in Indiana in 2006. Think of air hunger. Think of bleeding. Think of the preschooler waiting at home. Think of all the broken hearts.

15   Chicago

After we made our decision and found the hospital in Chicago, we had another set of choices to make. If I wanted, they could induce labor and I could give birth to him. We were told this could take days and there might be complications, particularly because of the hemorrhaging I'd experienced after Ella's birth. Because he was so small, and because of his heart condition, the baby would die early in my labor. In any case, our baby would be born dead.

At first, I thought I wanted birth, but Mark gently pushed me away from laboring. He was worried about me. While I'd been in and out of consciousness during my first postpartum hemorrhage, Mark carried sharp memories. He couldn't lose me. Now, when I ask him, he doesn't even remember that we'd talked about laboring as an option, but I do. In any case, we chose surgery.

During our consultation, our Chicago doctor hadn't mentioned injecting the baby before the surgery even began to stop his broken heart, but in my furious days of research, I'd learned that some doctors do that. I trusted this doctor. Dr. J was a lot like me (except, you know, smarter—and a surgeon). In her mid-thirties, she had a young daughter, and she wore the exact same closed-back Dansko clogs. In mahogany. When she talked to me, she looked me straight in the eyes, always and with what felt to me like true empathy.

When I asked her about the shot, Dr. J said, "Fetuses don't feel pain before twenty-six weeks. I couldn't do what I do if I didn't know that. That would be cruel." As she spoke, she held her hand on my arm, her own baby daughter waiting at home. "But we can do whatever makes you feel more comfortable. We could bring the nurse in right now to do the shot."

Dr. J listened to me. We were a team. My body was my own, and I knew I had choices.

I shook my head. I wasn't ready. "I didn't know," I said quietly, not able to quell my urge to apologize for not having done something to change this story, for not having known how to protect our baby. "Half a heart. I didn't even know there was such a thing."

"That's a good thing," she said, squeezing my arm tenderly. "You don't want to know everything there is to worry about."

I was too exhausted to take in the comfort she was holding out to me. "I didn't know," I repeated, lying back and putting my feet in the stirrups, scooting into position to begin the process that would end our baby's life. I could feel my warm tears filling my ears. Fight or flight or freeze had merged into one feeling. Boneless.

With her cool hand still touching my arm, helping to keep me attached to my body, Dr. J said gently, "This baby's fate has already been written."

Moving to the foot of the table, she unwrapped laminaria rods and handed them to the medical intern who was doing the insertion, giving my cervix the signal to open up and let my baby out. Too soon. I was looking at her over my draped right knee. The pain, rod after rod, intensified. The pain felt like labor. The two doctors marveled at my capacity to bear it, checking in with me with each rod, wider and wider. "Are you still okay? Is this okay?"

"Can you give me a count?" I asked. "How many more? If I know what I'm in for, I can take it."

And Dr. J told me it would just be two more, but that turned out not to be my question—or the answer. I had no idea what I was in for.

When I was up and dressed, Dr. J handed me a business card with her pager number written on the back. "Call me later and tell me what you decide."

IN MY WRITING classes, I advocate for a strategy I call "opposite world." This is just what it sounds like and can be a helpful tool even in good times, but especially when you're trying to tell a really hard story. When things have gotten dark, sentence after sentence, opposite world helps you find a way to turn on a light, a real light, even the tiniest of sparkles—a lantern, a star, a lightning bug. Anything. In the story of the two days we spent in Chicago for the abortion, opposite world comes in the form of a human—my friend Sherrie.

Sherrie and I had met in Minneapolis in the English Department of the U five years earlier. We were both staff members charged with solving other people's problems. We were also both writers, and exactly the same age. If souls travel in packs, Sherrie and I have been around this cosmic circle together quite a few times. It wasn't long—a week?—before we went for our first after-work Leinie, and not long after that, we were spending weekend nights drinking wine at her place or mine, talking and laughing and crying until the rising sun surprised us. "Oh shit. Is it *morning*?!" Sherrie is from Wisconsin—an identical twin adopted at birth along with her sister—and she is a miracle of a human. The hardest-working person I've ever known, she also believes in treats and beauty and the magic of a well-lit room—which is to say, not too bright, unless it's sunshine. Sherrie is fiercely loyal, can make anything out of fabric, and is a proud member of Packer Nation. Last year, because she loves me, she came to a reading I was giving in Chicago even though it inconveniently coincided with a championship game: She wore an earpiece under her hair and sweet-smelling scarf so she could be there for me *and* follow the game. The woman is resourceful.

So when we needed to find someone in Chicago to stay with

two-and-a-half-year-old Ella while Mark and I went back and forth to the hospital, I called Sherrie and not ten minutes after we checked into the Congress Hotel on Grand Park—the cheapest last-minute rate I could find—Sherrie burst into our dim, musty hotel room as if she were hope incarnate. Equipped with a Mary Poppins-esque bag that she'd made herself, naturally, Sherrie gave me a long hug and whispered, "Oh Jillian," in my ear before turning to Ella with a huge smile, opening her bag, and exclaiming, "Prizes!"

Despite our best efforts to protect her, Ella had endured four days of bearing witness to our pain, and now she looked as if we were receiving a personal visit from Santa. The first thing Sherrie pulled from her bag was a rag doll with big blue eyes and fuzzy, lime green pumps.

Love? *Love* is a resource.

Love is a light.

EVEN THINKING ABOUT the view from our seventh-floor window in the Hotel Congress on the night that our baby was dying in my womb catches my breath in my throat. The weather that day couldn't make up her mind—rain and sun, rain and sun—and so, looking across Grant Park toward the lake, I watched the arc of a giant rainbow climb across the sky. I put up my hand to support my weight, my tipping body, on the dingy wall. "Look," I whispered to Mark. "Look."

We were living in a storybook. Sherrie brought Ella back to us for the night and Ella reported that they'd been in the park, throwing coins in the fountain. "We made *wishes*," Ella said earnestly, a penny in her palm. "But the seahorses are kind of *scary*."

Whose story was this? I did not want it to be my own. I have never seen such a rainbow. Somebody took a picture. That somebody was probably me, but I can't remember pushing the button on the shutter. I felt numb, novocaine-limbed. Except for the cramps.

By eight o'clock, the cramps were coming hard. Labor pains, really. Labor pains working toward my baby's death, not his birth. I knew he could be dying right then. Not for the first time, my body was the scene of the accident.

Standing by the big windows in our hotel room on the dirty carpet, wearing only a T-shirt and underwear, I paged Dr. J and she called right back. We wouldn't have the shot to our baby's heart, I told her. He would die during the surgery. Or he would die before. "He's kicking less," I choked out. Far below, the people down in the park, so small, moved through the walkways, past the monuments. The people in the park walked dogs and hurried along carrying bags and stood talking by the fountain as if it were a normal evening—and this seemed wild to me. How was that possible? I held the phone to my cheek and listened for Dr. J.

Her voice was soft. "Some babies die right after we put in the laminaria. He could be gone already." The cramps were normal, she told me—and she reminded me to keep up with the pain meds she'd given me. (So hard to swallow after the months of nothing stronger than a prenatal vitamin.)

I rested my forehead on the cool window. The sun was down and the last of the light shimmered with pink. The sky. The sky was big enough to hold us all.

"Get some rest," Dr. J said. "Try to sleep."

And, somehow, I did.

BUT AT 3:00 A.M. I woke to the sound of rain, hard rain. Had I really been sleeping? Was it the painkillers? Was it supposed to rain again? I didn't think so, but it was really coming down. Swinging my feet over the edge of the bed, careful not to hit Ella sleeping down on the floor in her blow-up bed, I walked the three steps down the short hall to the bathroom. Stepping off the carpet and over the threshold, my foot splashed onto the tiles. Everything smelled like shit. I reached for the light switch.

I remember seeing my bloated face in the mirror—so horrified, so sad, inhuman almost. What was happening? Water streamed down the mirror like something in a horror movie. Like tears. Or the work of a poltergeist. The mirror was seeping, the mirror was crying, and there was my ruined face, looking at me. I stood there while the water breached the threshold, leaking out onto the carpet, pouring down the stinking walls.

My baby was dying. My baby was dying or dead. I had chosen for my baby to die, maybe he was already dead, and here. This. It was raining in the bathroom. Shit rain. A shit storm. A shit storm!

I don't know how long I stood there with my bare feet in the tepid, rising water, staring at that dripping mirror.

Who could tell what was real and what was not?

Not me.

What was happening?

Finally I found words, a voice. "Mark!" I called out. "Mark! It's raining in the bathroom. It smells like shit."

We called the front desk and they rushed up a bellhop with a luggage cart. While Mark piled our things on the cart, I threw a towel over Ella's sleeping head and ran through the dripping hall to another room to wait for the dawn.

EARLY THE NEXT MORNING, Sherrie arrived while Ella slept, and as if in a dream, Mark and I made our way from one echoing parking garage to another, and then onward through the labyrinth, past and through long hallways and registration desks and clipboards hanging onto their captive pens with clanking chains. There was not enough light and then way too much. My legs felt the way they so often do in dreams. Useless. The kind of legs I might call on to run, to take me away from a bad guy or slavering wolf intent on ripping out my throat, but when my brain commands *run, legs, run*, my legs are stuck, responding with only slow, leaden steps. My fingers felt the same.

Does this mean my fight or flight instinct was used up? Do we reach a point in crisis when all fear has leached away and we are left only with loss? A couple of years before, Mark had taken an antibiotic, a quinolone, for a lung infection, swallowing the first tablet while he was at work in the English Department building, just before the start of a class. His allergic reaction was immediate, like a monster's hands around his throat, and when Mark slumped to the floor, suffocating, his students called 911. I arrived before the ambulance and I will never forget the look in Mark's eyes—first, I saw his fear; then a kind of rage; and finally, just before he lost consciousness, the fear and the rage were gone and he seemed to be looking at something beyond this world. Afterward, when the beautiful doctor saved him, and he returned to the ER, opening his eyes and taking us all in, he couldn't say what he'd seen on the other side.

The place beyond the end is a secret land.

Later, on that night he almost died, Mark and I shared a carton of McDonald's fries in his hospital room. "I was sure I was going to die," he said, licking salt from his fingers. "I was seeing things, crazy things, and I knew I was going to die because nobody could see what I was seeing and still live. I knew the things I was seeing weren't things I would be allowed to live to tell about. I had to die because otherwise I would tell. If I lived, I could tell everyone."

Of course, I wanted to know what Mark had seen—but he couldn't remember. He was alive and he couldn't remember.

Those early morning hours in Chicago on the day Baby Brother died felt like this, as if I was seeing things I could never speak of again. I struggled to hang onto reality, but even before the anesthesia, my mind was up to her old tricks, slipping away, trying to find a dark corner where we could hole up and be safe. I moved in and out of reality. The lights were so bright.

USHERED INTO A CHANGING ROOM by a kind nurse, I fumbled for the silver hoops in my ears and the rings on my fingers, sliding them off, tucking them into my jacket pocket and rolling everything but my own naked body into a clear plastic bag. After I slipped my arms through the gown—a child's gesture, donning a smock for art—I allowed myself to be led into a crowded pre-surgery room with rows of beds separated by easily flung curtains sliding with an almost liquid violence on metal rings across metal rods. Mark stayed by my side as they prepped me, holding my hand, and reminding the doctor—again—how I'd bled when Ella was born. He didn't want to lose me too. I overheard a curtained conversation about a hernia operation and something else having to do with an ankle. I don't know. When the anesthesiologist came by to start the IV, he told me he would give me something to forget, and he didn't lie.

In the operating room, there was a lot of shining steel, and when I looked down toward where I could still feel my feet, heels tucked into stirrups, I saw the pale tent staked out by my spreading knees, and above that, floating, the eyes of my surgeon, that sweet mother like me whom I knew to be standing in her mahogany clogs.

"Are you ready?" she asked.

I nodded and in my final seconds of memory I felt something like ice water moving into my veins. I tracked the ice to my fingertips and was gone.

But I have learned about my anesthesia, and I wasn't gone, not really. With this kind of twilight anesthesia, I was conscious, as my mother was when I was born, but with no possibility of laying down tracks to find my way back to that room, to the memory of that morning. To return to the land of the living, to join the other parents in the circle around our preschoolers singing "Baby Beluga," I couldn't come back with this memory. I think of my mother and that sad thing I have heard her say over and over about her own twilight torpor: *My greatest regret is that I wasn't awake to see you kids born.*

My greatest regret. What is *my* greatest regret? This too? Should I have stayed fully present and born witness to every moment? If I tried hard enough, could I hear what the doctors said to each other? Could I catch a glimpse of my poor baby before he was gone?

I know this is crazy talk. I don't want to know everything there is to worry about. I don't want to see everything there is to see.

This is a choice my mind makes for me. I am always leaving and having to go back.

THE MOMENT around which every moment before or after revolves is the only one that matters to tell. In fiction, we call this moment the climax—the point after which nothing will ever be the same. Right before they wheeled me back to the operating room, they left us alone for a few minutes and we said goodbye to our baby. Still holding my hand, Mark bent over the side rails of the bed laid his face on my taut belly. "Goodbye, son," he whispered. "I love you."

And our baby kicked his father's cheek.

16   Between Heaven and Earth

Hours after they vacuumed our baby from my body, I waited in recovery with my hands on my empty belly while Mark drove back to the hotel to get Ella, our suitcase, and Sherrie. When Mark returned, I had finally peed, just a tiny bit, enough to get released, and he helped me up from the wheelchair and held my hand while I shuffled out to the parking garage. I remember turning the last corner and seeing Ella and Sherrie waiting by our station wagon halfway down the row, how beautiful and bright they looked in that dark garage, arms full of prizes—like creatures from another world.

Instead of heading home, we drove straight south to Champaign because the next day Mark's little sister, Juliet, was having a wedding. As Ella would tell you, Juliet looked like a fairy princess, married in a green park by a little blue lake. The kids ate Barnum and Bailey graham crackers out of the red boxes and blew bubbles.

In the few pictures I have of the day, I can't believe I am there—in a black dress, in case I leaked, with a face. An actual face attached to the front section of a head.

I was bleeding so much I felt weak, bloody pad after bloody pad. The doctor assured us over the phone that this was normal, my body emptying itself. Somehow, in the pictures, I am smiling. I am wearing a dress, I have a face, and the face is smiling. I didn't want our tragedy to ruin Juliet's big day. Grief would have her chance, but on Juliet's wedding day I let shock carry me through.

God knows, if there's one thing in this life I know how to do, it's fake it.

IN THE THREE DAYS after the surgery, we attended Juliet's wedding in Illinois, drove home to Indiana to pick up our stuff—how did we think about what to pack? stopping the mail? what we would need?—and made it to the airport to use tickets booked long before our lives had shifted. Somehow, we got ourselves onto a plane bound for Washington. The sane thing would have been to delay the trip, to wait—at least—for the bleeding to stop—but I needed to get back to the mountains, home to my mother. I remember almost nothing of the journey. A blur. We must have packed workbooks for Ella, snacks for the plane, a fresh outfit. We must have checked in, passed through security, found our gate. We must have changed planes in some city—Denver or Salt Lake or maybe Phoenix—and I must have watched the faces of the other travelers walking past us and wondered.

Wait. I have one memory: In the Indianapolis airport, I took Ella to the bathroom—to put her in a pull-up? to change my own pad?—and on the way back to our gate, I saw a family. They were beautiful, all of them. A dark-haired father and a daughter, Ella's age, looking as much like her own father as Ella looks like Mark—and then the mother. Her hair was long, a shining dark curtain, pulled apart to reveal her bright eyes—she sparkled—and hanging down and to the sides of her great, round belly. I stopped walking, Ella's hand folded into mine, and stared. I remember a knife stab of grief, and something like awe and jealousy. I tried to will the feeling away, to smile. Maybe I could look like a newly pregnant mother myself.

What did I look like? Could this other mother see me? If she did, she gave no sign.

And one more: In the air, Ella sat by the window with her forehead pressed to the plastic porthole. We had told her the baby wouldn't be coming to live with us as we'd hoped because he wasn't ready. We told her he wasn't in my belly anymore. Mommy and Daddy were sad, we explained—that much she could see—but the baby was okay. He was going to live in the sky. This explanation seemed to satisfy her, and on the plane she turned her face from the window and said, "I'm looking for my baby brother in the sky. He's going to peek at me from behind the clouds."

"Yes, sweetie," I said, "he'll be peeking at you," and then I turned my face away to cry hot, silent tears.

Mark squeezed my hand.

When I recovered, swallowing my grief into the place where our baby had lived just two days before, I turned back to help her look. Where was he? Where was our baby?

I remember nothing more until I saw my mother waiting at the first possible place she could stand and watch for us before security, her face sad and expectant. As soon as we funneled out with the crowd, as soon as she could reach me, she pulled my body to hers, my belly soft and aching between us.

"Oh sweetie," she said. "Oh my poor sweetie. You made it."

IN THE WEEKS after our baby died, Mark rarely touched me when we lay together in bed. I know he didn't want to hurt me. He knew I was sore and he wanted to be careful, but I felt as if my body was the site of trauma. Everything happened there. There, in my body, our baby was conceived, grew, missed a step in the folding heart, and died. Before the baby died, Mark loved my pregnant body. He would curl up behind me and touch my rounding belly, say hello to the baby. Afterward, when I pulled his hand around, he might give my top breast a perfunctory squeeze, but then skip over to my hip, a pat, and pull his hand away, leaving the loose flesh of my empty belly alone.

How could my body not be sad to both of us? I was a walking graveyard.

Ella used magical thinking to fill the empty place I presented with my deflated body that summer. Boldly lifting my shirt for a better look, she'd say, "My baby brother's not in your belly anymore?"

When I confirmed what she already knew, she'd nod and pat her own round stomach.

"Okay," she'd say. "It's okay. I have a baby brother in *my* belly."

EARLY ON, I began a behavior I revisited for years afterward. I snuck into my mother's tiny office and balanced my bleeding body on an awkward stool in front of her old Dell. Clicking the mouse, I listened to the atonal grasping of the dial-up modem trying to make a connection, waiting full minutes for an image to load horizontally, a shade closing to reveal a child HLHS survivor, maybe a three-year-old, his scars cloaked by a superhero T-shirt. Then I leaned in close to study his face.

This child looks like who our son might have been. This child looks like the miracle we couldn't believe was possible for us.

Mark didn't understand why I read the stories of hypoplastic left babies, pored over the survival stories and the obituaries, both. Why would I do that to myself, he wanted to know. "Why torture yourself?"

A valid question I couldn't answer. What was I looking for when I went to the health updates for these surviving children, or the memorial sites for those who didn't make it? Regret? Assuagement? A place to be in my grief? A glimpse of *my* baby in another baby's face? I carried a desperate urge to *check on him.*

I couldn't think this clearly then, but something I realize now is that the so-called "pro-life movement," designed as it is to be a mechanism of political power with its simplistic, easy-to-sell message that abortion is murder, had gotten into my head and lodged there like a parasite. I had to get those messages out. If I didn't push back, I couldn't grieve. I couldn't let the pro-lifers simplify abortion—or pregnancy, for that matter. Pregnancy doesn't equal baby. Abortion isn't murder.

Mark and I needed to grieve, and grieving didn't mean regret. Grief didn't mean I wanted to go back and make a different choice. Don't let them say that because we thought of our baby as a tiny person, our dear one—because we talked to him and read to him and called him "Baby Brother"—that it was murder to make the choice to end his developing life, to stop the awkward pumping of his broken heart. Half-hearted. HLHS couldn't be the source, could it? Half-hearted attempt. Half-hearted effort. Half-hearted baby boy I could hold curled in the palm of my hand.

Every story that ends in a baby—or no baby—is endlessly complex. When I leaned into the low-res monitor, peering into the sweet faces of babies living with HLHS, what was I trying to find validation that we'd made the right choice? Or was I searching for some kind of time-travel key that would take us back before the abortion to that moment when our baby's heart folded and the blueprint got it wrong? This is it, I think. This diligent magical thinking is closest to the truth. Sneaking into my mother's office, I felt frantic, as if I were on the trail of some secret knowledge that would make everything that went wrong *right*. I didn't want to make a different choice, but I did want my baby back.

HLHS stories have two beginnings—the bad news that comes before birth and the bad news that comes after birth—and from there each branch splits into two more branches: The baby struggles and dies or the baby lives and struggles. Of course, there are variations even within the fundamentals. I found no happy endings, but in some baby's stories I read about respites, breaks from the hospitals, lives being lived, and as one mom said, "You wouldn't even know what she'd been through if you didn't lift her shirt."

Years later, I come across a eulogy written by the doctor of a baby named Sean, born in August 2006, just six weeks before our own baby would have been born had we made that choice. Sean survived the first two surgeries, the Norwood and the Glenn, but died of complications when he was six months old. Sean's parents asked Dr. Michael Snyder (Columbia Presbyterian, New York), Sean's pediatric cardiologist, to speak at the memorial and explain their baby's medical history. Dr. Snyder said that the three-stage heart surgeries were meant to:

> convert his one strong pumping chamber, the right ventricle, which normally pumps blood out to the lungs, into the ventricle which pumps in the body, to take the place of his underdeveloped left ventricle. This may seem like a backwards way of fixing things. Why not just have the surgeon enlarge and fix his small ventricle so he could use it? It is just not that simple. In spite of all the advances in cardiac surgery over the years, our surgeons still can't make a ventricle.
>
> Only God can do that.

Dr. Snyder praised the parents for never leaving Sean's bedside, taking shifts so he would never be alone. Dividing her time between Sean's twin, a sister born with a whole heart, Sean's mother made two thousand paper cranes while she sat with her baby through surgeries, recoveries, and setbacks. Two thousand cranes. That should have been two wishes. I wonder how she used them.

I read stories of parents watching their children for every sniffle and cough, anything can lead to an infection of the heart—and this was many years before COVID. These parents have seen their children taped up with monitors, eating through tubes, breathing in bags. And yet, these parents say, again and again, how they sometimes forget their babies aren't normal. Jake or Jack or Avery: eating pudding, climbing the ladder to the slide, reaching up from a hospital crib to touch Mom's face. And then there's shoptalk about blue versus pink, heart catherizations, "satting" in the high 60s (blood oxygen saturation levels: You and I are used to the high 90s in our regular lives), and the intimate, daily knowledge of life at Children's.

I read the stories and cried. I read until the pain filled my veins like a drug and I went numb. And then I shut down the computer and went back to the living world.

When Colin died, my mother kept me alive during those first months. Now she was doing that again—for my whole little family. When Colin died, the thing I needed most was a way to communicate with him. I filled lab notebooks with letters. After the baby was gone, I needed the same thing, I guess. I started writing letters. Like this one.

May 23, 2006

Dearest Baby,

Time is playing her tricks again. Or maybe it's my mind in my grief. Today is Tuesday. Every day I have to wake up. Every day I wake up and remember. Last Tuesday was the first morning I had to wake up with the knowledge that we were going to lose you.

What did you know?

Half a heart. Was the blueprint wrong or was it something else? *Why?* I keep asking. *Why?* And nobody seems to know. Nobody can give us any kind of answer. I want to know when. *Early,* the genetics counselor says, *the heart folds early.*

I am not a young mother, Baby. That's why we had all the fancy tests. Risk factors. Numbers. Age. Time. And then this thing I'd never even thought to imagine in all my worst imaginings. Asking *why* isn't enough. I don't even know the question.

Your heart had nothing to do with my age, they told me. Just a fluke.

Your chance for half a heart? Less than .2 of a percent.

So many numbers. So many useless numbers, and still, I can't stop counting, measuring, searching for something, anything. I know I am searching for you.

Forty weeks from blood to blood. Nine months. Any mother who has carried a baby knows how time rebels and all the different ways we try to pin it down. Nine months, forty weeks, 280 days. I'm at 14 and 4, we say. Fourteen weeks, four days. We scour the internet, figure out the day on which our babies could emerge and still survive. I had these days all marked on my calendar, figured out. You were measuring big, of course, exactly a week, just like your sister before you, and they tried to tell me you would come early, October 5th, not the 12th, but I didn't believe them. I'm a skeptical patient. "I just have big babies," I told the doctor. "We were trying for this baby. My dates aren't wrong. I was writing everything down. I know my dates aren't wrong. I have big babies."

I was wrong. You were not big. Not yet. You were desperately small. You did come early. And in the end only one date mattered. "I'll be at 19 and 1," I said when I scheduled the appointment. For this, for the appointment, I have no language. We mothers measure time to pretend we have some control, to pretend there is something to know about what is happening within our bodies, what we can do to make our imaginations manifest and hold you. Hold you. Hold you.

I need you to know how much we loved you, Baby. Love you. I try so hard to make decisions from love, not fear, but this one is so hard to call. I was so in love and so afraid. Your father and I would have laid down our lives for you. But not yours. We could not lay down yours. We could not know you would come into this world with half a heart, just to be cut open, broken into, a blue baby under the knife.

I'm so sorry, Baby. This is not the letter I sat down to write. What's wrong with me? You are a baby. A baby!

I just want you to know how much we love you. I want you to know what your life was during those seventeen weeks you spent in my body. In a way, you were like a fish—happy in the waters of my womb, eating, swimming, growing—and doomed on the dry land of the world. No way to breathe oxygen to your organs. Nothing to do but be blue. But there I go again. One fish, two fish, red fish, blue fish.

Why can't I tell this story without beginning at the end?

This. Let me tell you how much your father loved you already. I did nothing at home. I dragged myself off to school, came home, and collapsed. Your father did all the shopping, all the cooking, brought me cereal to bed in the morning so I could put something in my stomach before I even lifted my head. After the amnio, the doctor said not to lift anything heavy for twenty-four hours. Your father put me on total bed rest for three days. He believed we should err on the side of caution. Prenatal vitamins, omega three, as much water as I could stand to drink, ten to twelve hours of sleep every night, nothing bad for you, not ever. You and I curled together and your father took care of all of us.

Also? You were a mover and a shaker, Baby. I felt you turn, a slippery flip, when I was not even fourteen weeks pregnant. This is the part of pregnancy I love. The quickening. Astoundingly, by the time I was sixteen weeks, your kicks were so thumping I could pull your dad's hand to my belly and he could feel you moving, too. Before you died, I got to share you with your dad. This was another of your miracles, wasn't it? I don't know how you did it, but I am grateful. We are both so grateful.

Near the end, when you kicked your father's cheek, my own heart split in half for you and for your daddy, Baby.

Remember, please, Baby: We would have laid down our lives for you. But we could not, would not, lay down yours.

I know there are people who will say we did the wrong thing. I will try not to listen to them. Whatever we chose, we were called upon to participate in your death. We were given the rare parental choice to pick the when and where. With your half a heart, we had three options, and none of them were good.

I wanted to hold you in my arms—even for an hour or two. But what was in it for you, Baby? The force and trauma of birth followed by the force and trauma of death? The pain of the beginning and the end with so little in between? Already, I was holding you. Already, I was feeding you from my body. Your sister loved to nurse, nursed until the very month you were conceived, and she asked me once, *Is the baby having ba-ba inside your belly?* And I laughed, because she'd gotten so close to the truth. *Yes*, I said, *the baby is having ba-ba. Ba-ba is for babies.* You did not have to be born for me to do these things for you. I was so tempted. I wanted to hold you on the outside, too, in my arms, but I know myself, I know your father, and if you'd gotten here, we would have tried anything to save you.

The best-case scenario was so bad, Baby. So bad. We could not put you through all that pain to have, still, just half a heart, to grow big enough for the transplant list. I want you to know how I will carry you forever, in my whole heart, for the whole of my life. I will never put you down.

Love,
Mom

WE HAD NO BODY to bury, but we needed to do something. Together we planned a memorial ceremony for June 11. That morning, my mom drove into town and brought home a beautiful pinwheel and six helium balloons in the colors of the rainbow—red, orange, yellow, green, blue, and purple. Ella was inspired, and so when we covered the picnic table with newspaper to paint river rocks to serve as our baby's gravestone, we stuck to the rainbow theme too. Mine looked like a rainbow—with a tiny red heart at the center of the arch—and Ella, well, she mixed her colors, thick and stirring. When her Baby Brother rock was wet, it looked black, but by the time it dried and we packed it into the box to take to the cemetery on the mountain, the rock shone a deep purple, and along the edges, here and there, some flashes of bright color peeked through. There was a rainbow in there after all. In those days, I lived for every sign, every stretched metaphor. *I look for you everywhere, Baby.* I was so tired. So sad. *Forgive us, Baby, it's so hard to know what to do on a day like today.*

I wanted to get something right. I asked Mark if I should write something on my rainbow rock and he said, "What would you write?"

I didn't really know. "Maybe 'Baby Neely May 2006'?"

"Why?" Mark asked. "We'll know it's his rock. It's not like we're going to forget it's his rock. What if the cemetery people see it and say, 'hey, they didn't get permission to bury somebody else here'?"

This was so logical I wanted to strangle him.

WE DROVE THE ROCKS and the balloons up to the mountain cemetery where my uncle Mark, my mother's only brother, and my grandparents are all buried in the same family plot. There's space for one more, and the plan is my mother will be planted there—that's the way she says it: *When you plant me . . .*—when she dies.

It's a beautiful place way out on a dirt road with long grasses, Ponderosa pines, wildflowers, and a stunning view of the valley. As cemeteries go, it's hip and funky. We know some of the other folks who are up there. Gabe was six when he was killed on

Halloween. The school bus went off the road on the way home and rolled. Most of the kids weren't even hurt, but Gabe's window was open and he fell out. The whole mountain went up in a wail that lasted months. His mother Karen, a Jew, converted to Catholicism. There are other babies there too. Tiny graves with shoes and rattles. One of our friends lost his baby one night in his bed. SIDS. And Valerie—the young woman who loved horses and whom everyone loved. She went off the road too. There's a bridle draped over her grave.

The vision of heaven our mountain cemetery paints is beautiful, a life in the sky better than anything we can imagine down here on earth. So many colors—trees and fields and horses and toys. Pinwheels and balloons. We're hoping it's better than here. Standing among the colorful graves on this mountainside, every part of me almost too heavy to lift, I felt lighter for the first time since the diagnosis. Here, in the breeze coming through the Ponderosas, sweet with vanilla and pine, I could believe in a world where my baby would be waiting and I would be able to hold him, finally, in my arms.

I didn't know what to say at the grave. I got a book at the library and there was a section on rituals divided up by prayers for special circumstances, and the prayers for ending a pregnancy all had to do with asking forgiveness and absolving guilt. This didn't do me any good. My guilt was more complicated than I could understand. I'm not even sure I would call it guilt. I wondered what guilt I would have felt if we had tried to see our baby through to birth and let his suffering begin. I have a hard time wrapping my mind around the intersection between "God's will" and prenatal testing and medical intervention. If we hadn't known about our baby's heart, and he'd made it to birth, we may have had a few hours before the valve closed—and then he would have begun his mortal struggle. With no intervention, he would have died, unable to get a breath.

But we live in an age of intervention—God or no God—so at the first signs of blue, our baby would have been taken from us, flown on a helicopter—would they, at least, have let Mark fly along with him?—to another hospital, another city. Then the first open-heart, if they figured it out, if the diagnosis came soon enough. So many ifs. On the day of the baby's memorial, I didn't want to take us there, the place I always landed with my rotaries whirring, stirring up dust and detritus, the landing pad of all the bad options. So many bad options. The time for choosing was over, and our baby was gone. It was time for grief, not speculation.

So I wrote our baby a love letter, and after Ella and I had nestled our rocks into the clover and my mom had planted the pinwheel, Mark and I stood shoulder to shoulder, propping each other up, and said goodbye.

Dear Baby, I read aloud. *We did not want you to suffer. Not ever. We made the choice to let you go out of love. We loved you in and out of this world. On the day I found out you were on your way, I danced. We loved you every week, every minute, you lived inside my body. We knew you and you knew us. And so we will miss you. We will cry and cry, but we will say goodbye because we know you're okay up there in the sky, busy with the dogs, your new friends, the making of rainbows. Send a sign when you can spare a moment and feel our love coming up to hold you. As your sister Ella says, we hug you and hug you and hug you. We do.*

I folded my letter into a plastic lunch bag and scraped a hole in the dirt under the rainbow rock, tucking the letter beneath for safekeeping.

Mark knelt to touch the rock. "Now cracks a noble heart," he quoted. "Good night, Sweet Prince, and flights of angels sing thee to thy rest."

We leaned into each other, and Mark cried. "Our baby," he said in my ear, his voice breaking. "Our son."

ONE DAY, a week or so after we had our goodbye ceremony for Baby Brother, Mark and I decided to drive Ella to the park for a picnic.

"I'm sad," she blurted out from the back seat of the station wagon. "I'm sad my baby brother didn't come to live with us." She'd been silent for a good ten minutes, and I'd been hoping she was napping, but instead she'd been thinking.

"We're sad, too, honey," I said, reaching through the space in our seats to touch her bare knee.

"But he's okay," Mark added, coming in with the part we all want to believe. "He's in the sky with your dogs. He can't come live with us, but he has lots of friends in the sky."

Ella tilted her chin up to the window and considered the sky.

I wondered if she was thinking about the rainbow balloons we'd brought to the cemetery. The helium lost its oomph in the hot car and by the time we cut the ribbons, the balloons sank into the air above the grave, bumping and rolling over the stones like puppies. Ella laughed and chased them. I'd pictured them rising into the sky, a glorious metaphor, but the bumping had seemed okay, playful. Only the red one caught a small breeze and lifted into the trees.

"I'm scared," Ella said next, returning her gaze to mine in the car. "My baby brother is going to come down and thump me on the head."

"What?"

"He's mad," she explained. "He's *mad* because he wanted to come live with us. He told me."

"Oh no, honey!" Mark and I cried out together.

"Your baby brother loves you," I said. "He might be a little mad, but not at you. He would never thump you on the head. He loves you."

She seemed to believe us, but she wasn't done. Not yet. Like me, she thought if she considered the problem long enough—the problem of our missing baby—she could fix it. He would be born just as we'd told her he would be born. Why should she believe this story of death any more than she did the one of approaching birth? Three weeks since the baby died and my belly was a collapsing balloon, still there, but losing air, leaking hope.

Ella asked a question she'd asked twenty times. "My baby brother's not in your belly anymore?"

"No, honey, he's not," I confirmed.

We couldn't explain the permanence of the baby's absence. We couldn't help her understand that there was no going back.

Ella persisted in making plans for her brother's return, his descent from the sky. In the park, eating our sandwiches, she pointed to a maple tree. "My baby brother can slide down that tree and have a picnic with us!" When we shook our heads, she got miffed. "Okay. Why can't he just grab onto a plane and meet us at Grammy's house?"

I wanted to believe that Ella remembered something we'd forgotten, some possibility of the spirit, but I thought she should know what we knew. Or think we knew.

"Your baby brother doesn't have a body anymore, sweetie. He's dead. Dead means you don't live in your body anymore."

For a long time, again, Ella said nothing.

"Okay," Ella said. "Okay. My baby brother can slide down the tree and I will *catch* him because he doesn't have any feet."

The wind picked up and shook the leaves. The whole world was a trembling green.

FOR WEEKS my dreams were drenched in blood. After the baby died, Ella had trouble with sleeping. At my mom's, in the loft, we're all in the same room, so when Ella struggled with sleep, fought her own falling into blackness, I lay beside her on the foam mattress on the floor and tried to help her with the fight. We tried everything, every night. We tried upside down or sideways, we took deep yoga breaths, we counted sheep in funny hats or rhyming names, we told the most boring, sleep-inducing narratives we could conceive about three little bunnies—Bop and Peter and Fluffy—"who lived in a cute little house at the bottom of a *beautiful* rainbow..." Almost every night, we cried. Most nights, sleep took me down before Ella who had more fight in her small body.

After restlessness came dreams. I wanted to see my baby in my dreams. I wanted him to come to me and tell me he was okay. I wanted something lucid, a message, but no messages appeared. Just the bloody dreams.

In the first dream, I am standing on a ladder in a dress and blood is splashing down from between my legs. My brain camera zooms and I see a close-up of thick, dripping blood clinging to a rung. I am making a mess. I have to climb down and clean it all up. I know the next person to climb the ladder will be freaked out by my blood. The others could slip. I have to hurry.

In the next dream I am naked in front of a full-length mirror and I am looking at my belly, grabbing handfuls of loose skin where my baby used to be. I am all flab and rolls. I start to sob and shake. The shaking is too much. Flesh flies until I am nothing but bones.

Three weeks after the baby died, I stopped bleeding, and finally I stopped leaking yellow milk, but my breasts still felt heavy and I had no idea how to live in that body. *My body*, I repeated to myself, trying to make it real, trying to find a place to live. *What's in there? What should I do? I am not young. I will need to make a decision. I am too scared to try again. I am too sad to never try.*

I was stuck between fear and grief, beginning to understand these two were one and the same.

I TRIED GOING INTO TOWN with Mark and babies were everywhere—waiting in cars at gas stations, riding in backpacks in parking lots, peering out of blankets in the grocery store. I kept looking at the tops of their heads. How soft they looked. Everyone seemed to have a baby. These mothers and fathers made it look so easy, nonchalant. But I knew I didn't know the real stories behind these babies, these maybe mothers and possible fathers. I was only guessing. We can't know just by looking. What children waited for them at home? What babies did not?

I am struck by all we do not know about the humans we move among, bumping elbows as we squeeze the avocados. Can you imagine? *Excuse me. Excuse me, Miss? Have you ever lost a baby? Miss? Miss? Are you okay?*

MARK AND MY MOTHER were doing most of the parenting because I was having such a hard time coping, such a hard time being with Ella—the very image of what we had lost. And not. And also herself, of course—and it was that collision of what truly was (Ella) and what would never be (Baby Brother) that crippled me in those early weeks, made it hard to look. So when my mother suggested we drive to her friend Dennis's on another mountain for a cookout, I signed on. I wanted Ella to have some fun. *I* wanted to have some fun.

To get there, we drove south along the river and as the fog from the morning rain lifted off the water, I saw our beautiful world. On the way there, my mom had to stop the car in the middle of the highway to let a mother pheasant with a trail of at least ten chicks cross. Highway be damned, this mama looked confident and proud. Her small sleek head lifted above a golden, feathered mantilla, and her high-stepping claws pulled a sloping train of elegant tail feathers to cut a path for her bobbing, fluffy chicks. Queen.

At the cookout, we played horseshoes, and when I walked with Mark to the opposite pit to check the points, probing the sand near the stake with the hook of the iron shoe, listening for the clang of metal on metal, lifting out the buried shoe and shaking off the sand to throw again—these physical steps of the game felt so familiar. I felt myself falling back into my body. We walked to the corral, and I showed Ella how to hold a carrot chunk flat in her palm, fingers arched down, to feed the horses. There was even a puppy who feasted on our ankles and made Ella laugh, but she liked the old dog, George, the best, and begged for more biscuits to carry to him in his hiding place in the shade of the house where the puppy could not harass him. We were pleased by her faithfulness to an old dog. In the end, she dubbed George the best part of the trip.

The drive home, at dusk, was like a video game. We barely missed a rabbit, a deer, and a calf, in that order, and when we reached the highway, we saw a black bear—Ella's first—lumbering up a hill behind a pasture of horses who had all frozen in place, nostrils quivering.

Ella was over the moon. I couldn't get her to sleep until after midnight.

ON JUNE 18, exactly thirty days after the baby died, my period arrived. Right on schedule—or almost. Neither Mark nor my mom seemed to understand how bittersweet this message from my body was for me.

"That's good, right?" Mark asked cautiously.

"That means everything's working, right?" my mom said.

I nodded and stirred half and half into my coffee, trying not to cry, wondering *And for what?* So we could try again. Part of me was glad of this, the possibility of another chance after what seemed like a complete upheaval of everything in my body. But there was also a feeling stronger than the relief of the cycle continuing, my body shedding the old and preparing for the new: betrayal. I felt as if I was betraying the baby we lost. It was too soon and I was too afraid.

Sitting on the toilet in my mother's little bathroom, I studied my own blood on the tissue, redder than red, and thought, *No, no, I can't do it again. I cannot.* And then: *I'm sorry, my sweet boy.*

Menstrual cramps are like labor pains—a kinder, gentler version, to be sure, but in the same family of pain—that low-in-the-abdomen, ovary-forward combination of nausea, gas, and back-alley knifing. With this same pain, dialed up or down, our bodies either make room to release our babies or wash out the monthly waste, that uterine cushion no one is using. No baby.

Instead of taking to my bed, bleeding and aching, I laced up my running shoes and hit the streets. My body was still made for my baby, and looking like a pregnant woman without *being* one was killing me.

The running was hard but good. I let my legs fall forward, releasing, down the big hill to the lake, and on the way back up, I looked down at my chest, watched my own heart pounding through the thin fabric of my T-shirt, pushing myself past comfort, thinking about how many times my body had borne what seemed unbearable—and pushing on, digging into my strength.

In the slow months after Colin's death, I had visited a volcano in Costa Rica. Arenal. How perfect she had been, erupting daily, her top glowing with fire, her flanks lined with the tracks of her fiery tears. I hadn't known then—just twenty years old!—how my body, too, would rise up in grief's heat, a collision of continental and oceanic plates, the solid I could touch, holding me together, and the liquid that was most of me, bubbling, carrying me along through another nearly twenty years in my changing form from grieving girl to lover, lover, lover, then wife, then mother, my baby girl thriving, then grieving again—the new baby in my womb damaged, my body opened up to take him out, my body the site of our loss and grief, my body the scene of the accident, my whispered prayer to Colin as I crested the hill, weeping: *Please take care of my baby. Keep him warm. Don't let him go hungry.*

THAT NIGHT Ella actually went right to sleep. Miraculous. I should have taken my chance—had a drink, watched a movie, read a book. But I didn't. Lying down next to her, I propped myself up on my elbows and watched her sleep. I watched her breathe. I put my hand on her chest, gently, and I felt her heart pumping.

How could she be so beautiful? How did I get it so right just that once? Please keep her safe.

I'm so sorry I could not do the same for you, Baby. So sorry.

OUR INSURANCE was willing to pay in-network rates if the procedure I needed wasn't available within a fifty-mile radius of our home in Muncie. This part was easy, but a couple weeks after the surgery, I checked our answering machine from my mom's phone and there was a message from the hospital saying we needed a "letter of necessity" from my primary care provider. This was not so easy.

As our cardiologist had said, St. Vincent's is a Catholic hospital—they cannot counsel abortion no matter what, no matter how dire or desperate. "You don't need to say the abortion was necessary," I explained, "you just need to state the diagnosis, hypoplastic left heart syndrome, and the prognosis for the baby—which is a hundred percent fatality in the first week, right? And then that there was nobody within fifty miles to perform the surgery."

The genetics counselor was sympathetic, but understandably cautious. Her job was on the line: She couldn't write the letter. Such a gentle version of what is happening now, post-Roe, with women in ban states waiting in parking lots until they're close enough to death that doctors who fear license revocation or even prison feel safe enough to make the call that an abortion is medically necessary to save her life. Some of these women are dying—how many is going to be hard to measure, but a 2023 study out of the University of Colorado estimates a 24 percent increase nationwide for pregnancy-related death (much, much higher for Black women). Women are showing up at hospitals for emergency care—bleeding out, going septic, crashing—and hospitals are turning them away. Pro-life?

"Try your regular ob-gyn first," she said before hanging up.

So I did. I called my regular ob-gyn and got a nurse I knew on the phone. "We're all thinking about you," the nurse said, so kindly. "I'll take care of it. Don't worry about it." And she did. Later, in some medical file, I see the letter written by the doctor in our own small city. The baby's condition, the letter stated simply, was "incompatible with life."

Incompatible with life. That phrase has never left me. Unbidden, randomly, this phrase pops into my mind—"incompatible with life"—and I shake my head, surprised each time.

17   What If It's a Myth?

By fall we were trying again. Mark and I both still felt ravaged by grief, and I alone had been taken over by a mournful, unruly magical thinking. Was there any way, I wondered, spiritually speaking, a new baby could *be* Baby Brother, but with a whole heart? No. A new baby would be a new baby, not the baby we'd lost, and I tried to force myself to accept this. If there were a new baby, she would be a girl, I decided, as if this were the way biology worked. As if this were the way the world worked. As if I had the power to decide anything, ever. As if a healthy baby were a decision to be made. As if.

I felt empty, hollowed, and I wanted to feel full again. Before we lost the baby, we might have been able to convince ourselves that what we really wanted was a family of three, but with Baby Brother gone, there was a vacancy in our family. We all felt this emptiness—in the station wagon, at the dinner table, in our future.

Someone was missing, and we were in the position to try to fix this emptiness, to fill his place. What a weird and complicated thing. I was going to say that when Colin died, he was just gone. I couldn't *make* another Colin. The place he filled as my mate was burned out, blackened, and there was nothing I could do to fill it. I was going to say this was the opposite of the situation we found ourselves facing in those horrible months after Baby Brother's diagnosis and death. But that's not really true, is it? Baby Brother cannot be replaced. Colin cannot be replaced. These are facts. I will always miss them. But I didn't die. I'm still here. And eventually I filled the place of mate—with Mark. And now Mark and I had the option to fill the place of a second child—with another baby.

WHEN COLIN DIED, there were no choices to be made. No uniformed officer came to my door in the middle of that horrible night and asked whether I wanted to keep him alive, knowing he would suffer and die, or whether I wanted to choose for him a quick death, likely instantaneous, painless, dead on arrival. No one asked me to weigh any options, play prognosticator or God, make a life-and-death decision. Colin was alive and then he was dead. There was no way I ever devised to truly blame myself for what happened. That morning he'd come to our bed where I was still sleeping and kissed me goodbye. I had kissed him back. I realize now my grief for Colin was the purest kind—a clear, hot flame.

With Baby Brother, we needed to make a choice, and our grief was a swirl of dark water, flotsam and jetsam, a mess of despair and rage and responsibility. All the hearts broken. For months I was mad at Colin himself. How could he let this happen? Why hadn't he been paying closer attention? And then, I felt guilt for even thinking that: How many times did I expect Colin to save me?

Once we were back in Muncie and reentering our lives, we had to figure out how to explain the obvious fact that I was no longer pregnant. I experimented with language—pronouns and nouns and verbs and degrees of agency—complicated by the element of choice. We chose to terminate the pregnancy. I got an abortion. I had to get an abortion. The baby died. Our baby died. Half a heart.

There is the birth announcement—and then there is the pregnancy loss announcement. Such different genres. My closest friends knew, of course, and so we all decided together to have them go ahead and tell other people and just let the bad news spread around the English Department and beyond into our larger community like a rumor. Using this method, I rarely had to speak. I received the sad looks and sad-looked my colleagues back, and if some brave soul, in the first week or so of the fall semester, said quietly in the hallway, "I'm so sorry," then I said back, "Thank you. I really appreciate that." And I did. And in this way, we all moved forward.

MOVING FORWARD did not mean never looking back, and sometimes I wondered if our decision to end the pregnancy was a failure of strength. Was I too afraid to feel the pain of holding my baby in my arms as I watched him die? Of *knowing* through those final months of pregnancy that I was preparing for birth and death in the same day? Could I not hack it? Was it really Ella we were trying to protect? I understand the choice to end a pregnancy, and I respect the parents, like us, who open their hearts to that kind of letting go, to that kind of love.

And the choice to continue the pregnancy and be prepared to fight the fight, through a lifetime of surgeries and intervention? I understand this too, and if we had decided this for our son, I would shout to the rooftops that every smile he smiled, every breath he breathed—every cupcake, painting, story—was evidence that we'd made the right choice in giving him a chance to be on this planet with us, his family.

All these choices are right choices, and none spares pain; otherwise, we would all have taken that pain-free path together. Say, if those three surgeries were truly reparative. If those three surgeries, even with all their inherent risks and percentages, could land a two-year-old firmly on his toddler feet with a whole, functioning heart, high oxygen levels, pink cheeks, and a full life ahead of him, we parents, in love with our babies, would make that choice.

We would not see a fire and choose to reach our hands in to watch our fingers burn.

MEANWHILE, Ella was already here, almost three, and needed her mother. In September I took her to her first day of school at the

Child Study Center. The discovery table was filled with navy beans, and measuring implements, and Ella got right down to business. A new student teacher plunked herself down on her knees on the other side of the table and started asking Ella questions, to get to know her. "Do you have any pets at home, Ella?"

"Yes, I have two dogs." She pulled a big cup through the center of the beans and the sound was as satisfying as rolling stones in a creek bed.

"Are they big dogs or little dogs?" (I spelled out D-E-A-D and the nice student teacher nodded her comprehension.)

"Big dogs." Ella held her short arm up high above the table and watched the beans rain down, a melody of small collisions.

The nice young woman didn't give up. "Do you have any brothers or sisters?"

"Yes," said Ella again, getting excited. "I have a baby brother!"

"Oh!" said the student teacher, happy to have hit on something good.

I considered letting this go, but it didn't seem quite fair to the new teacher—or to Ella. "Yup," I decided to say, as matter-of-fact and cucumber-cool as I could muster, even though I could feel the grief rising into my throat. "He lives in the sky." And then, while Ella concentrated on a particularly large and loud scoop of beans, I whispered to the teacher, "We lost him halfway through my pregnancy."

So I'm pretty sure folks thought we were crazy, but we didn't forget our baby. We weren't leaving him behind.

That month, once again, my period came right on schedule. I wasn't pregnant, and when I returned from the bathroom with this news, in tears, Mark changed his mind about going for a new pregnancy. Just up and changed his mind. "Are we crazy? Are we completely crazy? What are we thinking? We're not ready for this." He couldn't bear the thought of losing another baby. Neither of us could. Maybe we needed to just give up, grieve, pull ourselves together and be a family of three. Maybe we couldn't do this. Everything hurt.

One day, on the way to the grocery store, Ella shouted out the car window: "What if my baby brother's floating along behind us?" And then she did herself one better. "What if he's playing *chase* with us?"

WE DIDN'T, couldn't, stop trying, and by Christmas of 2006, I was pregnant for the fourth time, but I was feeling sensitized to this species of loss—pregnancy loss, the loss of new hope. I had built pain barriers I didn't know how to pull down. I couldn't make myself believe in a "good outcome" (perinatologist-speak for "healthy baby"). Pregnancy does not equal baby. And yet, despite my foreboding, the initial news was positive. At six weeks, in a small exam room at the infertility clinic we'd just begun visiting when we got pregnant naturally, I had a vaginal ultrasound—my first. Happily, I was somewhat distracted by the fantastic device necessary for such procedures. Ever the eighth graders, Mark and I laughed—in horror? fascination?—as we watched the tech roll a condom over the dramatically flashing plastic dildo that would do the good work of traveling up into my vagina to see what he could see—and there it was: the sac, the fetal pole, and a tiny, flashing pinprick of light. A heartbeat.

"This is big," our newly met reproductive endocrinologist had said, passing the flashing dildo to the waiting nurse. "This reduces your chances of miscarriage to around seven percent."

THE SEVEN PERCENT was delivered to us as great news. I remained wary. Odds and numbers and percentages had lost their capacity to comfort me. The chance that our baby would have just half a heart had been one in about four thousand. We'd beaten those odds, hadn't we? Still, through the nausea, I tried to feel a sparkle of hope.

But, then, at nine weeks, it happened again. That horrible silence in the darkened ultrasound room as the technician slid the wand around on my slightly curving belly, pressing the blunt plastic into my gut like a punch, a gentle punch. It was taking too long.

I closed my eyes. I knew.

"I'm so sorry," she said.

Mark's head fell into his hands.

"I'm sorry," she repeated, "but I'm not seeing a heartbeat here."

I thought, *I should feel worse than this*. But I was outside myself, looking down on my draped body, my husband's hunched figure crying into my thigh. "Why you, honey?" Mark said, holding onto me with both hands. "Why you?"

"It's okay," I said. "I'm okay." Was I? I think so. Something in me had known all along we would lose this pregnancy. Something in me already knew.

Before leaving the office, I scheduled the dilation and curettage (D&C) for that Friday and insisted I could drive myself home while Mark went back to work. At the intersection above our house, I watched a minivan drive over a cat. From half a block away, I could see the dark shape of the dying cat twitching spasmodically on the center line. The gray road, the black cat, the yellow line; the black ultrasound screen, the pale outline of another dead baby, an unmoving shadow where the blinking heart light had been.

This became the image of miscarriage in my mind.

THE FEBRUARY D&C in a hospital just blocks from our home for an already dead ten-week fetus seemed so simple and so sad after Baby Brother's surgery the year before. Both procedures clean out the uterus; both procedures are coded as abortions; both procedures *are* abortions. By way of reassurance, Dr. L told me that fetal death after a beating heart was commonly linked to anomaly. The idea was that this time, nature had made the hard choice for us. Of course we all wondered if this had been another heart defect, but the cells Dr. L sent to the lab for diagnosis never grew. We learned nothing, and the only number we had to go on moving forward was the catchall 3.4 percent chance of reoccurrence that gets attached to mysterious and rare congenital conditions. Again, the oft-cited numbers for good outcomes—or their opposite—had ceased to hold much meaning, flickering like a fetal heartbeat on a wavering screen.

All I remember of the February surgery is the moment I emerged from the haze of whatever light anesthesia they'd given me. I was only just coming to know him then, but I already understood that my dark-haired high-risk perinatologist with the kind eyes, cowboy boots, and fancy fountain pens liked to talk. As he and the nurses were finishing their work on and around my body under the drape of a sheet, they chatted about bowling. Apparently the doctor belonged to a Friday night league.

Bowling? Lying on my back with my eyes closed, I tried to see fresh possibility, another pregnancy, one more chance, but instead I thought about how Mark and I used to go bowling in graduate school on Cosmic Bowl night, circling one another under the pulsing lights, back when sex was sex for sex's sake. *I bowl*, I almost offered, but I realized that would be awkward. I was supposed to be sleeping. If I spoke, it would be as if I were sitting up in my coffin, speaking from the dead.

We'd moved quickly to clean out my uterus for three reasons: (1) I couldn't bear the thought of holding another dead baby in my body, waiting for the miscarriage to complete naturally, (2) I was a bleeder, and if I hemorrhaged I'd be in surgery already, and (3) there was no time. Months earlier, the fertility specialist in Indy from whom I'd never needed to accept anything more than progesterone supplements had said to me—*Normally we'd wait three cycles before trying again, but at your age, we can't waste time.* The faster we emptied my body of one lost pregnancy, the sooner we could try again. Grief was a luxury we couldn't afford, and in

2006 the D&C was medical care Dr. L could offer. (If this were all happening now? In 2025? I would have to wait for the bleeding.)

Lying on a gurney under the bright surgical lights, the bridge to a land where we would be a family of four stretched, diminishing, toward its vanishing point. I couldn't see the other side.

I GREW UP around bridges. Seeking another life, on the other side of a Miami faculty-wife supporting role that didn't seem to suit her, my mother drove Ian and me away from our little white stucco house in Dade County—and our father—when I was only two years old. First, she piloted the van south across the spectacular narrow bridges spanning the shining waters of the Florida Keys, and then she headed back up north over land and bridge to park, finally, on our little island off the coast of Newburyport, Massachusetts.

Mostly, I remember the Plum Island Bridge with great fondness. The bridge was green, *bridge* green, stretching a hundred thirty-five feet over the Plum Island River and her grassy fringe of marshes. This bridge of my childhood is the bridge by which I have always measured all other bridges.

Ours was a drawbridge, the kind with a guy in a booth at the top who waited for the boats with the tall masts to approach and blast their horns. One assumes the booth guy would check the middle of the bridge for kids like me hanging out on their banana-seat bikes, and when the coast was clear he would push a button or pull a lever or whatever guys in bridge booths do, and the white arms would snap down into their horizontal position, blocking motorists. The red lights would flash.

Warning. Any moment now, the bridge under your body will open a space big enough for a ship to pass through. Blink. Blink. Blink.

Then the huge metal teeth at the bridge's midpoint would grind and separate, pulling apart, gleaming, a spectacular gaping maw. Safe on one side or the other, we kids would wait and watch in wonder. *Holy shit*, we must have been thinking. *Wicked cool.*

AFTER THE THIRD LOSS, we came close to saying "never again." In fact, we *did* say it, but then we took it back, let in a surge of strength or hope, and recanted. Everybody was starting to wonder how much I could take. *I* was starting to wonder. Would we try and try and lose and lose until my grief drove me to an asylum? Or would the repeated pain make me hard? How much could I take before I failed to feel joy when three-year-old Ella slid her soft fingers into my hand before we crossed the street or presented me with a crayoned gift?

This much I had learned from losing Colin. If I stopped feeling the pain, I wouldn't get to feel the happiness either. When we shut down emotions, we shut down all the emotions. We don't get to pick and choose. Sure, I'll take that joy, but I'm going to keep grief stuffed down between my rageful spleen and heartbroken liver. Nope. Not the way it works.

At this point, we'd been trying for a second child for eighteen months. On the big scale of time, I understood, this was a flash, but I also realized that for a full half of Ella's life, much of my attention had been turned away from her as I charted temperatures, stretched cervical mucus, cried for a baby who wasn't here. Ella was right there and she deserved better.

And I didn't know how much more our marriage could take. Between thinking about dead babies and pregnancy, and faking it for Ella, Mark and I could barely see each other through the fog of daily survival. Sex wasn't sex because sex is fun and we loved each other, sex was a bridge to pregnancy, which could lead us, again, into the dark woods of loss. We were both exhausted and snappish, worn thin by the relentless oscillation of hope and disappointment. Why didn't we just give up? How long would it take us to accept our family of three and move back into happiness? What if we stopped trying for another baby and channeled our energy, and acceptance, into what we were already so lucky to have?

But there's always the chance that the next time will be the right time, isn't there? The risk was huge, but the payoff, my god, the payoff could be a *person*, a little beloved person. And without another baby, I worried, I might never heal. *We* might never heal.

THEN I FOUND Ella crying on the toilet. "I don't want you to die," she whimpered. "What if you die before me?"

Oh, please God, let me die before her, I prayed, but not yet, not too soon. "I'm not going to die before you grow up, honey," I said, touching her head, and knowing I had no real right to claim such a thing.

"What if you do?" she persisted. "Sometimes people die when they shouldn't. Sometimes people die when they're not old and sick."

"I know, honey, but that's really rare. That's not going to happen." I dropped to my knees in front of the toilet where she was still sitting. Tears gushed down her cheeks and dripped onto her Little Mermaid nightgown. "And if that does happen, if I do die, do you know what? I'll be waiting for you up in the sky. I'll be with Tango and Walt, and Baby Brother, and we'll wait for you together."

She shook her head, her whole body trembling. "But what if that's a *myth*, Mommy? What if that's just a story we tell ourselves because it makes us feel better and it's not really *true*?"

I had no answer, so I brought her back to bed with me for a snuggle, kissing her smooth forehead again and again until she slept beside me. One more time, I told myself, one more time. I would convince Mark I could handle it, and we would try again. I needed to draw in a little brother or sister to stand beside Ella at my grave, to put a loving arm around her.

18   Painting Faces

I am fearful, but I am also my mother's daughter. I am tougher than I look. Also, I am trying to connect the lines.

Like most abused children, when I was being molested, I bore the violation wordlessly—until the night I didn't. Perhaps because I am writing this with bridges on my mind, I have remembered a night I had buried deep, a night when my abuser—a teenager—was driving me (why just me?) home to the island from somewhere and instead of crossing the bridge, he turned his giant, floating American car down a dirt side road to a muddy lot in the marsh under the shadow of our bridge, troll territory. *Don't trolls steal children? Do they eat them?* There, this molester molested me, which was not unusual, but what I remember now about that night was how my mom was waiting at the door for us when he finally got me home, yelling at me for taking so long. Did part of her know something then she hadn't allowed herself to see? Had she glimpsed the troll lurking under the bridge? A flash of his hairy back, a waft of troll, reeking of fecund mud? That night, when I came in late, I was sure she would smell him on my skin.

I have told you this story, but it bears repeating: When I was twelve, I made this molester stop. I locked the door to the living room, braced the rough-hewn wood with my strong legs, and told him through the wide cracks I was finished with our secret. If he didn't go away, I said clearly, I would call my mother at the bar where she was working late, and I would tell her what he was doing. What he had done.

And that was that. My tormentor never came back to my room at night. He didn't kill me. He didn't even punish me. He just stopped coming over.

I wish I could say now that I took in the lesson of that closed door, those boldly spoken words, and hung onto the power of my own voice, the safety I could find in refusing to stay silent. But I wasn't finished with secrets. Not yet.

The bulimia began later that year. I didn't binge. Bingeing wasn't my thing. I was in it for the purging, the opening up and letting go. I tried not to eat, but if hunger got the best of me, or even if I quenched my thirst with a too generous glass of water and felt bloated, I'd throw up.

I'd open up a space and release from my open mouth everything I wasn't yet ready to speak. My goal, if I can articulate a motivation born of trauma and sickness from a distance of so many years, was emptiness. I wanted to scour myself from the inside out, feel clean and hollow, scraped out like a Halloween pumpkin before the cutting in of the shining face.

Only now can I see that my teenaged compulsion toward emptiness was the opposite of how I was feeling as we tried for another baby: I wanted to feel full again. I was done with emptiness.

The summer I turned thirteen, the same *month* I escaped my abuser and ran into the waiting arms of bulimia (the causal link is undeniable), my brother went to college and my mother moved us to our mountain in northeastern Washington state. We had no electricity, no indoor running water—no flush toilets. I was a bulimic without a flush toilet. I know this is dark stuff, but I appeal to you to see the comedy here too. Not only that, but we lived with a Vietnam vet who had taken to the woods, a man who hunted our food. This guy knew how to read signs in the dirt. I had to travel far and dig deep, but I didn't expose my disease. I mean, I don't think I did. Now I wonder if he knew and I didn't know he knew.

Nor was I stupid. I checked out books about eating disorders from the local library, learned to be better and smarter. After I read that stomach acid could eat away tooth enamel and many bulimics ruin their teeth, I made an appointment with a dentist, and used by own money to have my teeth sealed. I wasn't ready to be well, but neither was I foolish enough to sacrifice my nice teeth.

For three years in the latter half of high school, I dated the same boy, although technically—again, as I have mentioned—at nearly six years my senior, J wasn't exactly a boy. I thought I'd chosen him because he drove a Jeep and had his own apartment. He could make it up our mountain road in the worst of conditions and get me out of there. I needed reliable transportation to get to town. Even at fourteen I was a pragmatist, but I would need almost thirty years to recognize that J was the same age as the man who had molested me when I was a child. While I understand that unprocessed trauma camouflaged this startling parallel inside my own brain, I persist in wondering why one of the actual adults in my life didn't do something to intervene. I mean, such age-inappropriate dating may have been common in Washington state in the eighties, but it was still, you know, *illegal*. I don't remember thinking our relationship was weird in any way. I thought I had chosen. I needed someone who could drive up the mountain and get me out of there, after all.

And this sounds cold, but when my grandmother assumed I would marry J, I assured her I would do no such thing. Every evening, I popped one pill out of the round case (thank you, Planned Parenthood in rural Washington) and swallowed it when I brushed my teeth and then I woke up early to pore through college entrance materials, never doubting I'd drive away from that tiny town the summer I turned eighteen and never go back. Those were the days when pregnancy would have been the worst thing, when the blue plus on the pee stick would have meant the end of my dreams as I understood them.

When I first remembered the abuse, really let myself remember, I was nineteen, and so battered by shame I thought even Colin's encircling arms might not be able to save me. And then just weeks after he slid his ring on my finger, just weeks after I agreed we could do this thing, live this life together. I would allow myself to be adored, get healthy, be a team—Colin died. He had made me safe enough to remember, he had protected me over a summer I spent fumbling in darkness and fighting for healing, he had loved me when I was convinced I was unlovable. And then, in a flash of headlights and collision of metal, he had left me alone. This time, surely, I would follow him. I would die.

But I didn't die. Instead, I stopped throwing up. Instead, I honored Colin's love by taking care of myself. I fought for my own life—my lucky, lucky life—and won.

And here I was again: When Baby Brother died, I grieved. I was afraid. But also? There was nothing I was unwilling to face for my family. I knew my own capacity.

BY SPRING 2007, Ella was three and a half and I was investing in home pregnancy tests as if they were Microsoft stock. I was able to laugh at my prior naive wonderment, four years earlier, when I had passed over the double packs of pregnancy test kits at Walgreens. Why would any woman need *two*? Now I was a regular at the Dollar Store, where I picked up a few alphabet workbooks for Ella, and then hurried over to the Health and Beauty aisle, avoiding the off-brand toothpastes and bubble bath, but clearing the shelves of the stacked white boxes of one-dollar ovulation and pregnancy test kits. Twenty or more at a time. Sure, I had to play chemist and pee into a little plastic vial, use a dipstick, but it was worth it for the freedom to test at will. Five days before my period if I wanted. I'd sometimes collect urine a reckless six days before the period I hoped would never come was due to arrive. Just in case. I used first morning pee, naturally, and sometimes I would dig into the bathroom trash basket later in the day to extract the negative stick and then hold it up to the window, turning it like a prism in the sunlight, hoping to see a rainbow. Was that another line? Ever so slight?

This was nuts, I know, but although I was acutely aware that pregnancy did not necessarily equal baby, I needed to make progress. I wanted a baby, so on those crazy-making mornings, I wanted two undeniable lines on the damn stick.

Even now, finished with pregnancy, I sometimes feel a pull toward the test kits in the drugstore. What a strange compulsion. I equate my need to test to a recovering gambler's desire to buy scratch-off lottery tickets at the gas station. Despite the fear, despite the worry, despite the looming forty weeks that I would need to cross, double lines on a stick felt like victory—a burst of dopamine that felt, ever so fleetingly, like hope. *Look, honey, I won!*

In May, when the coveted lines appeared on the Dollar Store kit, I celebrated by splurging on a double pack of the fancy kind you can soak midstream to write "Pregnant" in a happy, egg-shaped window. I spelled out pregnancy two days in a row, with the goofy joy of a little boy writing his name with his own urine in the snow, and then, I pried the sticks apart to see if the double lines hidden beneath the plastic were darkening with each passing day, indicating the desired uptick of hCG in my urine. And then, since this was silly science and I was supposed to know better, I called Dr. L's office and scheduled a blood test.

The news was good. I was pregnant for the fifth time.

THIS PREGNANCY was fresh and secret when I volunteered to paint faces at Ella's preschool May carnival. My nerves were shot through, but with this latest opportunity for hope, I was trying hard to relax and enjoy being Ella's mom. Painting any kind of decipherable image on a wiggling cheek, already stained with punch and slick with frosting, is harder than it looks. I come from a family of artists; for heaven sakes, both my parents earned degrees from the prestigious Rhode Island School of Design. Surely I could handle preschool face painting.

My "booth" was actually a wooden raised playhouse. I balanced my already expanding ass on a minuscule plastic chair designed for three-year-olds in the corner, trying not to knock the water cup with my elbow, while the kids lined up on the sandpaper strips of the ramp. It was stuffy and claustrophobic. Through the single tiny window I could see Mark in his beanbag toss corner setting up the same pyramid of cans over and over and dodging wayward bags. I smiled. What's that proverb? Is it Slovenian? Mark tried to get his face away from the cans before the next hurled beanbag and perched on my tiny chair in my airless tower I thought: *At least my neighbor's cow is dead too.*

Responding to excited requests, I tried my hand at a couple of superhero cheeks, but the designs were too elaborate given the jiggling canvases, the too-large brushes, and my utter lack of skill. The disappointed faces when the superhero kids gazed into the handheld mirror I offered, shrugged, and pushed their way back down the crowded ramp, were more than I could handle in my body's progesterone flood. I needed to recalibrate.

In this case, choice would not be without limits. I painted samples of four designs on a piece of construction paper, like a menu: a balloon, a heart, a spider, and my specialty, a cat face. My one concession to variation was a heart-shaped balloon. Oh, and kids could choose any color for any art. A pink spider? Sure! A black balloon? Whatever floats your carnival. This worked. And so it went, face after face, until in some feat of spatial puzzling, a mother crammed her way up into my playhouse with her son, a classmate of Ella's—an odd, smart little boy with Harry Potter glasses I'd always enjoyed—and a baby in her arms.

I pressed myself farther into my corner. The baby was covered with spots. Her face, her exposed chubby legs, her creased wrists. Everywhere. This child, mere inches from me in what felt in that moment like a totally airless enclosed space, was dotted with oozing sores.

Shit shit shit.

I lifted a shaking pointer finger and croaked out, "Chicken pox."

"Yes," the mother said, as casual as if I'd said, "new tooth" or "cute haircut." She nudged her Harry Potter son forward. "You don't mind, do you? I'm sure you're immune."

"I'm pregnant," I whispered, terrified. "I'm pregnant. You need to get her away from me. You need to get *out of here*."

This pregnancy, if it continued, was going to be a long one.

19 The Heart Folds Early

Days after the carnival pox debacle, we flew to Washington state to get into the mountains and see my mom—one year, almost to the day, since Baby Brother's death. This time we hadn't told Ella. We would wait until we were sure this baby had a whole heart. That was the best we could do.

I needed a rest, and proximity to my doctors was not going to change any outcome. Mostly we stayed in my mom's little town of Marcus, population one hundred fifty humans and many, many dogs, on the banks of Lake Roosevelt, but just as the gestational calendar flipped over to six and a half weeks, my mom took us up to the old house on the mountain. Our newest baby was no bigger than an eyelash, but we knew it was a big week, the week the heart should start beating.

The words of our former genetic counselor at the Catholic hospital echoed in my head. *The heart folds early*, she had said simply when I called her with questions about hypoplastic left heart syndrome. But when? I had wanted to know. *When* did this happen? How did this happen? *Why?* What did I do? How can I make sure this doesn't happen again?

The heart folds early.

Through her words, more poetry than science, I'd found the significance in week six. If the embryonic heartbeat can be detected by six weeks and two or three days with the use of intravaginal ultrasound, then the heart has folded. If the fold is wrong, I reasoned, if the origami artist has made an error, sealed a crease in the wrong position, turned the materials wrong and made a break between halves, there may be just two working ventricles. If the maker forgot the left side of the heart, our baby's heart, then by week six the error would be locked in. Imagine the scale here, a fetus not even a quarter of an inch long, half the width of my pinkie. How small the heart? How minuscule the folded ventricles? How miraculous that any among us has a whole heart with four chambers.

Maybe those were the questions I should have been asking: How did I get so lucky? Me, with my whole heart? My daughter with hers? In the making of a human, there is so much room for error.

IN MAY 2007, having traveled all the way around the sun since Baby Brother's death—and also back across the country to spend another month with my mother in Washington state—I called my perinatologist's office in Indiana from my mother's kitchen table while Ella was on a walk with Mark to hear the results of my latest blood tests. I wanted to know if my numbers were doubling as they should. The nurse on the phone told me "everything looked fine," but I asked her for the actual numbers and jotted them down on a white sheet of scratch paper.

Before leaving Indiana, I'd had my blood drawn twice, almost, but not quite, forty-eight hours apart. The lab had analyzed the blood for hCG and progesterone. I worked out the math myself after I hung up the phone, scribbling out the sum. The number was indeed where it should have been, but barely. I took a short breath and explained my scribblings to my mother who was eyeing me skeptically.

"I know more about pregnancy than I ever wanted to know," I said.

"That's certainly what *I* was thinking," she said. I could tell she had been trying to resist comment, but I had opened the door for her.

My throat tightened. "You had two pregnancies and two babies. I've had four pregnancies and one baby. I'm one for four. It's different."

She nodded, holding her lips in a straight, restrained line, trying to be good.

A COUPLE HOURS after the kitchen table conversation, I was still steaming. These were the days when *The Secret* was everywhere—and my mother had been influenced. She had placed her order to the universe for another healthy grandchild.

Her faith was an act of love, and I couldn't have been more pissed off about it all. *If only it were that fucking easy*, I grumbled to myself, trudging back to the kitchen to help with the dinner. *Blame the fucking victim, that's the fucking secret.*

The Secret stoked my hormone-fueled ire like gasoline on a campfire. I felt defensive of fear, and of caution, and mad at all the wrong people. Pessimism is a tremendous protective measure. Not to mention the fact that it was all so much bullshit. I worked on the salad while my mother stirred the boiling noodles. We were talking about my niece's upcoming destination wedding in Mexico, nearly a year in the future, and I said, *Something, something, blah blah blah* "... if we have an infant."

And my mother turned from the boiling pot and set the wooden spoon on the counter, the steam rising up behind her. "Don't say '*if* we have a baby,' say '*when* we have a baby.'"

The serrated knife in my hands tore the red skin of the tomato and the slick orangey pulp inside didn't look nearly as good as the rosy outside had promised. "Whatever," I growled. "You think what you want, and I'll think what I want."

I'M MAKING MYSELF sound like a terrible person here, and maybe that's fair. I wanted this baby desperately. In the privacy of my own brain, I tried to picture him or her snuggled to my breast, the ways our lives would change with a baby around the house again, the unbearable sweetness of placing the baby in Ella's arms. A real live little brother or sister. She'd been waiting too.

I chanted affirming messages to myself. I called on Colin for help and protection. But I'd done these things before.

During Baby Brother's pregnancy, I'd finished worrying. I remembered vividly the moment I'd received the phone call from the genetics counselor with the results of the amnio. At home in Indiana, I'd walked with the portable phone toward the front door and I'd had my hand on the storm door, pushing it open to get some air, sitting on the front steps, braced for the absolute worst, when she delivered the unbelievable news that we had a "healthy baby boy."

After that, I wasn't worried at all. I typed up the details of my maternity leave.

So complete was my trust and belief in Baby Brother's safe arrival in the world that I'd done some spring cleaning the day before that fateful ultrasound appointment, the one we'd almost canceled because it seemed so unnecessary. I went through the plastic storage containers under my bed and sorted out all the most girly of the newborn wear—pink flowered onesies and tiny purple ruffled diaper covers. This would be our last baby and he would be a boy. I brought two garbage bags of girl clothes to the Muncie Mission. I believed.

Fewer than twenty-four hours later, the news was different. There would be no baby boy. In a rush of heart pain and superstition, I wondered if I'd brought this on myself with the hubris of my baby-pajama purge. I'd attracted the attention of the evil spirits somehow with my overconfident preparation. This species of magical thinking was my anti-Secret secret.

With this fifth pregnancy, we had decided there would be no intravaginal ultrasound. We wanted to be far away, in the mountains, and really, what difference would it make? In the last pregnancy, early detection had given us greater access to loss, our hope ticking up a notch with that pinlight flicker of an early heartbeat. This time, instead of racing to the endocrinologist's office, we would be bumping up the rutted road to our old mountain home.

The heart folds early. I tried to send our baby's heart a message: *Please be a whole heart, please be a whole heart, please be a whole heart.* I visualized a four-chambered pumping heart. Or I tried to. I didn't really know what such a thing would look like, so small, and it felt critical to get the picture just right. *Whole heart, whole heart, whole heart.*

SO PERHAPS our baby's heart was folding even as my mother steered the Subaru up the first long ascent of the three-mile dirt road to our mountain place. Just maybe. I gripped Ella's hand with the refrain *What was I thinking?* looping through my brain even as my mother-mouth narrated the landscape: "This is the road that Mommy and Grammy would ride up on Moona the Horse with our groceries after we went to town. Sometimes, in the winter, we pulled our clean laundry up on *sleds.* Isn't that cool? Look, honey! *Waaaaaaaay* down there? There's the river we drove past!" And so on, and bumpity bump, up the rutted, rocky, cliff-edged road.

I wanted our daughter to know her mother's story, how in my teens I had lived up here with my own mom—with no electricity, telephone, or indoor plumbing. I told Ella about the butane-powered curling iron I had used to mold my feathered bangs—the Clicker. Knowing nothing about curling irons or the Farrah-Fawcett hair of the 1980s, Ella's focus stayed on the bumpy road. Bumpity bump. Bump.

Seeing that Ella was doing fine without my ongoing narration, I turned my energy to not vomiting or panicking. That morning, on the mountain, there were things to scare the mother I had become, things that hadn't fazed me when I was a girl clinging bareback to Moona's mane as we picked our way down the hillside to the one-room schoolhouse in the driving snow. I tried to think of what I was afraid of then. Not the steep road, although I didn't like the dust in summer. Not falling from my horse, although I sometimes did. Not the dark, although in the shortest days of winter, I left for school in the dark and returned home in the dark. Not tick bites, probably because I hadn't yet heard of Lyme's disease. Not even bears, although they regularly visited to ransack this or that.

Turns out, my teenage self wasn't afraid of much. (That's not true. She was terrified of the loneliness and rejection she was sure would come of being not pretty, smart, or good enough. And also spiders.) The scaredy-cat mother in me shook my head and I squeezed the molded plastic handle on the door tighter with one hand and Ella's little knee with the other. *What had we been thinking? Why hadn't we just stayed down by the lake, where the road was paved and there was a telephone?*

As a teenager, I suppose I'd been a *little* afraid of Bigfoot (imaginary) and cougars (real), but this time, with Ella and my invisible heart-folding cargo, I struggled to weed the real fears from the imaginary and deal with them one by one. My three biggest real fears: the primitive road, the distance to the nearest hospital, and disease-carrying ticks. I'd already decided the tick-fear trumped my DEET fear, hands down.

When we cleared the final rise through the aspen grove and arrived at the house we discovered signs of a recent bear visit, things that had been pulled from the crawlspace under the house and ripped open: a black garbage bag full of pine cones, a burlap bag of sand, and finally, a large Tupperware storing powdered white lime for the outhouse. Because of the lime, it was easy to play nature channel. The bear's tracks, outlined in white powder, were as obvious as a child's crayon drawing on a wall.

This discovery was mostly exciting. "Look, Sweetie! See the bear paws?!?"

Standing next to a big, white paw print in her tiny sneakers, Ella looked vulnerable and small. *She'd be so easy to snatch*, I thought. *We'll have to keep her close.* When Ella overheard me and Mark consulting about this unlikely danger, she demanded some answers. "But *why* are bears scary?"

"No, no, honey, bears aren't scary. The bears are a lot more afraid of us than we are of them. This is where the bears *live*. These woods are their *house*."

Ella gave me the eyeball. She's never been anyone's fool. "Is that bear going to eat me *up*?"

"No!" Mark and I shouted together. I had given Mark my fear, and now, together, we were trying so hard not to hand it down to Ella.

Also, black bears were the least of our troubles.

BY FAR the most pernicious danger on the mountain that summer was the vigorous population of deer ticks, carriers of Lyme's disease—not something you want your kid to contract, not something you want to pick up during pregnancy. Over five years earlier, my mother had been stricken with horrific serial fevers, which put her into a 104-degree delirium every few weeks until the doctors figured out hers was probably one of the first documented cases of Lyme's in northeastern Washington and treated her with mega antibiotics. But that wasn't the end of it. The disease cycled through her body in the subsequent months creating other bizarre symptoms. For a time, she couldn't lift her arms above her head, she had some trouble with short-term memory, and she still struggles with pain in her knees. My mom's as wary of ticks as are the rest of us, but to give into that fear is to not go to the mountain anymore. And that would be much worse. That's not the way my mom rolls.

Outfitting for our visit to the mountain, we'd taken precautions. We bought white tube socks for everybody. Before we ventured out for a hike, we pulled our socks up over our pants and sprayed all the seams with DEET. Normally I'm not a DEET girl, but this mild exposure was, I figured, better than a tick bite—which, in turn, was better than being the kind of mother who was too freaked out to let her daughter climb a mountain.

In the morning, we hiked out to the ridge overlooking the old one-room schoolhouse and the Kettle River valley. Along the path, I stumbled across a steaming pile of rich, dark, berry-studded bear scat.

I pointed. "Bear poop."

My mother nodded.

Ella came up to take a look. "Wow," she said, admiringly. "That's a lot of poop."

AS A TEENAGER, all my encounters with bears had been innocuous enough. The black bears I'd seen were never that big—more like large dogs—and we'd always chased *them*, rather than the other way around. My mother likes to tell the story of the time we returned home to find a bear dragging our blue cooler down the bank and into the deep, dark woods. There were pork chops in that cooler, and I can't remember how my eating-disordered-self reconciled this apparent contradiction, but I loved pork chops. I skidded down the trail after the bear, yelling, "Hey! Hey, Bear! Give that back..."

When the bear saw me coming, she abandoned her quarry and lumbered into the brush. I snatched up the cooler. The pork chops were already gone, but I did get our cooler back.

My mother intends this story to document my fearlessness. *Remember the time you chased the bear into the woods?* Indeed, I did remember, and I kind of love that I did that. I probably wouldn't do that *now*, but once upon a time I'd been a bear chaser. I, Jill Christman—survivor of traumas, collector of fears, rebuffer of fat, renowned among scaredy cats—had pursued a bear into the deep dark woods to reclaim pork chops that were rightfully mine.

I wish the story ended with a feast of chops and crispy potatoes fried over the fire, but that's not the point, is it?

NOW HERE WAS A BEAR somewhere ahead of us—or behind us—on the trail. And on that beautiful morning, walking with Ella past that big pile of fresh poop and into the denser forest to get over to the ridge, my unrealistic fear grew like a fire in a gust of wind. Mark must have felt it too, and we held Ella's hands on either side. We made noise. We sang loud songs: *She'll be coming 'round the mountain* ... We pretended to be big and brave.

With bears—and children—it's all about the acting. You can't let them smell your fear. And you have to let them know you're there. I realized how Ella had saved my life—again—and here's why: I couldn't wrap up in my fear. I couldn't indulge it. Every day, on or off the mountain, I learned to pretend I wasn't afraid even if I was, and then, sometimes, I really *wasn't*. Sometimes, from deep down, I was as brave and curious as my wide-eyed daughter.

When we made it through the woods and into the clearing at the top of the ridge, we checked our legs for ticks. Then lifted our heads and looked around. Wow. On the cliffs, rich pink rock roses clung to the soft green lichen. The aspen trees rustled their silver dollar leaves, making music with the wind, and as the last of the morning fog lifted off the peaks, the sun warmed the fresh earth— the grasses, the wild roses, the pillows of fallen pine needles—and toasted the air into a luscious sweetness.

I smiled at Ella who stood with her hands on her hips, her chin raised, taking it all in. A pint-sized mountaineer at the summit, cheeks glowing with exertion and happiness.

To be able to give her this, I had talked down my fears.

"I'm not scared of that bear," she proclaimed, grinning.

BACK HOME, I asked Ella about the bear on the mountain. "So you're not afraid of bears, are you?"

She crunched on an oatmeal cookie. "No. I'm not afraid of bears when I can't see them or hear them." She gestured with the cookie around our cozy, bear-free living room. "I'm not afraid of bears *right now*."

"Me neither," I said, laughing. As an erstwhile mountain girl, this struck me as a good lesson in fear management.

Something about being pregnant again took me back to the mountain, not just with my family on the bear-and-DEET weekend, but forward through the slow-turning weeks. Clawing my way to the end, one test after the next, I found solace in this return to the beginning, a time when I'd never even heard the words now defining my every day: nuchal translucency, hCG, hypoplastic left heart syndrome. Hell, I don't even know if I'd ever heard of an ultrasound and I'm *sure* I didn't know there were transducers disguised as dildos.

On the mountain, I know a woman who was told she couldn't have a vaginal delivery after C-section, so she stayed home, many miles from any hospital, laboring in her own bed on the mountain. There was no phone, no running water, and no electricity. Her husband shined a flashlight to illuminate their daughter's path into their world. The birthing mother had learned that high-pitched screams impede progress, so through her long labor she vocalized her pain in moose-speak, deep and low.

This birth could have been beautiful, and it could have been hell. Likely it was both.

As a bleeder, I might not have lived through such a defiance of doctor's advice (as Mark once said, raising an eyebrow and looking at me over the spine of *War and Peace*: "Honey, you would *not* have fared well in nineteenth-century Russia"), but I like to know there are people, *my* people, who played it that way—and survived. I don't want to idealize an off-the-grid existence that was pretty much always a pain in the ass and often downright treacherous, but I do want to give my mom some credit for taking me there. From my knowledge of that place and its people, I draw sustenance. In my memories of the mountain, I find courage.

We made the trip that summer, despite the risks, because we wanted Ella to know the mountain, the real mountain. I wanted her to wake up in a place without other houses, with no noises save the rustling of the chipmunks and the mating calls of the songbirds. I wanted her to end a day in a place where there are no streetlights, no glowing storefronts, no interfering beams from passing cars. I wanted her to know real darkness, a place where she could look up into the sky and bask in the wonder of a galaxy of shining stars. I wanted Ella to stand, eyes up, in the full glow of the rising moon and know for absolute certain that she was lucky and loved.

And she did. We did. With one hand in Ella's and the other tracing constellations on my tightening belly, I channeled that starshine—luck and love distilled into pure, universe-crossing light—deep into the place where our new baby's heart was folding. *Lucky loved lucky loved lucky loved. Whole heart whole heart whole heart.*

20   L.B.

I am looking at my lengthy obstetrics chart and I can tell you exactly how a woman like me is classified in the eyes of a perinatologist. By way of diagnosis, putting me firmly in the high-risk club, I am a woman with a "previous child with congenital anomalies, previous hypoplastic left heart." In addition—and this is where the language starts to smart—I am an "elderly multigravida" and a "habitual aborter." Nice.

Who makes these terms up? No man who wants to get close to a woman without a gleaming set of metal stirrups intervening, but probably a man. Let's take a moment to consider a pair of particularly rich obstetrical charges leveled against women: "blighted ovum" and "incompetent cervix."

Seriously? You're going to tell a woman who's just learned her pregnancy is over, may have stopped growing weeks earlier while she allowed herself to hope, her egg is "blighted"? Or we're going to write on a woman's chart, a woman who has suffered premature labor, possibly lost her baby, that her cervix is "incompetent"? How about we label the guys putting up the low sperm numbers or the premature ejaculators with "blighted balls" or "incompetent cock"? Trigger-happy testicles? Mark points out that "erectile dysfunction" is not exactly a label a man wants tacked on his nether regions, which is probably why the commercials abbreviate the diagnosis to the almost sexy "ED" before going on to warn that any erection lasting more than four hours might require the dude to seek immediate medical assistance. You *think*? I know it's not exactly a fresh take to experience a kind of Bobbitian rage when I think about the ease with which Viagra can be acquired as compared with the restrictions on the full range of reproductive healthcare for women. I simmer.

Mark shrugs and says, "Well, you gotta have adjectives." Okay. You want to go tit for testicle here? I'll give you some adjectives. Keep your relatively benign "low sperm-count," but allow me to toss in bungling balls and clumsy cock.

Useless dick. Ham-fisted vas deferens!

Habitual aborter my big fat elderly multigravida ass.

LINGUISTIC QUIBBLES ASIDE, all these factors—previous congenital heart defects, multiple first-trimester losses, and the alarming maternal age of thirty-eight—gave the doctors and lab technicians a lot of numbers to feed into their risk formulas. As I've said, testing begets testing.

First, there was good news. On the day we returned from my mom's house in Washington, we'd seen our baby's new heart beating, a beautiful sparkle of light on the ultrasound monitor, Tinkerbell's jangling wand. This seemed miraculous, but we'd seen this before, a night-flight jet blinking red toward the dark horizon. We barely dared hope, but we couldn't help ourselves. Hope we did.

Also, we had kicked up our magical thinking to a new level on what was the first ultrasound day of many, many ultrasound days. Mark and I had both equipped ourselves with protective talismans: He had a lucky penny he carried in a tiny red pouch in his pocket, and I'd chosen my grandmother's lucky rabbit, which I'd recently uncovered in the jewelry drawer. The rabbit was a ceramic pin, glazed mostly with an opalescent blue, ears pointing up to hold in the luck, sharp whiskers cut from fishing line and glued in a touchable fringe around its nose. Even near the end of her life at the assisted living home, my grandmother had loved to play games, especially when there was a wager involved. She and my mother spent long hours playing canasta, and my grandmother, a sharp-witted retired librarian, was a formidable opponent as the lone woman joining the complex's weekly poker night. If Beatrice Ingraham was at the table wearing her lucky rabbit, you'd better watch your chips. Wearing my grandmother's rabbit to every appointment seemed like an excellent way to call the forces of good to help protect our baby.

On the same day as the ultrasound, a Wednesday, rubbing my lucky rabbit's rump, I'd driven across town for a blood draw to confirm my progesterone and hCG numbers. These tests mean nothing, really, when read in isolation, but the nurse on duty that day said that watching these numbers rise in a series of weekly tests would be "reassuring" to me. The doctor, to his credit, said that the blood tests weren't really necessary at this point. The heartbeat was telling us more about fetal viability than my blood ever could. He offered to let me skip the blood tests if I wanted, but the nurse had dangled the reassurance carrot before my twitching nose—and I bit down.

What happened to those reassuring numbers? Well, the progesterone level held steady (this was to be expected) at a robust 26.9. Okay, so it had gone down a single point, but progesterone fluctuates in the body depending upon the time of day: no big deal. But the hCG levels . . .

". . . and your hCG is 83,000." The nurse on the phone was Karen.

I swallowed panic. Karen seemed indifferent. Gripping the brochure for the birthing center I'd been using as scrap paper to record blood numbers, I could see that 83,000 was *not* reassuringly higher than the previous number: 108,000. I guessed the nurse wasn't looking at these numbers.

"Um," I said, "last week it was 108,000. It's going down."

I heard the pages of my chart rustling and Karen made an assenting grunt in her throat.

"That's bad," I said, as a statement.

More rustling and grunting.

"That's bad, isn't it?" I said, as a question.

"Well," she said, hedging, "it's not what we like to see. Let me talk to Dr. L and get back to you."

AND SO IT BEGAN. In the hours after phone call number one and phone call number two, Mark and I both hit the internet with a vengeance. Here we would find the answer. Could we find the cure? I've come to recognize something troubling about myself. Even when I'm controlling my urge to Google my worst fear, I don't turn to the internet for information alone. No. Somewhere, in a dim place in my brain, I must believe that if I locate just the right piece of information, I'll be able to change the course of whatever is happening. I know this is radically illogical, but for what other reason would the search for information feel so *urgent*?

Turns out, hCG (human chorionic gonadotropin—manufactured by the placenta, not the baby), which doubles every two or three days early on in a healthy pregnancy, slows down a bit as the weeks progress, plateaus, and then begins dropping around week twelve. But this wasn't week twelve. This was my week nine. Too early, but a possibility, right? We found a few references to this plateau coming early. Everything could be fine. It's not that the pregnancy is doomed, it's just that I have an overachieving placenta. She's a couple weeks *ahead* of the curve!

Dr. L was not of the A+ placenta spirit. That afternoon, he sent me in for more tests, blood clotting screens of every ilk and description, and ordered me to swallow a baby aspirin immediately after having my blood drawn. Blood draw *nothing*. I was leeched and drained, more of a blood *letting*. The tech filled her pocket with clicking vials of dark crimson blood. Eight total. I was woozy with worry. The kind receptionist who set me up for the tests, the one who said *Don't cry, don't cry, if you cry, I'll cry*, gave me a little card with a phone number and a code: "You can call and check your test results on the progesterone and hCG tonight. Probably by ten o'clock. Don't give up. Have hope."

That was a grim evening. Mark and I passed each other in the halls of our house like the walking dead. We avoided eye contact—fed Ella, bathed Ella, read with Ella—and prayed.

Not again. No. Please. Not again.

THE CODE WORKED. At 9:03 p.m., a real person in a lab somewhere read me my results: Progesterone 37 (up ten units!) and hCG 88,000. Wait. That's *up*. The hCG isn't continuing to drop. Now it was *rising*. Nobody had mentioned this possibility to me. I dashed to my computer. These are the two scenarios I discovered in which hCG levels fall and then rise again: ectopic pregnancy and a vanishing twin (one baby dies, so the levels drop, but then the placenta kicks in again for the surviving twin and the levels rise again). These two possibilities would have been ruled out by the ultrasound we'd had the week before: one baby, settled appropriately in my uterus. So what gave? Finally, I found two anecdotal stories—one by a mom herself and one by a sheepish family doctor without an ultrasound machine who had recommended a D&C on the basis of the initially falling hCG: In both instances all was well. This was internet anecdote, not science, but with two more days to wait until the viability scan, we were taking comfort where we could find it.

Those two days of waiting were pure torture—a slow drip on my wet forehead, the incremental turning of the crushing thumbscrew. I permitted myself a single call to Dr. L's office to put myself on standby for any canceled sonography appointments. Then I waited.

"That nurse thinks you're crazy," Mark had whispered during the previous week's appointment when the nurse stepped out of the room. I argued that she'd valued my sense of humor, an appreciation reflected in her odd expression. "No," he said, "she definitely thinks you're crazy."

When the nurse returned to the room, she told me she'd consulted with Dr. L and he'd be happy to write me a script for some anti-anxiety meds, totally safe for the baby. "We want you to *enjoy* your pregnancy," she said. She leaned forward and looked me in the eyes, compassionately but cautiously, the way you might approach an injured dog liable to bite. "You're not enjoying this pregnancy very much, are you?"

I snorted. *Enjoying* this pregnancy?

I declined the prescription, trying to appear as sane and well-balanced as possible, although I wasn't sure what this looked like or whether the snorting had supported the image I was trying to project.

Mark felt much affirmed. He grinned, and when the nurse stepped out for Dr. L, he waggled his forefinger in loopy circles at his temple, mouthing the word "crazy."

Funny man, my husband.

BY THE MORNING of the viability scan, medication free, I was one big, tangled fear knot. Walking in from the waiting room, Mark and I passed Dr. L entering another exam room.

"Jill!" he said cheerfully. "How you doin'?"

"Terrified," I answered. "How are you?"

"Terrified," he said, jokingly, and then took a better look at my face. "Oh, come on now. PMA! Positive mental attitude!"

"What about the hCG?" I wanted to know, from someone who might, you know, actually *know*. "Does hCG *do* that?"

He hedged around a bit, made some noises about an early plateau. "Come on, now," he said again, touching my shoulder, "LOVE your progesterone level."

And do you know what? As I climbed onto the exam table, I thought about his comment—so weird, and so *comforting*. "He *loves* my progesterone," I whispered to Mark, blushing a bit. "I guess that's something you get to say when you're an ob-gyn." But

I was pleased. He loved my progesterone. He had hope. Mark took his penny out of the bag and held it in his palm. I had pinned the lucky rabbit on the hip of my pants to bring him closer to the baby.

Becky, the sonographer, had barely touched the gelled-up transducer to my belly when she said, bless her, "Baby's fine. Baby's fine."

I burst into tears. Of course I did.

You know that feeling you can get in your veins after a period of intense stress or a really good yoga class? Blood warming and picking up speed, stress breaking into pieces and crashing into the channel like tiny calving icebergs? That tingling feeling as the stress-bergs make their clunky, iceberg way to the open sea? I had that feeling. I wanted to go home, drink a lot of water, and maybe take a warm cider-vinegar bath. Finish the toxin-cleansing this wonderful news had started.

I wept. "I feel like I could cry for a week," I said, grinning, and accepting the tissue Becky offered.

Because she'd given us the news of the baby's well-being so quickly, I forgave Becky when she launched into her story about—purportedly—the necessity of nurturing a PMA.

Positive mental attitude.

NINE DAYS AFTER the bloodletting I started to wonder what the lab had done with those extra vials of blood. I had been taking a baby aspirin every day, per doctor's orders, but I was *sure* I didn't have a clotting disorder. When I was twenty-two, I had all four wisdom teeth removed at once. I had Novocain, naturally, but was otherwise fully cognizant, declining the laughing gas or any other kind of anesthesia. Because I was so alert, I maintain a persistent and disturbing memory of the dentist's tight, round belly pressing into my right arm as he leveraged his grip on my stubborn teeth. Yeek. After the extraction, the dentist couldn't staunch the flow of blood, and the laughing nurse said, "You'd better not ever have babies. You'll bleed out on the table." Naturally, I resented her insensitivity mightily at the time, cursing her under my pained breath in the days after the extraction as I gingerly chewed my mashed potatoes, my still-seeping blood flavoring my soft meal like macabre gravy. But the wisdom-tooth nurse was some kind of witch. She'd cursed me and her postbirth bleeding came to pass: black wave, Ella slipping from my arms, *Take the baby take the baby*, doctors, nurses, panic, needles, a great ooze of humanity trying to get a line into my collapsing veins so they could pump me with fluids.

I was a bleeder, not a clotter. This much I thought I knew.

Right? Didn't I?

Still. Where was my blood? On the scale of test results, these ranked low, but in these trying days, there was no lab result for which I was not at least *curious*. I called Dr. L's office, fully expecting to hear I'd better stop with the aspirin.

"I don't know whether you're going to think this is good news or bad news," Bonnie, the nurse, said when she called back with my results.

"No news," I said, airing my smart-ass prediction. "Nothing. All the tests came back negative."

"No," Bonnie said, "they're *not* negative."

Now I was listening.

"You tested positive for something called MTHFR. It's a clotting disorder and Dr. L wants to start you on the Lovenox injections *today*. Karen and I are going to wait here for you to teach you how to do the injections. We'll keep the office open for you. Just knock on the back door."

A clotting disorder with five initials? Crap. MTHFR. I know the letters don't match up, but for the life of me, I think of methylene hydrofolate reductase's awkward acronym as the days of the week. Out of order. With no Wednesday and the "R" for Thursday (as we do in academic scheduling). I know this doesn't make sense. Nothing was making sense. The only part that seemed clear to me was also the only part that mattered: The nurses were staying late in the perinatologist's office to give me a shot that might save this baby. Time mattered.

At the office, Bonnie gave me an injection lesson, showing me how to move the bacteria away from the chosen injection site with an alcohol swab. My options were thigh or belly. On that first evening, I chose thigh because wasn't there a *baby* in my belly? Before inserting the needle—with a jab, with *conviction*, not a tentative push—Bonnie demonstrated how to find a good fold of skin to pinch. Because Lovenox is viscous, the needles were of an alarmingly hefty gauge. *We want to go under the top layer of skin, but we don't want to hit the fat. Make sure the needle goes in all the way, right up to the hilt, and then depress the plunger. Not too fast. It's thick.*

While we practiced, Bonnie explained that pregnancy is a hypercoagulable state. I found this word strangely comforting because it's fun to say. Hyper-co-ag-u-la-ble. What it means, of course, is that pregnant women are more prone to blood clots. And the clots they're particularly concerned about are the ones in the placenta that could potentially block oxygen to the baby. This was the clot the Lovenox shots were supposed to prevent.

My god. Could I be more afraid? Could I?

And my theory that being a bleeder would protect me from being a clotter? Wrong again. Sometimes, I learned, people are bleeders *because* they're clotters. What happens is that all the clotting agents scurry to a single location, causing clots there and leaving the rest of the body to bleed. While the cops speed to the riots downtown, setting up roadblocks with firehouses and tear gas, the looters flood the streets uptown, break windows, and raise hell. Fuck.

NOT UNTIL THE NEXT MORNING, when I was sitting bravely in the light of the dining room window with an alcohol swab in one hand and a prefilled syringe in the other, reconsidering the advantages of the less painful belly shot, did I study the packaging and notice what else I was dealing with: Lovenox, or "enoxaparin sodium," is derived from "porcine intestinal mucosa" (which contains natural heparin and is invaluable for its "antithrombotic action"). Good words.

I sat on the chair in my underwear, slumping, letting this all soak in. Terrific. Every day for the rest of this pregnancy until we got so close to a possible delivery that we had to stop, balancing the risk between me bleeding out and a clotting placenta, like a freaking Wallenda on a highwire, I would find an unskewered location on my stretching skin and inject myself with pig guts. Every single day. Guts from a pig. Fucking glorious.

I do have some good news. Here is something of which I am not afraid: needles.

Still. The poor pigs.

LIKE BABY BROTHER, this baby was a kicker. I detected flutters by twelve weeks, and by fifteen or so, the butterfly morphed into a goldfish and began to swim. That's what it felt like—I was the drunken frat boy on a dare and I'd swallowed the squirming live goldfish. My womb was the fishbowl and there was still plenty of room to move and so my fish would flip and spin and swim. This was such sweetness.

There were good days and bad days while we waited for our little fish to get big enough for a heart scan to tell us if the baby had a whole heart. Or not.

DR. L DEMONSTRATED his characteristic mercy and scheduled an investigative ultrasound in the seventeenth week. He couldn't promise, he said, that the baby would be big enough to see what was going on in the heart, but he would try. He is a compassionate man.

As usual, Becky was in the sonographer's seat for the scan. She was cheery, but serious. "Do you want to know the sex?" she asked as she typed in our information and clicked on her machine.

"Yes," I said. "If you can see, we want to know." I threw in my standard line leveled against those who argue we're ruining the surprise, somehow going against nature. "The way I figure it, we'll be surprised right here. Surprise!" I mustered a smile, but I considered asking Mark for a bag, in case I threw up. In my mind, I repeated, *Pleasepleasepleaseplease. Have a heart. Have a whole heart. Wholeheartwholeheartwholeheart.* I tried to pretend I was still the kind of pregnant lady who could care about her baby's sex, and in a way I guess I did. I was sure this baby was a girl. At home, swinging on her new play set was our little girl with her whole heart. I had given birth to a girl and she was alive. I associated live babies with girls and dead babies with boys, therefore this baby would be a girl. She had to be.

Becky turned on the machine and our three sets of eyes all turned toward the screen. The baby wriggled, so I didn't need to ask about a heartbeat. Babies without heartbeats don't dance, and this one was dancing. Becky laughed and said something about wishing she had a soundtrack. No doubt she'd used that line before.

Like her employer, though, Becky was merciful, and she'd been empowered to tell us exactly what she was seeing without waiting for Dr. L to come in and interpret. This is as it should be. She was uncharacteristically quiet for a moment as she concentrated, skidding the wand around my well-lubed belly. I didn't know what she was looking for, but I'd requested that she not leave the heart for last. I'd asked her to go there as quickly as possible because I couldn't bear the stress. I did not want to watch another doomed baby on the screen.

"Okay," she said. "Oh. Okay, I see a protrusion here."

A protrusion? Microseconds passed, but I was thinking: *Protrusion? From where? The skull? The heart?*

This is as far as I got. "Looks like a baby boy!" she exclaimed. "He's got a lobster roll between his legs!"

I gasped for air and reached for Mark's hand. Any fool would have known this is what she meant by protrusion. A penis! Of course. Duh. Of course. Anybody but somebody who's been in a dim room like this one when she heard the utterly unthinkable. Later, I asked Mark about that moment, and he confessed to a similar shock—not quite as severe as mine. "Well," he said, "I knew she was down by the legs, so I thought there was something wrong with his leg."

Even at seventeen weeks, the heart is no bigger than a legume, and the scan required long minutes, plus our dancing boy wouldn't stay still to let Becky get a good shot. She told us as soon as she had located all four chambers, and we breathed an initial sigh of relief, but that was not enough. We needed all four chambers with blood flow. Becky turned on the Doppler color, and we watched blue and red swish through our baby's magnified heart.

I held my breath. With our first baby boy, I remembered seeing the shadow of the heart, inscribed with the white spider web lines of the ultrasound, and when the color was switched on, only a half-moon of color. The other side had stayed black because there was no blood on the dark side of his tiny moon. This time, I saw color everywhere. I didn't know if there was blue where we wanted blue, and red where we wanted red, but I could see color.

Color in all four chambers.

The temptation is to link the Doppler's color to the diagrams of our high school biology texts: blue for oxygen-poor blood, and red for oxygen rich, but this color is all mixed together; played fast it might be purple. Here in Doppler world, I learn, the color depends on the blood flow in relation to the transducer: red coming toward the transducer, blue flowing away. Becky didn't remain silent this whole time. She told us things looked great, but she was trying to get a really good angle, to be sure.

And then she *was* sure. She got her shot. "I can see blood flowing through all four chambers," she said, smiling up at me through the dim light. "I can see the aorta, and the aortic valve. Everything's good."

I started to cry. For three days, I alternated grinning and crying, like the crazy person everyone believed me to be.

THE BLUE-AND-RED HEART gave us hope. At dinner the next night, we told Ella the secret we'd been keeping. She smiled. "A boy?"

"A boy," we confirmed. I wanted to cry. Again.

Ella sat quietly for a long minute, alternately smiling and frowning. "Well," she said at last, moving into her three-year-old-Ella-as-ancient-Yoda mode, "we are very happy we're getting another baby brother, but the new baby will not *replace* Baby Brother. We will never *forget* Baby Brother." Then she looked up toward the ceiling fan, through to the sky. "We won't forget you, Baby Brother."

At which point, I was undone, so deliriously happy and so unbearably sad.

Not long after, my friend Diane—Colin's big sister and Ella's beloved "Auntie Di"—came for a visit and was shocked to learn the baby didn't yet have a nickname. She and Ella came up with "Little Brother" together. "Our baby's name is L.B.," Ella would explain. "L.B. for short, Little Brother for long."

HERE IS A GLIMPSE at how my mind worked during the second half of my pregnancy with L.B. The date is August 28, 2007. L.B. is nineteen weeks and one day old. Exactly. As we enjoy our small cup of morning coffee, I feel him shift around a bit in the left hemisphere of my belly, but then he's pretty still. At first I tell myself he knows this is the gestational day his big brother, B.B., died. He's sleeping off this gloomy day.

But by 10:00 a.m. there is a war waging in my head. The insane, hormone-addled pregnant lady has managed to convince herself that today is L.B.'s last day on this earth. This makes sense to her because this is when we lost *Baby* Brother, and once again well over a year later, the loss seems unthinkable: *How did she bear it?* The insane, hormone-addled pregnant lady doesn't know. She's terrified. She explains her fear to the calm, writer lady with whom she shares a brain. I know, I know, but in this binary the writer *is* the sane one, and oh, by the way, she's on *sabbatical* this year, which means she's supposed to be writing a *book*. This book. Oh my goodness, the writer lady realizes: This book is like the old Sesame Street classic *The Monster at the End of This Book* ("starring lovable, furry old Grover"). She shares this realization with the pregnant lady, hoping to distract her. You remember, she prompts, the one where Grover tries everything to prevent the child from turning the page? He nails the page shut? Ties the pages with rope? He does everything he can do to avoid getting to the end of the book where the monster from the title is lurking?

The writer realizes that *The Monster at the End of This Book* was in fact her first real exposure to postmodern literature. "It's totally meta!" she exclaims to the pregnant lady, who is way, way too distracted to care. The pregnant lady gets up out of their writing chair for some juice.

The writer changes tacks and considers aloud how statistically remote the chance of the pregnant lady's fear coming to pass. How unlikely would it be, she proposes by way of comfort, for this baby to die on exactly the same day as our other baby? No. That would be statistically freakish.

The pregnant lady considers this, momentarily assuaged. But the writer can't help herself. She keeps talking. Much more likely, she goes on, that this baby would die on a *different* day of something altogether unexpected, something we don't even know we're afraid of yet. And we are back where we began, but this time we're both there together, the pregnant lady and the writer lady.

As the weeks crawl by, this is the way I live. I've stopped engaging Mark in these conversations because it's not fair and because I want him to love both of us, the pregnant lady and the writer lady.

Like Grover, *we* are the monster at the end of the book, and we're feeling sheepish because it's taken us so long to figure this out.

ELLA'S YODA MOMENTS often come when she's enjoying a meal. One day in November, dipping a Triscuit into a pink plastic bowl of lemon hummus, a pensive Ella looked up and asked, "Will Little Brother live a longer life than Baby Brother?"

She wanted to know.

"Oh, honey," I said—my answers to these questions always seem to begin there, *oh, honey*—"I certainly hope so. The doctor says he's very healthy." As with my own fear, I wonder where she got hers—too much for a girl of three. I guess it's obvious that despite my best intentions, I've done this to her.

But what else could we have done? Someday she'll know the whole story, but when Baby Brother died we kept the story simple: "He's not going to come live with us. He's not in Mommy's belly anymore. He lives in the sky." How could we have protected her from this loss? We were almost halfway there. We'd waited a reasonable time to tell her. I can't remember exactly, but up around twelve weeks, past what I had imagined to be the miscarriage point. We had every reason to believe we'd be bringing home a baby brother just as we'd told her, and when we knew that wasn't going to be the case, we had to tell her that too. She saw us cry, yes, but when the gut-strangling wails rose up, I left her with her dad or grandmother. She'd seen my grief, but not my dismantling.

Will Little Brother live a longer life than Baby Brother?

ON NOVEMBER 8, 2007, I forgot what day it was for the first time ever until my mother called that afternoon to tell me she was thinking about me. "Eighteen years. Hard to believe."

I felt a jolt of awareness and was too ashamed to confess I'd forgotten. "Hard to believe," I muttered back.

Eighteen years after Colin was killed and I almost missed the anniversary of his accident. What was I thinking about? I was thinking about Ella, who had turned four on November 6—how fantastically delicious her vegan birthday cupcakes were, how the new winter coat from Kohl's seemed a little snug in the arms, how much we should limit screen time on her new laptop even when the games are educational. I was thinking about L.B., and my various ailments—the urinary tract infection last week, this week's gardenella vaginalis, sounding for all the world like an exotic species of orchid ("What a lovely name!" I said cheerfully when Karen the Nurse called with the results of the swab). Infections like these in pregnancy can intensify early contractions, and mine did, so I was distracted, of course, by the menace of preterm labor. Never mind the flagyl they'd given me to treat the infection, which was nasty stuff with the twin side effects of a perpetual metallic taste, as if I were using dirty copper pennies as breath mints—plus, I don't know, a kind of unshakable hopelessness?

So I'd been thinking about my children, here and gone and not yet, struggling to be a passable mother to the little girl sitting across the dinner table from me, and I had managed to let Colin's day pass without remembrance. I said to Mark, "This is the day, eighteen years ago, that Colin d-i-e-d."

"What's d-i-e-d?" Ella asked.

I looked at Mark, he nodded at me, and realizing our spelling days were numbered anyway, I said, "D-i-e-d spells died. Mommy had a friend named Colin who went to live in the sky." I paused. "You would have liked him. Colin *loved* kids."

Ella grinned. "Yeah," she said, as if she'd known all about him all along.

"Yeah," I echoed, realizing I'd never thought about the day when Ella would be old enough to spin through the implications of Colin's relationship to me, and his death. If Colin hadn't been on that highway at that precise moment on the night of November 8, 1989, in the precise location that the speeding tow truck was on the highway, where would we all be?

If life, instead of ending, had marched on the way I had once imagined life marches on—that is, following some kind of predictable path—then Colin and I would have had the wedding we'd planned. I would have been a twenty-one-year-old married woman. We'd already talked about kids. How soon would we have had them? Listen to me, falling so easily into the role of my younger self. How soon would we have *tried* to have them? When the nurse wiped the vernix from my firstborn's slippery flesh, would Colin's olive skin have glowed from beneath the white? Would her infant blue eyes have changed and darkened into her father's chocolate brown?

In other words, would blue-eyed, blond-haired, quick-witted Ella never have been born? Another baby in her place? No flirting in a dark bar with her father almost ten years after Colin's death? A bummed cigarette, a game of darts, a discussion of the endlessly variable point of view in *Middlemarch* through the smoke, and presto, change-o, an opening for the possibility of Ella's very existence?

How long can we all stay with this thought? How do any of us know what to wish for? Whole lives never lived. All of us, every day, every turn, roads and roads and roads traveled—and not. "What's d-i-e-d?" Ella asked me, and I told her, as best as I knew how.

Mark and I never bargained for more than two children. So, if our first lost baby, that early miscarriage, had continued to grow, he would have been our family. Or she. But along came Baby Brother with his half a heart. If he had been born whole and healthy, well, there we'd be, with a one-year-old at our table, palming peas, with a face and a name.

But that didn't happen either, and there we were on November 8, 2007, thirty weeks pregnant with a new little boy, praying for a baby—*this* baby. And so each negation had carved the hole for the next to grow, each loss a possibility, and still a loss. I almost couldn't bear the beauty and the terror.

NEAR THE END OF NOVEMBER, finally free of the godforsaken flagyl, I felt funny on my way to pick up Ella from preschool, as if I had something in my throat. At a traffic light, I did what any good pregnant lady would do. I stuck my tongue out at myself in the rearview mirror to take advantage of the bright light. What I saw next is burned in memory, framed by the elongated oval of the mirror.

Aaaaaaaaaaaaaaaaaaaaaaaagh! There was a yellow kitten curled up on my tongue! What the hell?!?! Her thick, yellow fur rippled with the increasing rapidity of my anxious breath. I opened wider. What *was* that in my throat? Stalactites? Yes, "c" is for ceiling. Stalactites hang tight to the ceiling. These thick, creamy drips were heading down, like spilled milk . . . to feed the kitten!

I picked up Ella, saying as little as possible to her teacher, feeling as if I were hiding a forbidden pet in my closed mouth, and dashed home to call the doctor. Of course, it was 12:20. On Fridays, Dr. L's office closed at noon. For the weekend. I put in a call to his answering service, assuring the receptionist that I was *not* in labor, but asking that he be paged and call me at his earliest convenience. Before he headed out for bowling league night.

In the meantime, I typed my symptoms into the Mayo Clinic page and came up with an answer: thrush. I had a yeast infection *in my mouth*. My vaginal problems had moved north. Knowing Mark would never want to kiss me again, I reported my self-diagnosis to Dr. L when he called and ran off to the drugstore for the prescription bottle of antifungal "swish and swallow" he called in. Yummy.

Here is a self-portrait as I approached what would be my final month of pregnancy:

10:00 p.m. Bedtime. I stagger into the too-bright light of the kitchen, wearing only my somewhat sticky underwear because I've just brushed my teeth and performed my nightly hemorrhoid treatment. Always, I try scraping at my tongue with the tough bristles of my brush, but so far, the kitten won't budge. I am beyond disgusted and disgusting. I swish, gag, and swallow. Bleh. Be gone, yellow kitten.

I line up my medications and supplements: baby aspirin, prenatal vitamin, cranberry capsule, probiotics, Tums with calcium, vitamin B6, omega 3, and swallow them all down. I get out my icepack and Lovenox injection and try to find a piece of skin on the upper part of my abdomen that is not stretched into the drum of my growing belly. This proves difficult. Maybe it was from hanging my head down, pulling my heavy breasts up and away in my search for a needle-width of flesh that hadn't already been poked into the consistency of an elephant's hide, but drip, drip, drip. Here it is—red like a party, or a war—my nosebleed du jour. Lovely. I dash back to the bathroom, make myself a toilet paper nose tourniquet, and pull one of my precut paper bag strips from the kitchen drawer. I run the strip under the faucet and stuff the soggy brown paper into position between my gum and upper lip. If anyone wanted to talk to me—and why would they?—I would speak with a lisp, but the paper bag is the only trick that seems to staunch the nose blood these days. Thus adorned, I return to the kitchen's bright light to find some jab-able skin.

Finally, I locate a potential injection spot and hold the sandwich bag of ice to my naked flesh. The baby kicks at the bag. He hates cold things. "Well, too bad, baby." I say this last bit out loud, with a lisp.

Maybe it's because I expressed an uncharitable thought in the general direction of my longed-for baby, or maybe it's because I'm a bloated, hormone-charged, nose-bleeding, fuzzy-tongued pregnant woman standing naked in her kitchen with a giant needle—but I unravel. I lose it. I start weeping. I can't stop myself and I don't even try. My tears water down the nose blood and now the dark red splotches are running together, pink streams down the white globe of my belly, like . . . Like what? Oh god. I can't even think of a metaphor! I am painting myself in rosy rivulets of blood, snot, and tears.

Mark must hear my weeping, and he puts his head around the corner into the kitchen. Although he has the good sense to not step through the doorframe, I now have a witness to my disintegration and the image of what I must look like to him, this poor man who, for better or worse, has bound himself to me in holy matrimony, strikes me as terribly funny. I let out a snort of laughter. I am hysterical, laughing and crying, hanging onto the counter to keep myself from slipping in the mess I am making, and thinking: *Okay, okay. This is not so bad. If all goes well—pleasepleasepleaseplease let all go well—this deterioration of my body and mind will end, not in my own death but in the birth of a healthy baby boy. At which point, we will all tumble into balance: a family of four. A family of four!*

But in this moment, seriously, how must I look to my husband? I look up into his face and meet his eyes.

"Oh, honey," he says.

And then he backs out the door.

21   Vagina Will Find Vagina

Here is the birth story I like to tell pregnant women. It is not my own.

My friend Debbie had a pregnancy that overlapped with my last, but she was due much earlier—August. A couple of weeks before her estimated due date, Debbie, also an English professor, went into her administrative office to get some work done. In the midafternoon, Debbie began to feel "a little weird," so she said goodbye to her secretary and a wide-eyed student worker who confessed later to being glad to see her go (the twenty-somethings have watched too many movies and remain convinced, it seems, that pregnant women regularly let loose a seismic wave of amniotic waters on the tiles of places of business and deliver babies right there with nary a moment to boil water or locate clean towels).

Debbie went home and lay down on her couch, relaxing. Her two-year-old daughter, Sadie, was there with her, playing, and eventually her husband Tim started timing contractions, which did seem to be settling into a pattern, but they weren't hurting and the baby wasn't due for two weeks. Nobody got too excited, least of all Debbie. Debbie was chill. Around dinner, the funny feeling began to seem more like labor, maybe, and she continued to breathe and meditate through the contractions, using hypnobirthing methods she'd been practicing.

Hypnobirthing is rooted in the idea that birth is a natural, normal process we humans have been practicing for a good long time.

We needn't approach birth with fear. Fear creates resistance and resistance provokes pain. Debbie was down with this.

Around eight, Tim tucked Sadie into bed and called the friend they had on standby for just such a moment. He arrived, and around nine thirty Debbie and Tim headed off to the birthing center. Debbie was convinced they'd send her home, but the midwife had said to come in for a check, so off they went. Child number one was sleeping peacefully.

"It didn't even hurt," Debbie told me. "Seriously. I kept thinking I wasn't even really in labor." When the midwife did the exam, she told a "very surprised" Debbie that she was at eight centimeters and broke her waters manually—which, for those keeping score or beginning to hate Debbie just a tiny bit, "hurt like crazy." Nonetheless, reclaiming her hypno-mellow, Debbie climbed into the Jacuzzi to do the laboring she figured she had coming. But she felt the urge to push, the baby crowned, and swoosh, at 11:54 p.m. little Georgia Elizabeth entered this world, much wetter than her mama had planned.

At 6:00 a.m., the joyful, sleepy parents returned home to relieve their friend. When Sadie woke up in the morning, right on schedule, nothing at all amiss, her mother was sitting on the couch nursing the baby. There's a photo of this first meeting, and man, does the new big sister look surprised.

I *love* this story. I *wanted* such a story. Fear is a story we tell ourselves, and my brain excels in spinning tales of suspense, thrillers with ghastly accidents, horror with bad guys and boogie men of every description. I know this, I *knew* this, and so I understood that to survive this pregnancy I was going to have to work hard to tell myself different stories—pretty, painless, chill stories with happy endings.

What with the bleeding and the perinatologist and all, I wasn't a candidate for the birthing center, but by some trick of mind or faith, or just plain persistent optimism, I believed my baby's birth could unfold in the theater of the maternity ward without the high-level interventions of his gestation. Debbie passed on her hypnobirthing books and CDs to me, and in those final months the soothing female voice on my iPod shuffle became my regular nighttime companion.

My favorite meditation involved a rainbow. First, I saw red. Then I floated in red. I let my feet rise up in red, my head fall back, neck soft, supported by red. The red held me in a pillow of redness until I melted into red. I became red. I *was* red. I sank farther into the rainbow and became orange. "Deeper down," my hypno-friend intoned in my ear. "Deeper down now." And down I would go. *I can do this*, I thought, breathing deep and slow, fingers exploring my smooth belly like a new planet. *We can do this. We can be okay.*

THIS STORY is still missing a key character. During my pregnancy with Baby Brother, I'd worked with a midwife at my regular ob-gyn's office. Blonde-haired and coiffed, tanned neck adorned with a tear drop of gold, Shane was not the Birkenstocked, goddess-pendant-wearing midwife of stereotype. In her well-heeled, clicking pumps, Shane seeming to fear neither a slip in effluvia nor the conservative administration in our small Midwestern hospital. She walked the walk for a woman's right to own the experience of birthing, and for this—and the way that teardrop glistened in the seashell divot of her throat—I was a little in love with her.

In the early, brutal days after Baby Brother, Shane called me and told me she *knew* our story wasn't over, making me promise to call her when I was pregnant again. She insisted on a narrative I wasn't ready to believe in, but instead of making me angry with her positive thoughts, she had given me a distant hope. And when her words came true, and I was halfway through my fifth pregnancy, I kept my promise and called Shane. And so it came to pass that my high-risk perinatologist, Dr. L, with his gleaming tech and better-living-through-pharmaceuticals grin, formed an alliance with the midwife who fought to get our hospital's labor and delivery floor a real laboring tub. In their shared desire to help me, they were all in—an unlikely and frankly adorable team. The partnership between Dr. L and Shane was strange and wonderful. My L&D mom and dad.

Because I want to offer a concrete example of the work my two birthing professionals did together on the palate of my body, I need to talk frankly about vaginas. The subject arose organically during a conversation at a Mexican restaurant where Shane and I met when I was about seven months along to discuss my dreams for the birth.

We all know this restaurant: Inside, the air-conditioning is pumping and the light is dim—womblike, if wombs were chilly and enjoyed piped-in mariachi music. The high-backed, womb-within-a-womb wooden booths are shellacked to such a high gloss that when my hard plastic water glass started sweating, it moved across the slick table on its own volition to knock against the book-like menu featuring blurry, garishly colored shots of chimichangas and enchiladas in spreading pools of refried beans and melted cheese. I made a crack about the advantages of hiring a professional food photographer, but it wasn't long before Shane and I were getting down to the nitty-gritty.

She hadn't herself attended a hypnobirth, but she was excited to hear about what I was learning and read up on hypnobirthing methods. She was sure the brand-new laboring tub at our hospital would be ready for action by January, and she thought the water labor and hypno-methods would be compatible, if that's what I chose to do. We talked at length about clotting and bleeding, and reviewed all the precautions: This time there would be a hep-lock and post-birth Pitocin. I didn't want to get the baby out safely and then die myself. That wasn't a lesson I needed to learn twice. I reminded her about the bad vaginal tears from Ella's birth and she assured me that she'd massage and stretch the perineum with olive oil throughout my labor to get ready for my baby's head. I nodded happily, rolling another fajita. With every word she spoke, my hope grew. Maybe there would be no tearing at all, she told me, but if there was, she didn't plan to stitch up any second-degree tears.

"Really?" I put down my fajita. "But will that . . . *work*?"

Sweeping a yellow chip across the green surface of the guacamole and popping it into her mouth, Shane smiled, chewed, swallowed, and said, "The recovery without stitches is *so* much more comfortable." She wanted to spare me that postpartum feeling of being perched naked on a porcupine and told me that the latest midwifery literature established that up to second-degree tears would heal just fine *without* suturing. Shane's gold bracelets flashed against the dark wood of the booth as she raised her hand, winding up for the pitch. "You could throw some vagina way over there—" she said, releasing her imaginary projectile toward a shuttered window on the opposite side of the restaurant, "and on the wall up there." She pointed above our heads at an oil painting of a vase of sunflowers. As I did the work of picturing "some vagina" on both the wooden shutters and the bright blossoms, I felt a bit less well, a smidge less hopeful. "You could throw vagina over there and up there," she repeated, "and they'd meet in the middle of the room. They'd come together again. Vagina will find vagina," she said, taking a definitive bite of her taco salad.

I held my ice water to my suddenly warm cheek. "Really?"

"Really," Shane said.

At my next week's appointment, I relayed the conversation and the no-stitch plan to Dr. L, finishing with Shane's unforgettable pronouncement: "Vagina will find vagina."

Dr. L raised his eyebrows, a smile playing the corners of his mouth, before he got serious. His protocol, he explained, was to stitch anything beyond first degree, cinch her up tight. But, ever amenable, he scribbled a note on my chart, and nodded, once again acquiescing to any hippie-dippie plan that wouldn't put me or the baby at risk. If I wanted excruciating labor pain, I could have excruciating labor pain. If I wanted a saggy vagina, well, that was my choice. He may have said something about consulting with my husband on this important decision, and in response I may have shot him a look like the glint off the blade of Julia Child's cleaver. In the end, though, he said, choosing equally unforgettable language: "Suit yourself. I hope you don't end up incontinent."

Yee-ikes. There are fears that paralyze and fears that kick in the grit. Incontinent? *Hell* no. Now I had a new something to occupy my mind and body. I Kegeled like a madwoman. In the weeks leading up to the due date, I worked those pelvic floor muscles like a teenager in a basement with a free weight set. A kid determined to get stronger so he wouldn't wet himself when the playground bully kicked sand in his face. When I tightened and released, tightened and released, I heard Rocky's song as he sprinted up the step of the Philadelphia Museum of Art. *Da na na, da na na . . . Da na na, na na na na NA!*

The plan that Dr. L, Shane, and I massaged and stitched together for the gestation and birth of this longed-for baby was a microcosm of my own fear—represented by Dr. L and his many monitors—and my fierce desire to harness the power of my own female body to deliver my baby safely into the world. That's where Shane, Kegels, and my hypnobirthing rainbow training came in. I stood with one foot on each shore, my body a bridge between the land of fear and the volcanic island of power I was building, my determined vagina in training to kick some vagina *ass*.

AND YET—every week of L.B.'s gestation, save those three when we escaped to the mountains, had been scrutinized. I had so many ultrasound close-ups for the fridge, I'd begged them to stop printing them out. "Please," I told the sonographers. "We've got plenty of pictures. Just see what you need to see and turn off the waves." The more I saw, the more we knew and charted, the more afraid I became. Dr. J's words from that sad afternoon in Chicago played in my head: *You don't want to know everything there is to worry about.* I did *not* know, but I felt as if I was trying to know, searching and vigilant. This pregnancy reminded me of the months when I was grieving Colin, still healing from years of childhood abuse, writing out the horrors as I remembered them in longhand, page after page, memories stacking up on each other like broken furniture in a rickety session of can't-touch-the-floor in a dark basement, me teetering at the top. If I could just know *everything*, was my thinking, I could climb to freedom. Then I would be safe.

During that time, my mom started taking me to one of her friends, a healer and therapist who also happened to channel an angel by the name of Divine Grace. Divine Grace had perspective I lacked. She guided me through my grief, helped me also with the unfinished and now fully exposed work I had to do around the sexual abuse. Every day, it seemed, I would remember some new horror, a moment, a flash of something, and on the days I didn't remember, I would revisit the old ones, turning over clues in the dark, sifting through the wreckage of memory with my fingers like the child I'd wanted to be, letting sand run through my fingers in search of polished beach glass or shark teeth. I spent a lot of time in the dark, straining my eyes into the scariest corners of my folded brain. I wanted to get better. I wanted to live. And I thought to do that I would need to look the perpetrator right in his bloodshot eyes, step out from the protection of the deep brain shadows where I'd hidden every time I'd been held down, spread open, or shut up. I was weak with the effort of this remembering—the day I was home sick from school and he came over to fix a burst pipe and stayed all day, the afternoon he and a friend took turns with me on top, the late night he gave me peppermint schnapps and played dealer in a game of strip poker I would always lose, and on and on to exhaustion.

But there was too much to know. Who could tell me when I was finished remembering and could get on with living? Divine

Grace laid her hands over my shoulders where I was holding my grief, carrying sadness like a backpack. Pressing gently, she said, "Jill. You're in a dark room. You need to touch everything in the room, but there is no light. When will you know that you're finished? When will you know that you've touched everything?"

"I won't."

"Why don't you turn on a light?"

Now eight months pregnant, I thought about Divine Grace and her simple question.

As the gestational days clicked forward, I reached for the light. I tried so hard to picture a live baby safely delivered to my arms. I studied his face on the photos—his nose and lips just like his sister's, and my breaking heart, like his brother's—but I couldn't make the mental leap to *born*, to *safe*, to *here*. Not really. Not in any way that brought me real comfort. *Why don't you turn on a light?*

THE LIGHT WAS MINE to turn on. Because I was still processing the trauma of losing Baby Brother, still grieving, I couldn't fully bend my mind into the light and I wasn't going to beat myself up for that. I had traveled dark roads before. Grief doesn't get easier with practice, but I knew I carried the tools I'd found to navigate those other roads here to this one. There was so much I couldn't control, but I knew I had to figure out what I *could* do and focus my energy there. The act of birthing became my light.

All through December, the month that was to be the last full month of this pregnancy, I set myself up each afternoon like a queen on a palanquin of bed pillows, breathing in the color purple, watching the color purple move through my own veins in my mind's eye, and then blowing out the color purple, my exhalation a lavender cloud, *deeper down now*, feeling so relaxed I couldn't tell where my body stopped and the pillows began.

I'd written myself a letter right after Ella was born, lest I forget— and still, I forgot. I forgot because I wanted to forget. *I need to get it all down before I forget the pain,* I'd written to my future self, the self I was in my last month of pregnancy, breathing purple. In the letter, my stitched up, bleeding, postpartum former self had ranted. *Transition, my friend, is not a time in life to be fucked with.* And how did the deeper-down Jill respond? She didn't believe that other Jill. She smiled. She didn't remember it being bad at all. Purple-clouded Jill knew that letter-writing-postpartum Jill was likely prone to hyperbole and shushed her. Purple-clouded Jill was afraid of a lot of things—but she wasn't afraid of birthing pain. She wanted to remember what came next.

I've watched videos of laboring women on twilight sleep tied down to their beds, flat on their backs, thrashing and screaming, sometimes gagged. Horrific. If I've learned anything in this life it is that not remembering pain doesn't mean there was no pain. Not remembering traps pain. I thought of my mother's anger, her body's fury: "My greatest regret is that I was not awake to see you kids born." Our births were taken away from her, done *to* her, and she never put down that regret.

I, too, have pushed pain deep into the back of my brain closet, behind the hanging dresses. I didn't know how to clear out what had hurt me, but I didn't want to look at it every day either. My strategy worked: I forgot my own hidden pain. Before I let myself remember, during the years when the memory of what happened in that dark garage was stored in my darkest corners, I lived my life in the exhausting, perpetual effort to purge something I didn't know was there, something I couldn't access, no matter how many times I vomited, no matter how sick with emptiness I made myself. I lived this way until I was nineteen years old and Colin made a safe place for me to remember. For me, there were no work-arounds. I learned this. I could go through the middle or spend my life empty, feeling nothing. With no outlet, the memory of pain gains purchase deep in our cells, held by muscle and nerve, furious with the brain's betrayal. To come out the other side of the harm that was inflicted on my body when I was a child, I had to pull the trauma out of those dark closets and hold it in my hands.

My anguish after Colin's death was head-on and I know this deep grief, this Kübler-Ross style of digging down, saved my life. Some days I was so weak with the pummeling of his loss that my muscles ached like the flu and the light hurt my eyes. Until one day it didn't. Until one day, four months after the accident, walking through a rain forest on the Pacific side of Costa Rica, I looked around and realized I could see again. I could see beauty. I could see the way the morning's hard rain had left a perfect pool of water on a banana leaf that lit up like a diamond in the stream of sunlight that wriggled through the canopy. My heart felt the adrenaline rush from the howler monkey's scream. I saw my first three-toed sloth. What a world.

When we lost Baby Brother, I was in agony—and I knew my job was to grieve as hard as I needed to grieve. When we love, we lose. That's our heart contract. And here we were, again on the edge. This is all to say that I approached what I hoped would be the birth of this baby with clarity—perhaps only the size of that Costa Rican banana leaf pool of pure light: I wanted to *be there*. Fully present.

If a block in my spine prevented my pelvis, the center of my laboring work, from telling my brain about the pain, would that be a kind of betrayal? Here is another choice that belongs solely to the person giving birth. So much had been done *to* me, and my baby, during my pregnancy—with my consent. But I wanted L.B.'s birth to be something I participated in, something I could train and prepare for, something I could *do* with my mind and body.

This was my dream: With Dr. L's support, Shane would watch over us while I slid down the rainbow Baby Brother had painted in the sky above Grant Park in Chicago almost two years before. I would travel the arc of his vibrant, hopeful colors, my bridge over fear, my bridge to a land where we could, at last, hold L.B. in our arms.

22   The Angel and the Umbilical Rope

Fear of bridges? It's a thing. Not *my* thing, but one of those phobias with a name: gephyrophobia. As with great heights—the Mall of America's ridiculous escalators, Embassy Suites' column of open-concept potted-palm horror, the Space Needle—I am not afraid exactly. And yet when I cross a bridge, my mind plays through scenes of slipping off the edge or sudden wrist-jerking seizures that jack the wheel to the right and send my car crashing through the railing. In my imaginings, I fly into that empty space between the solid ground that held me safe and the crushing impact of whatever lies below. Those weightless moments are another species of bridging, an open and free rushing nothingness between something and something else.

Even in dreams, I never really fly. Like a gawky, featherless bird, I flap my arms, never soaring, never catching an easy updraft. Even in dreams, I work my sleeping mind to summon a parachute to soften the impact between my out-of-control body and whatever I am rushing toward. The parachute never comes. Even in dreams, I can't stop the fall and I have too much time to consider how I will feel when I stop falling, how I will feel when I hit solid ground—or water—at the bottom of all that air.

Maybe I'll escape with just a broken limb or two. Maybe there will be only nothing.

Get me to that childbed with a living baby in my womb, I thought, and I will do the rest. I will bring us home. Please let me have some agency to help my babies. I am stronger than I look.

SOMETIMES THE BRIDGE spanning the river to our house would close for days at a time in fierce New England storms, cutting us off from the mainland. If our mother was on the side with us when the bridge closed, this was a good thing since *school* was on the mainland.

But bad things happened on that bridge.

Bad things were always going down on or under that bridge, but the worst accident happened the summer I was ten and my brother and I were with our dad in Connecticut. During our weekend telephone call, Mom told us the gas tank had dropped out of her friend George's truck as he drove home over the Plum Island Bridge. We'd known George—as my mother's best friend's boyfriend—for years, and I thought we all agreed he was a jerk: the kind of guy who expected his woman to bring him a beer with his hoagie and keep the kids in another room. For this, she might get a slap on the ass.

But then George's gas tank dropped, dragging along the pavement, metal on rock, until the truck became a kind of two-ton flint stone and hot sparks ignited the tank. Boom. Traffic stopped on both sides. "No one came up the bridge to help him," my mother told us over the buzzing phone line, crying, and by the time my brother and I got home to the island in September, my mother was in love with George. "I think this is it, kids."

I'd never liked George and I didn't like him more after he was burned, but my mother sure did. My mother loved him and I think I know why. George was burned on July 22, the same day—here's my mother's miracle, the amazing thing—the very same date my older brother, at thirteen months old, had turned on a scalding shower and burned almost to death. But not to death. The burn doctors gave my brother a 10 percent chance of survival and he took that chance. He survived and he was a teenager with thick scars by the time George's gas tank ignited on the Plum Island Bridge. George's miracle was our miracle, our miracle was George's.

"He's a changed man," my mother said when she told us George and his big-balled tomcat, Fritz, would be moving in. She believed that George had literally seen the light and because of the trick with the dates—"July 22! Can you believe it? July 22!"—the light must have something to do with us.

Our domestic time with George was short—a few months, maybe less—but thinking about bridges today, I realize how my mother must have been looking to salve wounds she hadn't yet healed. From the outside, my mother seems fearless—or, at least, she hasn't moved through her life, like me, stuffing her pockets with the sandy shells of terrors she has known and survived.

For example, my brother's burning. I would think she would be afraid of the potentially deadly combination that is scalding hot water and soft-skinned babies, but when she visits our house (where we keep the thermostat on the hot-water heater set below the warning line) she wonders glumly at the impossibility of running a really steamy bath. She loves a good soak, and when she soaks, she doesn't smell the burned flesh of her toddling son; she luxuriates. She relaxes.

So who's the nutty one? Her or me?

Before you answer that, think about George and the bridge. She invited him into our home to live with us because she loved him. She loved him because he was burned on the same day that Ian was burned, and maybe, just maybe, there was healing on the other side of that burning bridge—for George, for Ian, and for herself—in our coming together. One afternoon, George invited Ian to join him at a support group for the burned, and my brother scoffed. His scars didn't bother him, Ian told George and my mother. He didn't need no stinking support group.

Fear is a story we tell ourselves. This is also true of shame, and healing.

For the record, my mother is the kind of person who would have run up the bridge toward the burning truck to help. She is also the kind of person who lived in a ratty studio apartment near the hospital where her burned baby needed treatment eating the skins of hot dogs for protein—and never asked for help.

PREPARING for the most natural birth possible, I needed to recalibrate my terminology and tell myself a different story. From the books Debbie passed on to me, I learned a new vocabulary for birthing, one in which the etymology for every word would not bring us down to a root like "pain" or "excruciating." First of all, the Braxton Hicks contractions making my abdomen rise up like a giant fist? Such violent metaphors. No. First, these are *not* "contractions," and nothing to do with that nineteenth-century British chap John Braxton Hicks, who first described these "false" tightenings that have no effect on the cervix. (I feel the need to remove myself from my rainbow here to say, *Fuck you, Hicks. I'd like to falsely tighten your balls.*) Okay, maybe not super helpful. Breathe, Jill. Back onto your rainbow. Deeper down now.

Contractions are "surges," my books told me, and since nothing the preparing woman's body does is false or wasted, these early surges are "practice surges." Yes. Better. And babies aren't "delivered" by doctors, they are "received." So true. I would do the delivering. And what is pain, I asked myself, but another sensation. Pain, by any other name, could be something else entirely.

Also? Language matters.

MEANWHILE, four-year-old Ella was making her own preparations, psychological and otherwise. One afternoon in December, she shuffled into the living room with a bulge under the belly of her T-shirt. She shook her head sadly, dramatically—I could see she was acting—and pulled out a tiny, hairless doll by its molded plastic toes like a magician yanking a rabbit from a hat. Delivery. The doll was about six inches long, the cheap kind she collected from her visits to the allergist with the cloth body and the loosely attached plastic arms, legs, and head. She laid the baby on top of a stack of coloring books as if she were preparing the funeral pyre and looked up at me, mournfully, still shaking her head. "She was in the first tri-mes-ter." She pronounced trimester so carefully I wanted to smile, but this was clearly no time for humor. "So sad."

And then she turned and walked away, leaving her dead baby on the stack, and me with my third-trimester baby still inside, sitting silently on the couch.

Ella did not wait long to try again. The next morning, she watched me while I smeared cocoa butter on my tight stomach after a shower. She patted her own belly through her pajama top and held a baby—a different, bigger one—aloft with her other hand. "This baby came out of *my* stomach last night. When she was still in there, she was stretching and stretching and stretching my skin *and* the umbilical rope . . ."

"You mean the umbilical *cord*?" I interjected.

"No!" she said. "I mean the umbilical *rope*. Mine is different because *I* am a *young* mother."

Thanks a lot. *Et tu, Brute?*

She squeezed her baby to her chest, patting her back, keeping her safe from the silly geriatric mother who didn't even know the right words for having babies.

WHAT WERE THEY THINKING giving me the new sonographer in my thirty-fourth week? After all those months with Becky?

I was used to Becky. Becky understood me.

Besides, any fool knows measurements differ depending on the operator, so why subject me to these vicissitudes? For example, according to the new sonographer (who, to be fair, seemed quite competent and friendly initially), L.B. was weighing in at a hefty six pounds twelve ounces. Now, this seems like the stuff of rejoicing, but wait. Just two weeks prior, *Becky's* measurements pegged him at four pounds fifteen ounces, meaning he'd gained a whopping two pounds three ounces in just two weeks.

Then she measured the amniotic fluid level and came up with twenty-three. Twenty-three! Shit. A range of five to twenty-five is considered "normal," but of course, twenty-three was way too close to the top of that range for comfort, especially since it was such a rise from the nice, cozy mid-range of fifteen the week before. *Aaaargh.*

"Do you have gestational diabetes?" this new sonographer asked gently.

"No!" I answered, considerably less gently.

"Oh, well, I just thought with such a large baby and the high fluid levels ... both of those things are common in women with gestational diabetes."

Thanks a lot. That's very reassuring *because I don't have fucking gestational diabetes*!!!

"You know ..." (she was still talking) "at this stage of gestation, babies average a gain of half a pound every week, so with six more weeks to go ..." She paused. "How big was your first baby?"

"Eight pounds five ounces."

"Yes," she finished, finally, "this baby could be *a lot* bigger than that."

Thank you. Thank you again. I was an English major, but I can do basic math. *She's turning this around on me*, I thought. *For months, I've prayed for every hope-giving ounce on this baby. I should get to be happy about these numbers.* "*If* I make it to term," I added curtly. "Which I doubt."

She slid in the last word, reminding me vaguely of my mother in conversations like this. "Well, *I* certainly wouldn't want to."

All the while, she continued to wave her gooey wand over my belly, saying things like, "C'mon, baby, c'mon, breathe."

Had she taken a *class* in bedside sonography for the high-risk mother? Honestly.

That morning, I'd experimented with skipping my once-daily self-prescribed cup of coffee. L.B.'s heartbeat had been a bit high during the ultrasounds, and I wanted to see if perhaps this was a result of the caffeine. I was always worried about his heart.

Initial findings from my low-tech, low-sample experiment seemed to support the hypothesis. At the no-caffeine appointment, L.B.'s heart was a beautifully average 146. But, like me, the poor kid was jonesing for his morning java. Usually it was Saturday Night Fever in there, but that morning just an occasional, drowsy stretch.

And—the issue—he wasn't practicing his breathing. Which is why this sonographer—whom I'd decided at this point I did not, in fact, like all that much—kept intoning: "Breathe, baby. Come on, baby."

Seriously? But L.B. would not. As I watched the loathsome sonographer wave her vicious wand, I traced the well-glazed rump of my lucky rabbit.

"Come on, baby," the sonographer pleaded while my own heart rate surged like a hound on the trail of a decidedly unlucky rabbit.

By the time Dr. L came in, over forty-five minutes later, L.B. still hadn't taken a "breath" and I was on the edge of hysteria. The distinct feeling was that our dad was coming in to end an argument. The new sonographer and I were glaring at each other openly when Dr. L strode in wearing his snappy boots and a big smile. He plopped down on a rolling stool and patted my knee. I never minded Dr. L's knee-patting, for reasons that probably had to do with the fact that I thought him smart, competent, and genuinely comforting. Pat pat.

"I can't get this baby to breathe for me," the sonographer whined, gesturing toward her screen.

"Babies don't *breathe*!" I squeaked, but now I didn't know what was true, all that *breathe-baby-breathe* crap had me doubting my own name. "Is the baby okay? Is he okay?"

"They can have sleep cycles of up to two hours," he said. "It's nothing to worry about."

"He's not asleep," I said, pointing to a gently waving fist on the monitor. *Me too, L.B. I feel you, kid.*

Dr. L sighed, turned to the sonographer, and like something out of *Pulp Fiction*, said simply, "Bring out the stimulator."

The *stimulator*?

And that's how it came to pass that my concern for L.B.'s wellbeing, fueled by hypervigilance and the new sonographer's *breathe* chant, resulted in Dr. L holding this thing, this "stimulator," to my belly, somewhere near L.B.'s rump, and giving the poor kid a vibrating, electric jolt. I yelped. And that baby *jumped*. He leapt, insofar as leaping is possible in such a confined liquid space, rebounding against the edge of his sac like a kid bouncing back from a trampoline's net.

And, yes, he seemed to gasp. A practice gasp.

The "stimulator," it turns out, is a cattle prod for the unborn.

"There he goes," said Dr. L, smiling, passing the stimulator back to the sonographer, and patting my knee again. "Next time, eat a candy bar before you come in."

ON JANUARY 6, 2008, I went in for a nonstress test. Speaking of medical terms, here is one that made no sense to me. Nonstress? Are you kidding me? At Dr. L's, the NSTs were held in a room with four stations, so a single nurse could monitor them all from a central location. Because the wide elastic belts the nurses used to strap on the dual monitors for the baby's heart and for the contractions (nobody was going "surges" with me in the nonstress room) touched our skin, we were supposed to remember to bring our own pair to every appointment—which lasted for about thirty minutes, recording the strength of contractions and changes in L.B.'s heart rate. Near the end, I was going in every few days, so I kept my gigantic belts in my purse.

There was plenty of time to chat with the nurses, so I asked about the name. These sessions are called "nonstress" because they don't place any stress on the fetus—as opposed to its sister procedure, the contraction stress test (CST), which introduces a flow of contraction-inducing oxytocin through an IV line to observe how the fetus reacts to the reduction of blood and oxygen from the placenta during a contraction. This usually happens earlier in a pregnancy and was not something I had to do, thank goodness. Here in the ninth month, I was just a pregnant lady chilling. Living that nonstress dream a few times a week. Watching the lines on the monitor zig and zag as if they were writing the story of whether our son would live or die.

That morning, Karen congratulated me for remembering my belts, baby blue and pink, and she hooked me up. "Did you bring a book?" she asked, flipping a few switches, and I had, but on the day of my last NST I never even cracked the cover. Instead, I stared at the screen with its two sets of Etch-a-Sketch lines, top and bottom, as they scribbled out the strength of the contractions (mild, intermittent) and the baby's heart rate (130–150, moderate variability, accelerations). The overall assessment was, and I quote, "reassuring." L.B. was tolerating the contractions just fine. He was okay.

I was not. My heart felt rubber-band tight and my brain's film reel whirred through disaster scenarios: cord strangulation, unexplained stillbirth, the oxygen-blocking placental clot we'd been guarding against all this time. I'd stopped the Lovenox shots two weeks before to play the balancing game between the risk of a clot (that could kill the baby) and the risk of postpartum hemorrhage (that could kill me): There was nothing nonstress about this game. My nerves, it seemed, were shot. *L.B. is fine*, I told myself. *Look. You can see for yourself. His heart rate is perfect. He's perfect. Look.*

Those thirty minutes felt like hours. Alone in my mind, I could not talk myself off the cliff. Here was my fear, so much bigger than me. Something snapped in me that morning, shattered, and I couldn't glue the pieces back together again. Maybe a panic attack, maybe a legitimate presentiment. *I need to get him out of there before he dies. He's going to die if I don't get him out now.*

"I need to talk to Dr. L," I told Karen as I squirmed out of the belts, not bothering to wipe off the gel, trying to make the band on my pants and my shirt meet in the middle. "Please. I need to tell him something. Right now."

L.B.'s gestational age was thirty-seven weeks and six days. In theory, we still had time to wait for labor to come on naturally. Since I'd stopped the Lovenox, Dr. L had stripped my membranes twice, but the contractions continued per usual, doing nothing, and with regular monitoring, he was willing to let me and Shane take the lead with the birth. Obviously, an induction would reduce my chances of having the birth I wanted—as testing begets testing, intervention begets intervention—but as Karen led me down the hall toward Dr. L, I didn't care about pain or no pain, contractions or surges, forceps or laboring tubs, epidurals or rainbows.

I just wanted to get my baby out before he died. Right now, this moment, he was okay. L.B. was alive with a beating heart. I needed to get him out before it was too late. What if I waited and he died in there? I didn't even make it to a consultation room because we ran into Dr. L in the hallway. As soon as I saw him, I started to cry. "We have to get this baby out," I said. "I'm afraid he's going to die in there!"

Dr. L put a gentle hand on my arm and said, "Okay, okay. Let's have a baby. Tonight? Tomorrow?"

And then they ushered me into a room so I wouldn't scare the other high-risk pregnant women, who were probably already plenty scared all on their own. Perhaps mine was a failure of courage. Perhaps my capacity to endure the stress, even with rainbows and meditation and so-called reassuring nonstress tests, had just dried up. Ended.

Or maybe my baby was telling me something: *Get me out. It's time.*

We'll never know. We'll never know what would have happened if I'd waited for labor to come on naturally. "Way leads on to way," wrote Robert Frost—who lost four of his six children during his lifetime. I made a choice to induce labor and now I would follow that choice to the next thing. The only way was forward.

SHANE HAD ANOTHER BIRTH the next morning, so we scheduled the induction for 8:00 a.m. on January 8. I would have to wait another thirty-six hours. I charted L.B.'s every kick and turn, haunted by my jolt of premonition that his life-clock was ticking, wholly convinced I had been given a warning—either spiritual or through some subtle change in L.B. my body noticed but hadn't articulated to my conscious brain. Terrified, I'd even let myself consider calling Dr. L to tell him I needed an emergency C-section. I just kept thinking: *He's alive now. We know he's alive now. Why would we give him a chance to die?*

I spent a sleepless night moving my stretched fingers across by naked belly—a dance, a massage, a laying on of hands, a language. I found his head right down where he needed to be, and held my cupped hands there until I knew he would feel the warmth of my touch, the heat of my love. He was so big now I could identify most of his parts in their cramped readjustments. I traced the bulge of his foot across the North Pole of my belly, palming his heel through my taut skin like a warm egg. *Hang in there, baby. Hang in there.*

On that intervening morning, Ella climbed up in our big bed, adding her small hands to my big ones, and told us she'd dreamed she was at the hospital holding the new baby.

"What was his name?" Mark asked.

"Baby Jo Jo," she answered without pause.

"Great name," Mark said, pulling her into a hug. "Perfect. Baby Jo Jo."

Ella's dream was a comfort to me. Her hopeful vision would have to carry us all across.

I REALIZE NOW that what I'd been trying to do was map out everything scary, chart all the ways in which my baby might die. Not to be grim. Oh, how I wanted to live in hope, slide down my rainbow in a great, cleansing wash of love, but because somewhere deep in my reptilian brain I'd learned that the thing that would harm me, the thing that would take away the one I loved—that speeding tow truck on the night Colin was just rolling across town to pick up a pizza, that glitch in Baby Brother's making that left him with half of the heart he'd need to live, that capsule of antibiotic that had blocked Mark's breath—was something I hadn't considered as a source of danger. I hadn't thought of these things before they happened. I hadn't pointed to them and said: *There. You. You scare me. I won't let you get us*. And then *another* thing, that least expected, unconsidered thing, had risen out of the muck. I never saw the dripping maw coming.

To guard my family, therefore, I had become the Cartographer of Fear. The Mapmaker of the Horrible. The Information Specialist of the Scariest Shit. If I considered everything, if I left nothing unidentified, then there would be nothing left to hide in the mud.

Of course, it turns out this is impossible. It's also no way to live.

> **The Chicago surgeon**: "You don't want to know everything there is to be afraid of."
> **Divine Grace**: "You are in a dark room. You have to touch everything. How will you know when you are done?"
> **Me**: "I won't."
> **Divine Grace**: "Why don't you turn on a light?"

Twenty years earlier, I'd listened to an angel and my life was saved. In the final hours of my pregnancy, I thought hard about what Divine Grace had said. I remembered about turning on the light and I reached for the switch.

23   Give Me Your Hands

During Ella's birth, I hadn't wanted anyone to touch me, not even Mark. January 8 would be a different kind of day. At 8:00 a.m., right on schedule, we met Shane on the labor and delivery floor. She grinned, crochet-hooked my bag of waters in dramatic, celebratory fashion, handed me a giant diaper, and said, "Put this on and get moving."

The induction plan was that simple: Break water and walk.

Dr. L was in the building, Shane told us, and he'd be checking my monitors throughout the day. He would represent my fear and guard against danger and harmful spirits, a gargoyle on the castle stronghold. Shane would be my hope, made manifest, staying with me on the labor and delivery floor until we got this baby born. In those first hours slow hours of cajoling labor that wasn't even labor, a labor demanded of a body that hadn't yet said it was time to go, my job was to change my body's mind, get her on board with the program, see what I could do to establish some strong, regular contractions—and the best way to do that was by walking.

At first, I was giddy with something that felt like relief. I hadn't given up on the thing I wanted most in life because I was afraid. I had tried and tried and tried, and now the waiting was over. There was nothing left to do but have a baby. I winked at Mark as I led him out into the hall. "Let's get this party started."

THE EARLY HOURS were like a kind of dream—a good dream. I wore my grandmother's nightgown—white flowered cotton, sweet buttons at the neck, lucky rabbit pinned on the breast. I spun my hair up into a loose bun to stay cool, but also to keep it out of my face if I threw up and out of the water when I got my chance in the brand-new laboring Jacuzzi. I must have looked like a round, eccentric old lady, but Mark seemed to love me anyway, and he'd remembered to put his lucky penny pouch into his pocket, of course. We walked, often holding hands—which is not something we typically do.

Because we were on the labor and delivery floor, there wasn't much to look at on our loop. All the doors with anything interesting happening behind them were closed tight. There were very few sounds, even. The whole day I think I saw just one real baby, held in her mother's arms, pink-capped, both being wheeled down to the maternity ward. The pale walls were decorated mostly with large-format, framed infant portraits. A black-and-white shot of a tiny baby boy with his legs curled up under him, lima-bean style, his sleeping hand draped up over a little inked-blue teddy bear, the only color in the frame. Or a baby girl with her cheek on a satin pillow, pinned there by the giant pink faux flower balanced on her wispy hair. The babies on the wall looked so cherubic—and gendered to the level of satire. You, little boy, have come into this world to play with blue toys. Your sweet head, little girl, has been pinned to your satin pillow, a lushly petaled symbol of femininity the size of a dessert plate. How did the photographer keep them sleeping while he manipulated their loose limbs into angel poses? More incredible, I pointed out to Mark, stopping before a close-up of a naked baby's face, her father's giant hand reaching into the frame to touch her soft shoulders, how did the photographer get this baby to *look* at the camera, so open-eyed and wise? And was that a smile? Couldn't be, right? Were they Photoshopping smiles onto newborns? Isn't it kind of incredible that even in the most extraordinary moments in our lives, the ordinary is still right there? Our bodies with their unending hunger and thirst, our needs to pee or have someone love us? I thought about this, shared random observations with Mark, and shuffled around the indoor track we'd made of the fourth floor of Ball Memorial Hospital in Muncie, Indiana, leaking a steady stream of the amniotic fluid that had been home to our baby.

I discovered a giant scale at one of the corners of our L&D track and on every lap, I'd step on and check the number. "I lost another pound! Two pounds!" Water weight is a tremendous thing. I stopped at my room and changed my diaper regularly to make my weigh-ins more satisfying. I know how to make my own fun.

I started having regular contractions, and we tried hard to call them surges, if we called them anything at all—"Here comes one..."—and I was happy this time to learn that I *wanted* Mark to touch me. I needed his hands on my body, and when I stopped walking for a contraction, pressing my palms against the wall, Mark would do a hypno-tickle method, running his fingers lightly down the fine hairs at the back of my neck, scratching my back with fine, light strokes. All my energy went to the nerve endings where Mark was touching me, rising to my skin, and insofar as such a thing is possible for a woman forty-five pounds over her skinny-jean weight and dressed up like her dead grandmother, I felt *sexy*. I was having *fun*. I kind of wanted to make out with my hot husband right there by the drinking fountain.

This was a feeling that would pass.

AS WE WALKED, we talked about names. With Ella, we'd had the whole business down by twenty weeks along, penned into the baby book, and here we were, laboring, or trying to, and all we'd done successfully was *eliminate* good choices. "Sam" was out because my mother pointed out that our children would be "Sam and Ella."

"So?" I'd said over the phone. "Ella and Sam. Sam and Ella. What's wrong with that?"

"Sam and Ella," she said, then repeated, faster and faster. "Sam and Ella! SamandElla. Sam an' Ella. Salmonella! They'd be a *disease*!"

Geez. Jasper and Oscar, both family names from my father's side, were also on my top-ten list, but the first couldn't shake its friendly-ghost associations and my mother had strong opinions about the latter. "What are you going to name the next baby," she said, with an uncharacteristic comic joust in her tone, "*Big Bird?*" I don't know who remains naive enough on this difficult planet to need to hear this, but if you're having a baby and you like a name, don't tell your mother.

So while I was otherwise occupied, convincing my cervix we were having a party and she should loosen up and join us, Mark came in the side door to name our son. "What about Huck?" he said as we moved down a long stretch of white tile, both of us wary of the cracks. "Huck's a great name."

True. I liked Huck. But can you name a kid just "Huck"? I didn't think so. "Okay," I said. "Huck. But we can't name him 'Huckleberry,' can we? I mean, we can't do that to the kid. What's he going to do when he grows up and wants to get a job or something?"

"No," Mark agreed. He obviously had a plan. "But we could name him 'Henry,' and *call* him 'Huck.' Then he'd have options."

I put my hands up on the wall for another contraction and Mark stood behind me. He had me just where he wanted me. If I could get this baby out, he'd have a name. Two names. And naming is one of the most powerful weapons hope can wield.

"KEEP IT SHORT," Mark advises, years later, on the subject of writing the birth. "Nobody wants to read about that." Pause. "I don't even like to *think* about it."

At first, this makes sense to me. This prohibition is a cultural assessment about birth narratives we've all taken in. Nobody wants to read about that. Keep it quick. Better yet, use white space, as we do with the naughty, sexy bits that usually aren't that interesting unless you're there in the bed or up against the wall between floors on the elevator. *Afterward* . . . The reader doesn't need to hear about all the wet bits. If you've heard one story of a stuck head or three hours of pushing or a cervix that "fails to progress" (naughty cervix), you've heard them all, right?

Okay. But why? Why, then, do we return again and again to stories of war, of boxing, of football, of teenage testosterone brawls against clanging lockers? Why are we drawn to these battle stories, stories of terrible pain, and not to the ones we can hope will end in birth? Is it because we tell ourselves the men's stories are really about strength and courage? Strategy and perseverance? Character and human connection? (Even when, say, Karl Ove Knausgård is writing about buttering toast, mowing the lawn—or, yes, holding a baby.) The thrill of victory and the agony of defeat? Why, then, not the women's stories as well? The birth stories that gave each of us, every one, homemakers and gladiators alike, our very breath? Our whole lives.

Here's something I know for sure about pain: You can't make pain go away by pushing it under—and also? My god. In this world, just past and far beyond my little corner, there is so *much* pain and we're making more every day. In my own life, I had moved into and through the catastrophes I have survived—the years of having my child body misused in that dark garage, the agony of Colin's death at those crossroads, the excruciating choice to release our broken boy before he was starved for air. Determined to hang onto what joy remains in the world—and to love more deeply, I have healed. Where I've lost power, I've reclaimed the force of my body and mind as mine. Where I've lost beloveds, I've taken them into me. I hold my missing boys in my cells, in my whole heart. Whatever pain was coming my way in this final stage of transitioning a living L.B. from my womb to my arms—almost there almost there almost there—was pain I believed I could handle. To live in the light, we must sometimes travel through darkness.

And there I go with all my talk of pain. So much for every surge is a good surge because it brings me closer to my baby. I still believe, I do. It just didn't work out that way for *me*.

Here's what happened: The hypnobirthing techniques worked. They worked so well I had to stop using them. That morning, when the contractions became so strong and so regular that the hallway laps had ceased feeling like a weird date with my husband, I returned to the room, sat on a birthing ball, sucked a lemon drop, and imagined I was red, then orange, then as yellow as the lemon drop. I was the color and flavor of lemon. When I sunk down into yellow, there was no pain. Mark tickled the arches of my bare feet.

Shane came in to check my contractions. They were slowing. Because I wasn't *really* in labor in the first place, apparently I could relax myself right out of labor. "You have to get up," Shane said, nudging the ball with the toe of her pretty shoe. "You have to get up and walk."

Progress was slow. Then progress was slow *and* painful.

Science still cannot point to one thing that brings it on, but from the inside, labor is fantastically elemental, a pull of the moon on the body's tides, pushing and receding. Labor crashed me and my boy against the packed sand and then lifted us up again, cradling our nested bodies in the soft, rocking waters. And there was pain, the deepest pain I have ever known—a fiery pain burning in what felt to me like the perfect center of my body, boiling lava pooling behind my pubic bone and flowing out through my limbs, down my arms and into my wrists and ankles, curling my fingers and stiffening my toes. The pain was a fire, then a knife, a slaying, finally I will be killed, and then many knives. How could I not yet be dead? *Shouldn't I die now?* And then, for two minutes, or near the end of a transition that lasted nearly five hours, just a few seconds, a respite: The pain stops, disappears. A stillness, complete. What other pain is like that?

Many survivors of sexual abuse suffer terribly during childbirth—the vulnerability and ripping open too much like another ripping open, the birthing like another assault—but this was not my story. I was nineteen when I fully remembered the abuse of my childhood, when I was clear enough on the details that I told, and I experienced no second betrayal. Colin believed me. My best friend believed me. My mother believed me. My brother believed me. Not a single soul who loved me denied what had happened. No one in my life tried to take away my power. And, now, finally, in too much pain to walk the halls, I was able to stay present. I did not have to betray my own body as she did the hard, hard work—the laboring. I know how easily I could have been gone, slipping into dissociation, my mind's best trick, honed as sharp as a boning knife, the abuse survivor's twilight sleep, but I didn't leave. I stayed. For me, hard labor was like the grief work I did at the Kübler-Ross camp on the mat with the rubber hose, every muscle and nerve pulled taut and then cracking down onto the heavy phone book, a rupture in the space-time continuum, breaking open, setting all the versions of myself free.

It hurt like bloody hell.

Where there had been rainbows, now there was only pain, and both versions are equally true—the beautiful one and the story that got really ugly. I was liberated and I wanted to die.

I've asked myself why I didn't give up, cry uncle, insist they do something, anything, to stop the pain. "Just kill me," I whimpered. "Please." How Dr. L must have been checking in at my monitors, shaking his head, thinking how it didn't have to be like this. I could have said the word, called him in, changed the course. I remember coming close, spitting out the word "epidural" to Shane by way of a threat. Together we would fail, but by then it was too late, and even then, I know I wouldn't have really done it. I just needed Shane to understand how close I was to my breaking point. I wanted to communicate to her I was as close to death as I'd ever been.

Through it all, L.B.'s heart on the monitor remained strong and steady. I would stay the course. If I could do this, I could do anything. Instead of giving in to the fear, I defied it. At Colin's grave, I had told him *I am taking you into me*. At Baby Brother's grave, I had promised *I will never put you down*. Now, delirious with pain, I felt them both there with us, and I asked for strength. Here was a thing I could fight for. Power would beget power. I would keep my baby safe and breathing.

Nearly twelve hours after it all began, after seven that night, Shane finally said I could stop walking and try the laboring tub if I wanted. This was the moment I'd been waiting for. In my mind's story, I would find relief in the tub's warm waters. Here is where my memory is vivid. The birthing tub had a swinging door, like a horse's stall, and to enter—or exit—the tub had to be empty. I stepped into the tub and waited for it to fill. Too tight, too close. *When the water rises above my belly*, I thought, *when the water covers my chest, then I will be able to handle this pain*, but I was wrong. The higher the water, the more frantic I became. I felt caged, trapped. "Drain it," I gasped between contractions. "Drain it. I need to get out of here."

I rattled the top of the door, waiting for the water to swirl down the drain.

I fell forward and out.

"What if I couldn't get out in time?" I wailed at Mark. "What if I was *stuck* in there?"

"I would have pulled you out," he said. "I could have gotten you out of there with the door closed."

Out of the tub and back in my own room, it was nine o'clock now and I was finally at eight centimeters. Transition. Finally, transition. Let me cross that bridge. Between the hours of nine and ten I worked as hard as I could, screaming now, watching myself scream and thinking how I didn't scream at all during Ella's birth, humming and moaning, yes, but never screaming, and now I didn't give a shit who heard or how a much lower pitch would better serve my labor. I just wanted this pain to end. I begged for mercy, never cursing or blaming, just please, please, kill me or release me. Please. And so at ten, when I insisted on a cervical exam, needing to hear I was almost there, the home stretch, and there had been no change, nothing at all, still right at eight centimeters and nothing more, I reached my low point.

"No," I said to Mark.

"No," I said to Shane.

"No," I said to the nurse whose name and face I cannot even remember. "No. That can't be. That *cannot* be." During the next contraction, my wails echoed off the walls of labor and delivery. In my thirty-second respite, I was lucid enough to remark, "I bet all the other women are going to be glad when I have this baby and shut the fuck up."

LABOR IS NOT PASSIVE. Labor is something a mother must do. Fuck it. *Fuck it*. I was going to get this *done*. I got up on my feet in the bed and leveraged my pain on the birthing bar. I lay on my side while Shane reached in with her hands and turned L.B.'s head in the canal, the canal of my body, using her gloved fingers to wedge my cervix over his enormous skull like a too-tight turtleneck. The pain was a black wave as I came close to getting my wish for oblivion. Mark tells me I tried to get away from Shane's hands. I clawed the sheets to pull myself up the headboard and escape. I screamed a mighty scream, not at all moose-like, and while my eyes were on the ceiling, Mark says Shane gave him a little wink and a smile, mouthed, "This is good, this is good," and he hated her in that moment for looking happy when I was in so much pain. Shane had heard that sound before, she knew what Mark did not, what I could not. We were close. With every contraction I turned or moved, on and off my feet, trying to get that giant head down and through.

At 12:48 a.m., Dr. L appeared at my bedside. I remember everyone's position from this moment like a photograph caught in a bright-white flash. He stood near my left knee. Shane stayed between my feet at the end of the bed. Mark leaned in on my right side, holding up my head and shoulders.

"I see his hair," Shane said. "It's time."

I had nothing left. I couldn't push any more.

And then Dr. L said, so simply, "Push past the burn. Feel the burn and push *through* it."

This made sense. I knew just what he meant. I pushed. It burned—nothing, really, in the big picture of those long hours. I felt the burn and pushed through.

"Give me your hands," Shane said. "Give me your hands."

I did.

Shane held my hands in hers and guided them down until my fingers touched hair. "Okay," she said, "Okay, here is your baby's head."

My god. My hands were on our baby's head. I could feel his thick wet hair and round, solid skull. I walked my fingers down to his ears. His ears! Mark put his body behind mine to hold me up so I could see. Our baby was in my *hands*. I felt a surge of power, a rush of joy. Like love, or God.

"Now push one more time and pull him up onto your chest," Shane instructed.

And I did. I delivered my baby with my own hands. I received him. I pushed and pulled as one effort and slid him up and into my arms, our chests naked and touching. We were wet and bloody and eye to eye. Henry looked right at us, me and his father. He blinked and took us in, flawed and dripping and generous with love.

"You're here," I whispered. "You're here."

Acknowledgments

Thank you from my heart to smart, generous editors everywhere, but especially at the following magazines and presses where excerpts or shared memories from this memoir previously appeared (in altered forms, snippets, and/or previous incarnations): *Barrelhouse*; *Brain, Child*; *Fourth Genre*; *Iron Horse Literary Review*; *Literary Mama*; *Longreads*; *River Teeth*—plus, the University of Nebraska Press (*If This Were Fiction: A Love Story in Essays*) and the University of Georgia Press (*Darkroom: A Family Exposure*).

Imagine this book as a table. We are sitting around the table before a meal and we join hands to make a circle. The heart folds early—that's a fact—but *The Heart Folds Early*, this book, took a ridiculously long time to gestate. Longer than you might be imagining. Decades. First, I tried very hard to write it and then I tried very hard to *not* write it, but after the Dobbs decision in 2022 overturned Roe v. Wade, eliminating the federal constitutional right to abortion, I rewrote the whole book like my skirt was on fire and only the book would put it out before I burned.

I am complicating a gentle metaphor with flames. We are still sitting around the table. *Thank you*, I am saying, feeling the love and energy of our human circle, *thank you to all the hands who helped to make this meal.*

There have been so many.

Thank you to my mother, Martha Christman, who made the choice to "have a baby that matched"—to grow me in her actual body, sweat through a pregnancy in Miami in the summer of 1969, miss Woodstock, miss labor, and then love me and my brother Ian so fully that we learned how to love as a foundation for everything else in our lives. Thanks, Mom.

As this book went to press, Ian died just shy of his sixtieth birthday. Our parents separated when I was two and Ian was six, so when we were kids, we were a traveling unit, the two of us like one word, "Ian and Jill" went here, "Ian and Jill" went there. Ianandjill. We grew in the same womb. We—and only we—shared the collective memory of our childhood. Losing you, E, feels like a kind of amputation, but this is a thank you, not a eulogy. Thank you for teaching me to be smarter. For giving me that look when I wasn't funny, but for laughing with your whole self when I was. For believing in my toughness. For choosing me again and again. For never ending a call without telling me that you loved me. I am carrying you in my heart and I will hold your beloved family—Jutta, Amber, and Jade—close.

Thank you to our late father, Pete Christman, for teaching all of us that what we do each day is get up and make art like our lives depend upon it. Because they do. And to Dad and Paula together for making a whole other family of siblings for me so that we could put our arms around each other: India, Sierra, and Max. I love you.

Thank you to my teachers—all the good ones—but especially Mr. Cosmos, my fifth-grade science teacher who taught us to really *look*. Diane, my ninth-grade teacher of everything (for real, we're talking one-room schoolhouse), but specifically for introducing me to Steinbeck, for handing back my first terrible story unmarked and telling me to try harder, and for being the very model of a woman who doesn't take any shit. Miss Chase, my high school English teacher: First you taught me to be humble and then you saved my fool ass by giving me a place to live that summer after high school when it didn't work out with my boyfriend. If you didn't *literally* save my life, you at the very least cleared the road for me to get out of town and onward to the rest of my life. Monza Naff: Thank you for introducing me to Toni Cade Bambara, Maya Angelou, and Toni Morrison. First you cracked my mind open and then you taught me what it feels like to really open my throat and use my voice. I needed that when I was writing this book. Jennifer Freyd, my first and forever mentor: You showed me (and also, you know, the *world*) what it means to live courageously. It was kind of you to offer me a job in your lab when I had zero experience in psychology: Thank you for seeing something in me I didn't know was there. And Sandy Huss? Shew. You challenged me to ask harder questions, pursue deeper truths, and write better sentences. When I thought maybe I couldn't do it, you wrote in my margins: "Keep going, Jilly." I live with your voice in my head. It's a good one.

Speaking of teachers, thank you to the thirty years of students who have learned with me in classrooms and editing labs with our heads bent together over the words. Keep going. You've got so many stories to tell.

Thank you to my mother-in-law, Carol Thomas Neely: Your feminism and fight drive me forward. Thank you for blazing a trail. (And thank you for making Mark—no small contribution to this book!)

Thank you, friends. Diane Downey, aka Auntie Di, sure you can be a bad influence on the kids, but they love you the most, with good reason and like their mother before them. Jackie Grutsch McKinney and Debbie Mix, my Muncie coven: sometimes I feel a little sorry for folks who don't have the smartest, funniest, fiercest, kindest, witchiest besties. Raising our kids together has been one of the greatest gifts of my life. I can't even imagine how I would have done it without you. I don't want to imagine. Sherrie, you feature prominently in this book for the simple reason that when the shit comes down, sometimes pouring from the actual ceiling, you are always there to pull me out and hose me off. I'm not even sure how you manage to be there in all the right moments. It's like you're some kind of angel from Wisconsin.

Also, my goodness, in no order and with a heart full of gratitude for everything from a much-needed workout or a bouquet of flowers to picking up a kid from school or a kind note: Pat Collier, Cindy Collier, Molly Ferguson, Todd McKinney, Tim Berg, Lauren Onkey, Bob Nowatzki, Kecia McBride, Katy Didden, Sarah Domet, and Sean Lovelace. And thank you to my nonfiction writing pals, near and far: Sonya Huber, Ander Monson, Beth Nguyen, Dinty W. Moore, Brooke Champagne, Silas Hansen, Ashley C. Ford, Steve Harvey, Dan Lehman, Joe Mackall, Alysia Sawchyn, Kate Hopper, Sue William Silverman, Abigail Thomas, Nicole Graev Lipson, BJ Hollars, Ana Maria Spagna, Brittany Means, Nicole Walker, Kelcey Ervick, Ira Sukrungruang, Jan Shoemaker, Kathryn Winograd, and Jill Talbot. And so so many more. I love writing and reading with y'all.

We're still around the table, and I'm beginning to worry my patient publisher is going to send these acknowledgments right back to me to cut for space. When I completed the post-Dobbs version of this book, there was only one press I wanted. Thank you from my whole heart to all the incredible people at the University of Nebraska Press for being that publisher, especially my amazing editor Courtney Ochsner who made me feel safe enough to send this book out into the world. You get me. To the whole Nebraska family—so many busy hands!—but particularly Sara Springsteen, Tish Fobben, Leif Milliken, Rosemary Sekora, Rebecca Jefferson, Sarah Kee, Abbey Frankforter—and my new pal from the NonfictioNow table in South Bend, Madison Wigley.

Thank you to Ball State University, many times over, and the National Endowment for the Arts for granting me the precious gift of time to work on this manuscript over the years.

Thank you to the patient librarians who helped us to fill our book box to bursting each week. Thank you to the gentle, kind caregivers at Ball State's Child Study Center—and to every babysitter who sang or played or painted downstairs while I hid upstairs, writing. Thank you, therapist of many years, for keeping us talking. Thank you to the medical professionals who appear in these pages, and especially to my A-team, Dr. L and Shane, who married high-risk technology and vagina-will-find-vagina philosophy to get our boy here safely. To the doctor I call Dr. J in this book: thank you for your skill and compassion. I'm sorry we live in a world where I cannot say your name for fear of putting you at risk. I am indebted to you and your colleagues for providing vital medical care. You are heroes.

I am not a person who could write a book without dogs. Tango, Walt, and Lola: thank you for keeping me moving and never letting me get lonely. I miss you all. Maggie May, you're a nut, but you're our nut, and you do your job with the fiercest and flooffiest love.

My deepest gratitude, always, is reserved for you, Mark. Everyone says marriage is such hard work, but that hasn't been my experience. Over a quarter century into our partnership, I can attest that being married to you is the easy part. A handsome, brilliant, funny poet who can cook? In my house? Sign me up. I'm a lucky woman. Thanks for doing life with me.

Sweet Ella, even before you were born, you transformed me. You made me a mother, and in doing so changed my life forever. Best daughter in the world. For *real*.

Dearest Henry, I chose you and fought harder for you than I've ever fought for anything. I am so proud of everything you are and wildly grateful that you are here with us, making every day better.

Thank you, Baby. I will never put you down.

And thank you all for coming on this journey with me. Love and light and grace to your many hands and hearts. I am so grateful.

IN THE AMERICAN LIVES SERIES

The Twenty-Seventh Letter of the Alphabet: A Memoir
by Kim Adrian

Fault Line
by Laurie Alberts

Pieces from Life's Crazy Quilt
by Marvin V. Arnett

Songs from the Black Chair: A Memoir of Mental Interiors
by Charles Barber

This Is Not the Ivy League: A Memoir
by Mary Clearman Blew

Body Geographic
by Barrie Jean Borich

Driving with Dvořák: Essays on Memory and Identity
by Fleda Brown

Character Witness: A Memoir
by Jason Brown

Searching for Tamsen Donner
by Gabrielle Burton

Island of Bones: Essays
by Joy Castro

American Lives: A Reader
edited by Alicia Christensen
introduced by Tobias Wolff

The Heart Folds Early: A Memoir
by Jill Christman

If This Were Fiction: A Love Story in Essays
by Jill Christman

Get Me Through Tomorrow: A Sister's Memoir of Brain Injury and Revival
by Mojie Crigler

Tell Me about Your Bad Guys: Fathering in Anxious Times
by Michael Dowdy

Should I Still Wish: A Memoir
by John W. Evans

Out of Joint: A Private and Public Story of Arthritis
by Mary Felstiner

Descanso for My Father: Fragments of a Life
by Harrison Candelaria Fletcher

Homing: Instincts of a Rustbelt Feminist
by Sherrie Flick

My Wife Wants You to Know I'm Happily Married
by Joey Franklin

The Perils of Girlhood: A Memoir in Essays
by Melissa Fraterrigo

Weeds: A Farm Daughter's Lament
by Evelyn I. Funda

Autumn Song: Essays on Absence
by Patrice Gopo

Shift: A Memoir of Identity and Other Illusions
by Penny Guisinger

Falling Room
by Eli Hastings

It's Fun to Be a Person I Don't Know
by Chachi D. Hauser

Borderline Citizen: Dispatches from the Outskirts of Nationhood
by Robin Hemley

And You Will Call It Fate: A Memoir
By Timothy J. Hillegonds

The Distance Between: A Memoir
by Timothy J. Hillegonds

Opa Nobody
by Sonya Huber

Pain Woman Takes Your Keys, and Other Essays from a Nervous System
by Sonya Huber

Hannah and the Mountain: Notes toward a Wilderness Fatherhood
by Jonathan Johnson

Under My Bed and Other Essays
by Jody Keisner

Ravelings: Essays on Love, Loss, and Wonder
by Lisa Knopp

Local Wonders: Seasons in the Bohemian Alps
by Ted Kooser

A Certain Loneliness: A Memoir
by Sandra Gail Lambert

Bigger than Life: A Murder, a Memoir
by Dinah Lenney

What Becomes You
by Aaron Raz Link and Hilda Raz

Queen of the Fall: A Memoir of Girls and Goddesses
by Sonja Livingston

The Virgin of Prince Street: Expeditions into Devotion
by Sonja Livingston

Anything Will Be Easy after This: A Western Identity Crisis
by Bethany Maile

Such a Life
by Lee Martin

Turning Bones
by Lee Martin

In Rooms of Memory: Essays
by Hilary Masters

Island in the City: A Memoir
by Micah McCrary

Thank You for Staying with Me
by Bailey Gaylin Moore

Between Panic and Desire
by Dinty W. Moore

To Hell with It: Of Sin and Sex, Chicken Wings, and Dante's Entirely Ridiculous, Needlessly Guilt-Inducing Inferno
by Dinty W. Moore

Let Me Count the Ways: A Memoir
by Tomás Q. Morín

Shadow Migration: Mapping a Life
by Suzanne Ohlmann

Meander Belt: Family, Loss, and Coming of Age in the Working-Class South
by M. Randal O'Wain

Sleep in Me
by Jon Pineda

The Solace of Stones: Finding a Way through Wilderness
by Julie Riddle

Works Cited: An Alphabetical Odyssey of Mayhem and Misbehavior
by Brandon R. Schrand

Thoughts from a Queen-Sized Bed
by Mimi Schwartz

My Ruby Slippers: The Road Back to Kansas
by Tracy Seeley

The Fortune Teller's Kiss
by Brenda Serotte

Gang of One: Memoirs of a Red Guard
by Fan Shen

Just Breathe Normally
by Peggy Shumaker

How to Survive Death and Other Inconveniences
by Sue William Silverman

The Pat Boone Fan Club: My Life as a White Anglo-Saxon Jew
by Sue William Silverman

Scraping By in the Big Eighties
by Natalia Rachel Singer

Sky Songs: Meditations on Loving a Broken World
by Jennifer Sinor

In the Shadow of Memory
by Floyd Skloot

Secret Frequencies: A New York Education
by John Skoyles

The Days Are Gods
by Liz Stephens

Phantom Limb
by Janet Sternburg

This Jade World
by Ira Sukrungruang

The Sound of Undoing: A Memoir in Essays
by Paige Towers

When We Were Ghouls: A Memoir of Ghost Stories
by Amy E. Wallen

Knocked Down: A High-Risk Memoir
by Aileen Weintraub

Yellowstone Autumn: A Season of Discovery in a Wondrous Land
by W. D. Wetherell

This Fish Is Fowl: Essays of Being
by Xu Xi

To order or obtain more information on these or other University of Nebraska Press titles, visit nebraskapress.unl.edu.

www.ingramcontent.com/pod-product-compliance
Lightning Source LLC
Chambersburg PA
CBHW020831160426
43192CB00007B/611